Sustainable Development Goals Series

The **Sustainable Development Goals Series** is Springer Nature's inaugural cross-imprint book series that addresses and supports the United Nations' seventeen Sustainable Development Goals. The series fosters comprehensive research focused on these global targets and endeavours to address some of society's greatest grand challenges. The SDGs are inherently multidisciplinary, and they bring people working across different fields together and working towards a common goal. In this spirit, the Sustainable Development Goals series is the first at Springer Nature to publish books under both the Springer and Palgrave Macmillan imprints, bringing the strengths of our imprints together.

The Sustainable Development Goals Series is organized into eighteen subseries: one subseries based around each of the seventeen respective Sustainable Development Goals, and an eighteenth subseries, "Connecting the Goals," which serves as a home for volumes addressing multiple goals or studying the SDGs as a whole. Each subseries is guided by an expert Subseries Advisor with years or decades of experience studying and addressing core components of their respective Goal.

The SDG Series has a remit as broad as the SDGs themselves, and contributions are welcome from scientists, academics, policymakers, and researchers working in fields related to any of the seventeen goals. If you are interested in contributing a monograph or curated volume to the series, please contact the Publishers: Zachary Romano [Springer; zachary.romano@springer.com] and Rachael Ballard [Palgrave Macmillan; rachael.ballard@palgrave.com].

More information about this series at
http://www.palgrave.com/gp/series/15486

Ezra Chitando • Ishanesu Sextus Gusha
Editors

Interfaith Networks and Development

Case Studies from Africa

Editors
Ezra Chitando
Department of Philosophy, Religion
and Ethics
University of Zimbabwe
Harare, Zimbabwe

Ishanesu Sextus Gusha
Anglican Diocese in Europe
Palma de Mallorca, Spain

ISSN 2523-3084 ISSN 2523-3092 (electronic)
Sustainable Development Goals Series
ISBN 978-3-030-89806-9 ISBN 978-3-030-89807-6 (eBook)
https://doi.org/10.1007/978-3-030-89807-6

© The Editor(s) (if applicable) and The Author(s), under exclusive licence to Springer Nature Switzerland AG 2022
Color wheel and icons: From https://www.un.org/sustainabledevelopment/, Copyright © 2020 United Nations. Used with the permission of the United Nations.
The content of this publication has not been approved by the United Nations and does not reflect the views of the United Nations or its officials or Member States.
This work is subject to copyright. All rights are solely and exclusively licensed by the Publisher, whether the whole or part of the material is concerned, specifically the rights of translation, reprinting, reuse of illustrations, recitation, broadcasting, reproduction on microfilms or in any other physical way, and transmission or information storage and retrieval, electronic adaptation, computer software, or by similar or dissimilar methodology now known or hereafter developed.
The use of general descriptive names, registered names, trademarks, service marks, etc. in this publication does not imply, even in the absence of a specific statement, that such names are exempt from the relevant protective laws and regulations and therefore free for general use.
The publisher, the authors and the editors are safe to assume that the advice and information in this book are believed to be true and accurate at the date of publication. Neither the publisher nor the authors or the editors give a warranty, expressed or implied, with respect to the material contained herein or for any errors or omissions that may have been made. The publisher remains neutral with regard to jurisdictional claims in published maps and institutional affiliations.

This Palgrave Macmillan imprint is published by the registered company Springer Nature Switzerland AG.
The registered company address is: Gewerbestrasse 11, 6330 Cham, Switzerland

CONTENTS

Part I Interfaith Networks: Conceptualisation and Examples of Pan-African Organisations   1

1 **Interfaith Networks and Development**   3
Ezra Chitando

2 **Exploring Interfaith Networks in the Context of Development: Key Considerations**   27
Sokfa F. John

3 **Faith to Action Network: A Permanent Balancing Act**   47
Ahmed Ragab, Emma Rachmawati, Grace Kaiso, and Matthias Brucker

4 **KAICIID: An Emerging Significant Player in Global Interfaith and Development Initiatives**   65
Ishanesu Sextus Gusha

5 **The Programme for Christian-Muslim Relations in Africa (PROCMURA) Work in Building Peaceful and Inclusive Societies**   81
Florence Iminza and Esther Mombo

vi   CONTENTS

Part II   Interfaith Networks and Gender in Africa 97

6   **Women of Faith Working Together as Mothers of a Culture of Peace: The Women's Interfaith Council in Northern Nigeria** 99
Kathleen McGarvey

7   **An Interfaith Body for Gender Justice in Tanzania: An Overview** 117
Klaudia Wilk-Mhagama

8   **Interfaith Approaches to Violence against Women and Development: The Case of the South African Faith and Family Institute** 131
Fungai Chirongoma

9   **Interfaith Collaboration, Sexual Diversity and Development in Botswana** 149
Tshenolo Jennifer Madigele

Part III   Case Studies of Interfaith Networks and Development in Selected African Countries 173

10   **The Inter-Religious Council of Uganda and Development** 175
Andrew David Omona

11   **Religion and Sustainable Development: The Role of the Zambia Interfaith Networking Group (ZINGO) in Contemporary Times** 199
Nelly Mwale

12   **The Role of the Council of Religions and Peace in Mozambique (COREM) in Peace and Reconciliation, 2012–2019** 215
Júlio Machele and Mário Jorge Carlos

CONTENTS   vii

13 **Colonial Marginalities and Post-Colonial Fragments: Inter-Faith Networking for Development in Ghana**   231
Samuel Awuah-Nyamekye and Simon Kofi Appiah

Part IV   Diverse Themes in Interfaith Networks and Development   253

14 **Education and Interfaith Development in Northern Nigeria**   255
Ezekiel Abdullahi Babagario

15 **Addressing Environmental Issues Through Interfaith Dialogue: A Case of the Southern African Faith Communities' Environmental Institute (SAFCEI)**   273
Tapiwa H. Gusha and Ishanesu Sextus Gusha

16 **Interfaith Networks, the African Diaspora and Development: The Case of the United Kingdom**   289
Nomatter Sande

Index   303

Notes on Contributors

Simon Kofi Appiah is a senior lecturer in the Department of Religion and Human Values at the University of Cape Coast, Ghana. His areas of research include Method and theory in the study of religions and the study of values

Samuel Awuah-Nyamekye is a Professor of Religion and Environment in the Department of Religion and Human Values in the University of Cape Coast in Ghana. Prof. Awuah-Nyamekye holds a doctorate degree from Theology and Religious Studies Department of the University of Leeds, UK. His current research interests are focused on religion and the environment, environmental ethics, religion and development, religion and politics, and religion and gender issues. Prof. Awuah-Nyamekye serves on the Editorial Advisory Group of Cambridge Scholars Publishing Ltd. and is currently the Editor-in-Chief of three journals in the Faculty of Arts of University of Cape Coast.

Ezekiel Abdullahi Babagario is the Director, Programmes at the International Center for Interfaith, Peace and Harmony (ICIPH) Kaduna. He is also an adjunct lecturer at the Baptist Theological Seminary Kaduna Nigeria. He holds a doctorate degree from the University of Massachusetts Amherst USA. His research interest includes Comparative World Politics, Peace building and Reconciliation, National Security Policy, Diplomacy & Conflict Resolution and Interfaith Dialogue/Education.

Matthias Brucker He is Faith to Action Network's regional director in Europe. He holds a Master in International Relations from the London

School of Economics. In his current role, he focuses on building bridges between European, African and Asian faith organizations and stakeholders, advancing interfaith dialogues and collaboration in the areas of peaceful coexistence, women's rights and sexual and reproductive health and rights.

Mário Jorge Carlos is a Postgraduate in Rural Sociology and Development Management, Faculty of Arts and Social Sciences, University Eduardo Mondlane and Postgraduate in Education and Development, Technical University of Mozambique. Currently he works in non-governmental organization, ADPP-Mozambique, as a senior Grant Administrator.

Fungai Chirongoma She recently finished her PhD studies in the Department of Religious Studies, at the University of Cape Town. Her PhD research focused on the interventions of faith based organizations in addressing violence against women. Fungai's research interests include religion and gender, religion and development and African Traditional Religion.

Ezra Chitando He is a Professor, History and Phenomenology of Religion at the University of Zimbabwe and Theology Consultant on HIV for the World Council of Churches. His research and publication interests include religion and: development, security, gender, sexuality, climate change and others.

Ishanesu Sextus Gusha He is a holder of PhD in New Testament from University of Pretoria, South Africa, Masters in Theological Studies, Nashotah House Theological Seminary, Wisconsin, USA, MA in Religious Studies (New Testament), BA in Religious Studies, Diploma in Religious Studies, University of Zimbabwe, and Diploma in Pastoral Studies, Bishop Gaul Theological Seminary, Harare, Zimbabwe. Formerly a senior lecturer from University of Zimbabwe and now parish priest in Palma de Mallorca, Spain in the Anglican Diocese in Europe, his research interests are in Interfaith Dialogue, Peace Building and Biblical Theology. A fellow of CEDAR, KAICIID and SAFCEI.

Tapiwa H. Gusha He is a PhD student at the University of Stellenbosch and an Anglican Priest in Canada. He is passionate in New Testament, Interfaith Dialogue, Peace and Reconciliation. He is also a founder member of Southern Africa Interfaith and Peace Academy-SAIPA.

NOTES ON CONTRIBUTORS   xi

Florence Iminza is a PhD student at Kenyatta University in the Department of Philosophy and Religious Studies (PRS). She has a master's degree in Islam and Christian—Muslim Relations, a bachelor's degree in divinity, and a diploma in theology, both from St. Paul's University in Kenya. She is currently the Project Officer, Women and Peace building with the Programme for Christian-Muslim Relations in Africa (PROCMURA). Her research interests are interfaith relations, Christian-Muslim dialogue, and women and peace building.

Sokfa F. John He is a postdoctoral research fellow and research manager at the DSI/NRF SARChI in Sustainable Local Livelihoods, at the University of KwaZulu-Natal. He holds a PhD in Religion and Social Transformation and a masters in Gender, Religion and Health. His research interests are in digital religion, digital cultures, ethnic and religious conflicts, and peace building.

Grace Kaiso He serves as the Senior Advisor to the Anglican Alliance and Chair of the Faith to Action Network. He is a theologian and a graduate of St. John's College Auckland, New Zealand, and St. Stephen's University, Canada. He has been actively involved in the issues of urban Ministry with focus on empowerment of low-income communities, and has played a key role in advocacy for human rights and good governance in Africa.

Júlio Machele is Researcher and Assistant Lecturer, Master Student, History Department, Faculty of Arts and Social Sciences, University Eduardo Mondlane (UEM), Maputo Mozambique. Areas of interest: Social Medicine; Traditional Medicine; Public Health; Environmental History; Poverty; Development; Urbanization; Music; Religion, War.

Tshenolo Jennifer Madigele She is a lecturer at the University of Botswana in the department of Theology and Religious Studies, Faculty of Humanities. She obtained her PhD in Practical Theology at the University of South Africa in 2020 with a dissertation focusing on Pastoral Care to the elderly caregivers of HIV and AIDS Orphans. Tshenolo has been involved in various initiatives serving women in Botswana as a member of the Circle of Concerned African Women Theologians, Botswana Chapter. She published several academic articles in peer-reviewed journals and chapters.

Kathleen McGarvey She is a Catholic Religious Sister of the Missionary Sisters of Our Lady of Apostles (OLA). Originally from Ireland, she has worked in Argentina, Italy and Nigeria. She holds a Doctorate Degree in Missiology with specialization in Interreligious Dialogue from the Pontifical Gregorian University, Rome. From 2003 to 2005 until 2013 she lived in Kaduna, Nigeria. She is the founder of the Interfaith Forum of Muslim and Christian Women's Association (a.k.a. Women's Interfaith Council) which is based in Kaduna. During these years she was also a lecturer in the Good Shepherd Major Seminary, Kaduna. She is author of the book Muslim and Christian Women in Dialogue: The Case of Northern Nigeria published by Peter Lang, Oxford/Bern 2009. She presently is the Provincial Superior of her Religious Congregation in Ireland.

Esther Mombo Professor at St. Paul's University in Limuru, Kenya, where she serves as a Lecturer in the faculty of Theology. she is A graduate of St. Paul's, University, university of Dublin and University of Edinburgh, In 2007 she was awarded an honorary doctorate by Virginia theological seminary for her work in bringing to the fore issues of gender disparity and gender justice in Church and society. She teaches courses in fields of Church History, Interfaith Relations, and Theology & Gender. She serves as trustee of Programme for Christian-Muslim Relations in Africa (PROCMURA). She is coordinator of the Circle of Concerned African Women Theologians in East Africa.

Nelly Mwale is a lecturer in the Department of Religious Studies at the University of Zambia. She holds a Doctorate in Religious Studies and her Research interests are religion and education, religion in the public sphere, church history and African Indigenous Religions.

Andrew David Omona is a Senior Lecturer in the Department of Public Administration and Governance and Dean of Faculty of Social Sciences at the Uganda Christian University—Mukono. He holds a Doctorate of Political Studies focusing on International Relations and Diplomacy from Kenyatta University. His research interests include Ethics, International Relations and Diplomatic Practice, Conflict and Peace Studies.

Emma Rachmawati She is a Lecturer at Public Health Department, Faculty of Health Sciences, and also Head of Ethical Health Research Commission at University of Muhammadiyah. She is a founder and steering council member of Faith to Action Network. She is a Coordinator of Public Health Program of Central Board of Muhammadiyah, and member of Central Board of Muhammadiyah Covid-19 Command Center. She has written various papers and is actively advocates for better public health programmes.

Ahmed Ragab He is a Professor of reproductive health at the International Islamic Centre for Population Studies and Research, Al-Azhar University. He is the Vice Chairman of Faith to Action Network. He is holding three master degrees (OB/GYN, population and bioethics) and a PhD, reproductive health. He was awarded the National High Academy of Scientific Research Family Planning Award, 2004. Egyptian medical syndicate awarded him its annual award for his work in the area of promoting the health of women in 2006. He has extensive record of research and books addressing family planning, reproductive health and gender issues from faith perspectives.

Nomatter Sande He holds a PhD in Religion and Social Transformation from the University of KwaZulu Natal (South Africa). Nomatter is an African Practical Theologian and practicing Reverend (Apostolic Faith Mission International Ministries UK). He is a Research Fellow at the Research Institute for Theology and Religion (RITR) in the College of Human Sciences; University of South Africa (UNISA).Research interests include theology, disability studies, and missiology and gender issues.

Klaudia Wilk-Mhagama She holds a Doctorate of Cultural Studies, Faculty of International and Political Studies, from Jagiellonian University. Her research interests include social, political and cultural changes in Tanzania, as well as the activities of non-governmental and religious organizations in Tanzania.

LIST OF FIGURES

Fig. 2.1 Affiliation network of URI Cooperation Circles and Action Areas in West Africa. (By the author) 33

Fig. 2.2 Religions associated with more than 8 Cooperation Circle in each country 35

PART I

Interfaith Networks: Conceptualisation and Examples of Pan-African Organisations

CHAPTER 1

Interfaith Networks and Development

Ezra Chitando

A video of an interfaith prayer outside a hospital in Cape Town, South Africa, went viral in early 2021. People from diverse communities of faith, who were observing the COVID-19 protocols, were praying for those who were in hospital, and for those who had died because of the pandemic (News24, 10 January 2021). This interfaith solidarity and presence in the middle of a devastating pandemic reminded many viewers of the role of religion and spirituality in human life. Putting aside their religious differences, they came together to be present with those who were lonely, as hospital visits were restricted, and to inspire those who were losing hope. In the video, one patient waved a white cloth, expressing appreciation and acknowledging the initiative. The capacity to transcend religious differences and collaborate is one of the most powerful contributions of the interfaith movement.

Despite the importance of the interfaith movement globally, it continues to be neglected in scholarly discourses. While there is a growing realisation that religion is strategically placed to contribute towards development, there is still some hesitation among scholars to invest in

E. Chitando (✉)
Department of Philosophy, Religion and Ethics, University of Zimbabwe, Harare, Zimbabwe

© The Author(s), under exclusive license to Springer Nature Switzerland AG 2022
E. Chitando, I. S. Gusha (eds.), *Interfaith Networks and Development*, Sustainable Development Goals Series, https://doi.org/10.1007/978-3-030-89807-6_1

researching and publishing in this area. However, the gradual emergence of a sub-field or discipline called religion and development bears testimony to the need to highlight the interface (see among others, Deneulin and Rakodi 2011; Swart and Nell 2016, Bompani 2019, and, Spies and Schrode 2021). Consequently, there is a steady growth of the literature on religion and development in different settings (among others, Lunn 2009; Ter Haar 2011; Carbonnier et al. 2013; Fountain et al. 2015; Tomalin 2015; Heist and Cnaan 2016; Hasan 2017; WFDD 2018; Tomalin et al. 2019; Blevins 2020; Chitando et al. 2020; Kraft and Wilkinson 2020). Whereas most developmental discourse and programming has assumed a secular orientation, falsely believing the secular to be superior to the religious (Tarusarira 2020), it has since become clear that religion remains a major and relevant variable in development. Thus, the rigid separation between religion and development is being overcome. As Clarke and Jennings (2008: 2) rightly observe, "there has been a gradual movement from estrangement to engagement." Olarinmoye (2012), and, Feener and Fountain (2018) also provide valuable insights into the convergence between religion and development.

Very few publications, however, have paid attention to the role and impact of interfaith networks in the quest for development. Yet, interfaith networks are critical players in the quest to meet the United Nations (UN) Sustainable Development Goals (SDGs) Agenda 2030. For example, the volume by Marshall and Van Saanen (2007) features a very important case study, the Inter-Faith Waste Management Initiative (IFAWAMI), in Ghana. The initiative has done a sterling job in environmental waste management in Ghana. Numerous other examples, including chapters in this volume, illustrate the key role of interfaith initiatives in meeting the imperative of holistic human development. In particular, this volume addresses the theme of interfaith networks and development in Africa, paying attention to SDG 10 (addressing inequalities), as well as other SDGs.

The World Faith Development Dialogue (WFDD) (see for example, WFDD 2017) has emerged to respond to the interface between religion and global development. The International Partnership on Religion and Development (IPRD) has the same interest. UN agencies have been collaborating with religious actors to foster development (The UN Inter-Agency Task Force on Engaging Faith-Based Actors for Sustainable Development/UN Task Force on Religion and Development 2018). It is, therefore, critical to appreciate the contribution and challenges of interfaith networks in the discourse on religion and development.

This volume seeks to add to the scholarly literature on interfaith networks and development. Utilising reflections by practitioners of interfaith collaboration and development, as well as scholars within this field, the volume presents new data and fresh case studies from diverse African contexts. It draws attention to the increasing importance of interfaith networks in the quest to improve the quality of life for the world's citizens. This volume, therefore, is a call to researchers, policy makers, activists and others to invest in researching into, and capacitating, interfaith networks and development in Africa, but also, globally. By highlighting the contributions of different types of interfaith networks in diverse African settings, the volume underscores their role in the quest to meet the SDGs. However, there are critical voices (see for example, Winkler 2008) that contend that religion's contribution to development is being overstated. The case studies in this volume, nonetheless, confirm that religion remains well placed to contribute to sustainable development.

Interfaith Networks and Development: An Overview

In the Arts and Humanities, definitions tend to be heavily contested. In this section, I will not claim to provide an exhaustive and binding definition of the two key concepts, namely, "interfaith networks" and "development," since each one of them demands a lot of space for elaboration. Instead, I will draw attention to only those dimensions that are relevant for understanding the deployment of these concepts in this volume. Further, I will not engage with the issue of the history of the interfaith networks and their various activities in different contexts, although this is important (see for example, Behera 2011; Halafoff 2013; WFDD 2017; Fahy and Bock 2019). Instead, the focus is on interfaith networks and development in a more direct way.

Interfaith Networks

First, "interfaith networks" represent initiatives bringing together actors from more than one faith tradition or community to pursue joint action that seeks to address a felt human need in a specific context. Essentially, this volume focuses on people of different religious orientations coming together for cooperative action that has the aim of improving human

6   E. CHITANDO

circumstances.[1] Contributors have preferred "interfaith networks" to "interreligious dialogue" (see for example Cornille 2013; Cheetham et al. 2013; Chia 2016; Orton 2016). David Lochhead (1988) referred to "the dialogical imperative." However, the focus in this volume is not on the theme of interreligious dialogue, important as this is. Others have used the term, "multifaith movement" (see for example Halafoff 2013 and, Fahy and Haynes 2018). Although this is a legitimate term, I contend that "interfaith networks" expresses the focus of this volume better in that most of the initiatives are more formally structured than would be expressed by the idea of a movement. Yet others have made reference to "multifaith spaces" (Biddington 2013; Religions 2019 and 2020). While the idea of "multifaith spaces" is quite relevant, we are of the view that the "interfaith networks" concept articulates our central motivation more effectively.

Contributors have chosen to concentrate on the social action (Knitter 2013) that has been either precipitated by interreligious dialogue, is an expression of interreligious dialogue or constitutes material that can animate or inspire interreligious dialogue or multifaith interaction. They are more interested in how interfaith networks of diverse histories, forms and geographical coverage are contributing to development. Whereas "interreligious dialogue" comes across more as cerebral, "interfaith networks" has a sense of movement, connectedness and dynamism. For the purposes of this volume, the focus is on concrete, formal interfaith networks that are working in the area of development. This is not to minimise the importance of informal or grassroots initiatives, but to declare the remit of this volume in advance. Indeed, a separate volume could explore the achievements and challenges of the grassroots interfaith initiatives when engaging in development work. Admirand (2019) expresses the focus of this volume when writing:

> We also have the dialogue of action, especially pronounced in cooperating together in striving for justice, peace, and the good of the most marginalized or poor, or the protection of the environment, and other pressing concerns.

[1] The WFDD (2017: 5) refers to, "interfaith, interreligious, multifaith, or intercultural dialogue." It is also possible to add, "cultural diplomacy" to this list. See for example, http://www.culturaldiplomacy.org/academy/index.php?en_historical-example, accessed 11 December 2020.

On Networks

The choice to concentrate the idea of "networks" is quite deliberate. The concept of a network has now been dominated by the concept from information technology where it expresses the idea of two or more devices or nodes that can communicate. Thus, the emphasis is on collective action that is undertaken when two or more faith groups communicate and bring their gifts together. As one Amharic proverb puts it so lucidly, "When spider webs unite, they can tie up a lion." Inspired by African collectivist thought and action, the call for chapters for this volume drew attention to the need to explore how different interfaith networks are engaging in collaborative efforts to promote holistic human development. However, there is an appreciation that interfaith groups also precipitate individual political action (Todd et al. 2017). On the other hand, Khan (2015: 47) identifies six areas of interfaith engagement: "neighbourhood interfaith, institutional interfaith, scriptural interfaith, campaigning interfaith, pastoral interfaith and women's interfaith." The various chapters in this volume address these different types of interfaith engagement.

The key consideration has been documenting and reflecting on the contributions of interfaith networks in different parts of the world. The emphasis is on identifying the challenges that they face as they seek to make effective contributions towards development. In this sense, the volume must be read as responding to the recommendation of the United States Institute of Peace (2004) to evaluate interreligious dialogue initiatives.

Although our direct focus in this volume is on interfaith networks, we appreciate that there are ecumenical bodies that do a lot of interfaith work. As shall become clearer in the section on typologies, there are some ecumenical bodies that do not limit their activities to members of their faith community but collaborate with others. For example, while the World Council of Churches (WCC) is a Christian ecumenical organisation, it engages in many interfaith collaborations. One of areas where the WCC has been actively promoting interfaith collaboration is through its role in responding to HIV and AIDS (see for example, UNAIDS 2019). Key African organisations such as the African Union (AU) and the All Africa Conference of Churches (AACC) have also promoted interfaith dialogue as an enabler of the continent's development.

8   E. CHITANDO

Having provided an overview of the preference for interfaith networks, it is important to draw attention to some of the major factors relevant for establishing a viable interfaith network. Thus:

Key pillars for establishing an interfaith network:
1. Have a *clear purpose* for forming the network
2. Create a *common space* that is neutral and respected
3. Set *common rules* such as respecting and listening to one another
4. Let all members feel *ownership* over the network
5. Set the *parameters* for conversation and action.[2]

Development

Second, there is need to discuss the term "development," albeit briefly. It is a term that elicits different reactions among different scholars, practitioners and participants in the development process. It has a long history and has been severely contested (Sapkota and Tharu 2016), with questions emerging as to how to measure it (Soares and Quintella 2008) and whether it is a neutral term. On the radical side are some scholars and activists who contend that the term is either vacuous, ideologically constructed or woefully inadequate (see for example Chitando et al. 2020). This is because the term has often been used to categorise and rank human societies in a descending order, with the West usually on top and Rest at the bottom. Due to historical factors such as the slave trade, colonialism, racism and neo-colonialism, there is a contention that it is intrinsically unfair to compare levels of development across different countries and contexts. On his part, Metz (2017) contends that the dominant understanding of development is characteristically anthropocentric, individualist and technocratic and, therefore, does violence to the African understanding. Cognisant of the challenges associated with the term, there have been proposals to embrace alternatives such as "human flourishing" (Green 2019).

We contend that dropping a concept because of its problematic character represents the ultimate failure of nerve. Given that there are no guarantees that any alternative that we will develop will not be contested, we are persuaded that the onus must be upon those using particular concepts to simply clarify their own understanding of the concepts and proceed to

---

[2] https://www.multicultural.vic.gov.au/images/stories/pdf/fact%20sheet_establishing%20and%20maintaining%20an%20ifn.pdf. Accessed 04 December 2020, italics original.

deploy them. After all, successful communication depends on functional (and not detailed or exhaustive) understanding of the key concepts in use. Although different religions have different understandings of development (see for example, Saggiomo 2012), they mostly do call for an improvement in the social, economic and political lives of citizens.

Development must be understood in holistic terms. Although economic growth is integral to development, it is not its totality. Rather development includes the social, economic, political, cultural, ecological and other dimensions. Holistic and sustainable human development takes into cognisance the cultivation of peaceful environments, gender justice, responsibility for creation and social justice. Crucially, it also entails acknowledging and according capabilities (Sen 1999; Nussbaum 2011). Chitonge, an economist with keen interest in African development, contends that development must be understood in holistic terms. Thus:

> The social, political, economic and cultural transformation which the term 'development' embraces is not limited to how many kilometres of roads or railway have been built, or how many people have access to clean water—it also includes changes relating to how many people are able to live lives which they value. ... Development in this broader sense includes changes in the way people perceive themselves; improvements in self-confidence in the general population; overcoming a general feeling of despondency and despair in the general population. (Chitonge 2015: 9)

There is a close relationship between religion's emphasis on salvation or liberation (Cohn-Sherbok 1992 and De La Torre 2008) and holistic human development. Most religions, including those with a sharply defined eschatology, are keen to promote health and well-being in this life (Prozesky 1984; Shoko 2007), as well as securing salvation in the future. In this regard, the earlier distinction between "world-rejecting" (and therefore not socially engaged) religions; "world-affirming" (and therefore, socially engaged) religions, and "world accommodating" (balancing the extremes, but also socially engaged) religions (see Wallis 1984) needs to be revised. Religions are not absolute, completely closed systems. In many instances, one religion can express all the three dimensions on different occasions. In the case of interfaith networks, the focus on addressing pressing human needs has highlighted the "world-affirming" dimension of the world's religions. Through networking, collaborating and sharing a common vision, different religions have come together to promote development. For example:

> Malaria was reduced in Nigeria once Muslims and Christians agreed to fight the same mosquitos—through the distribution of nets—that were biting the Muslims on Friday and the Christians on Sunday. (Seiple 2016: 5)

Having a common approach characterised by tolerance, mutual respect and collaboration is integral to development. Consequently, it is vital to adopt a more holistic approach to development. Development entails both the hardware of constructing concrete bridges, as it is about generating and nurturing the software that facilitates the bridging of divisions among people. Contributors to this volume have embraced expansive approaches to development, appreciating the interfaith networks' commitment towards joint action as critical to development. While most contributors have focused on interfaith networks and SDG 10 in Africa, the interconnectedness among the SDGs implies that this volume also addresses how interfaith networks have promoted the achievement of other SDGs.

Interfaith Networks and Development: Summarising Areas of Engagement

More space would be required to try and do justice to the areas in which interfaith networks are contributing to development. In this section, I shall highlight only some of the major areas where interfaith networks are contributing to development. I should hasten to add that this section is closely related to the next section where I shall attempt a typology of interfaith networks in the context of development. There is a logical connection as most interfaith networks have emerged with the express intention of addressing one or more issues related to development. One can combine the analysis, but separating the themes appears to be more effective. Further, there are also considerable overlaps across the themes described below.

Peacebuilding

Peacebuilding has emerged as a major theme in interfaith activities contributing to development. There can be no development without peace

(SDG 16). While there is debate on the history of religion and violence (among others, Armstrong 2015), but more particularly in the contemporary period, the need to focus on religion and peacebuilding (see for example, Irvin-Erickson and Phan 2016), as well as human security, has become more acute (Ter Haar and Busuttil 2005; Shannahan and Payne 2016; Tarusarira and Chitando 2020). Consequently, many interfaith networks have invested in peacebuilding. Indeed, one might rightly argue that the very formation of an interfaith network itself is part of breaking down barriers and laying foundations for peace. Nigeria, where religion is constantly being deployed to achieve political and ideological goals, represents one context where interfaith networks have sought to promote peace (see, among others, Ojo and Lateju 2010; Omotosho 2014). The Interfaith Mediation Centre in Nigeria serves as a powerful reminder of the commitment towards peace (Christian Aid 2014). The Inter-Religious Councils of Sierra Leone and Liberia have been central to the quest for peace in the two countries (Featherstone 2015: 19). The interest in interfaith networks and peacebuilding, is, however, global (see for example, Bamat et al. 2017).

The focus on, and contribution towards, peacebuilding by interfaith networks cannot be overemphasised. It was Hans Kung who famously remarked that, **"There will be no peace between the civilizations without a peace between the religions! And there will be no peace between the religions without a dialogue between the religions"** (Küng 1998: 92; emphasis original). Kung's insights have appropriated by many interfaith networks throughout the world, with peacebuilding becoming one of their major engagements. Indeed, the SDGs themselves are predicated on the world being peaceful for them to have any chance of being fulfilled (SDG 16). In this regard, the interfaith networks are making a critical contribution to development by striving to create a conducive environment in which development can take place. Although religious extremism remains a threat (Adogame et al. 2020), the reality is that the situation could have been much worse without the sterling work being done by interfaith networks. Such is the quest for harmony among the religions that in Nigeria there is a movement bringing together aspects of Christianity, Islam and Indigenous Religions, namely, 'Chrislam' (Williams 2019. See also Atiemo 2003 for Ghana). The role of women in religious peacebuilding (Marshall et al. 2011; Al Qurtuby 2014) requires further reflection than can be provided in this introductory chapter.

Women's Issues

The intersection of women's issues in general, and sexual and reproductive health and rights (SRHR) constitutes a significant area of interest for many interfaith networks. The underlying reality is that religion has generally sponsored deeply problematic and oppressive gender ideologies, across history. To say this is not to deny that there are many redemptive dimensions in religion when it comes to women's rights. In practice, however, it is often the ultra-conservative strand within religion that has enjoyed an upper hand (see for example, Sharma and Young 2007; Pereira and Ibrahim 2010). Many of the interfaith networks that have emerged seek to promote gender justice by recovering positive ideas and practices that are found within the different religions.

The empowerment of women and girls is central to the achievement of the SDGs as whole. In particular, however, Goal 5 speaks of the need to, "Achieve gender equality and empower all women and girls." The long history of women's exclusion is a blot on humanity's efforts to improve its quality of life. Although religions have often been regarded as a stumbling block towards the realisation of women's SRHR, particularly around family planning, contraception and abortion (Maguire 2003), many interfaith networks are seeking to mobilise faith communities to be more realistic in their responses. There is, therefore, an increase in interfaith networks that are addressing women's issues in more accommodating ways. This has seen greater investment around reflections between religion and human rights. The Office of the UN High Commissioner for Human Rights (OHCHR) has been playing a prominent role in this regard, promoting the "Faith for Rights" approach. This is where the different religions of the world serve as resources for promoting the human rights of all. Here, interfaith networks.

Health

Goal 3 of the SDGs is, "Good health and wellbeing." This is a major aspiration, as no development can take place in contexts dominated by diseases. Many interfaith networks focus on health and wellbeing in general, or seek to address a specific health challenge in particular. The devastation caused by HIV and AIDS in sub-Saharan Africa precipitated the emergence of interfaith networks that sought to mobilise the faith community to offer effective responses to the pandemic. For example, the African (later, International) Network of Religious Leaders Living with or Personally Affected by HIV or AIDS (A/INERELA +) emerged out of the quest to support religious leaders from diverse communities of faith to respond to HIV and AIDS (Byamugisha 2019: 134–146). As Gideon Byamugisha, the first African religious leaders to publicly disclose his HIV positive status reiterates in his messages, there is no virus for a particular religion or denomination: the virus does not discriminate on the basis of religious affiliation. The Asian Interfaith Network on HIV/AIDS espouses a similar conviction and seeks to galvanise united and coherent action among diverse communities of faith to respond to HIV and AIDS.

Various UN agencies have warmed up to the role of faith-based organisations (FBOs) in promoting health and wellbeing. It is in the same vein that they have been more forthcoming in collaborating with interfaith networks that focus on health (see for example, UNFPA 2009). UN agencies and other development partners have acknowledged that the coordination provided by interfaith networks facilitates greater effectiveness. The COVID-19 pandemic which wreaked havoc in 2020 and whose effects will continue to be felt in the foreseeable future, also required joint action by diverse actors from within the faith community. Recognising the importance of FBOs, including interfaith networks, to the quest for health and wellbeing, some academic institutions have invested in analysing this neglected dimension. For example, Emory University in the United States has the Interfaith Health Program and has undertaken research into the interfaith between religion and public health globally. The International Religious Health Assets Programme (IRHAP) at the University of Cape Town, South Africa has published on the role of FBOs in health provision in Africa and beyond. These initiatives have highlighted the contribution of interfaith networks to health.

Children and Youth

There are some interfaith networks that have a specific focus on either children or youth, or both. This emerges from the realisation that when children and youth catch the vision of interfaith collaboration, there is a much greater likelihood that they will become more effective global citizens in future. This is not to deny that children and young people are full, autonomous human beings in their own right. However, interfaith networks that focus on children and youth are motivated by the prospects of having a brighter future as there will be more actors who uphold the values of tolerance and collaboration. Such individuals are well placed to promote peace and unity in multicultural contexts. For example, Kusuma and Susilo (2020) have described the impact of interfaith youth networks in Indonesia. These groups are making effective contributions to peace-building. Thus:

> Having grown up in multifaith societies in a globalised world, young people are in an ideal position to play an important role in normalising pluralism and in spreading an awareness of interdependence and global responsibility in ultramodern societies. Multifaith engagement among young people provides opportunities for increased contact and to form friendships, thereby building mutual understanding among previously divided communities. Youth-led multifaith initiatives focused on both local and global concerns have the added benefit of empowering young people to have a critical voice and to take non-violent action to effect social change. In this way they can provide alternatives to extremist movements that advocate violent processes and feed off feelings of alienation. (Halafoff 2013: 104)

Recognising the importance of religion for securing children's rights, the Global Network of Religions for Children (GNRC) seeks to end child poverty, among other goals. It brings together actors from different faith communities to work for a better world for children. UNICEF has collaborated with the World Council of Churches (WCC) to develop the Churches' Commitment to Children. Other ecumenical and interfaith networks also address various issues relating to child protection, education, health, nutrition; water, sanitation and hygiene; early childhood development, humanitarian action, gender equality and child participation (see for example, UNICEF 2012). Development is only meaningful if it allows children to thrive and many interfaith networks have sought to uphold this vision.

Climate Change

Although there are some denialists, it is fair to say that climate change is now recognised as a global emergency. Goal 13 of the SDGs states the need to, "Take urgent action to combat climate change and its impacts." Interfaith networks have been actively involved in the response to the climate emergency. For example, they have been present at global meetings on climate change, namely, the Conference of the Parties (COP), where they seek to play an effective advocacy role. A review of their statements (see for example, Rautenbach et al. 2014) confirms their creativity and dedication. In different settings, interfaith networks have emerged that prioritise responding to the climate emergency.

The Interfaith Rainfall Initiative, the United Religions Initiative's the Environmental Network, Green Faith and other initiatives demonstrate the resolve of the interfaith networks to contribute towards addressing climate change. Further, the presence of faith-based actors at UN conferences on climate change (see for example Glaab 2017) shows their growing influence. The interfaith response to climate change confirms the importance of joint action to address a pressing need. There have been global, continental, regional, national, and local interfaith activities to respond to climate change, demonstrating the critical role interfaith networks are playing in this sector.

Other Themes

Combining other themes that interfaith are addressing in the context of the SDGs is not to undermine any one of them. It only serves as confirmation of the fact that there are diverse themes that interfaith networks are focusing on. These include mental health, disability, addressing population and development, refugees and migrants; water, sanitation and hygiene (WASH), housing, emergency and development programming, and others. Interfaith networks are actively involved in combating extremism, fighting poverty, as well as promoting global freedom of religion and belief (Fahy and Haynes 2018: 1). Other interfaith networks are involved in food justice, supporting employees at the work place, deepening their city councils' engagements, fighting child trafficking and upholding sexual diversity. In reality, therefore, interfaith networks are involved in extremely diverse activities. Their overriding concern is to contribute to development.

DEVELOPING A TYPOLOGY OF INTERFAITH NETWORKS CONTRIBUTING TOWARDS DEVELOPMENT

Having outlined the guiding framework in the foregoing sections, in this section the chapter provides an analysis of the types of interfaith networks contributing towards meeting the SDGs. It must be reiterated, however, that central to the construction of a typology is flexibility. This means that the categories described below must not be approached rigidly and that there is need to accept overlaps. Second, the examples deployed are only for the purposes of illustration. The inclusion or exclusion of an interfaith network within a specific category is not a comment/ary on its status, effectiveness in delivering development or level of visibility. In an earlier study, Halafoff (2013: 110–111) provided helpful insights into interfaith networks. She indicated that these included: "religious organisations headed by religious leaders; faith-based service organisations; faith-based women's organisations; faith-based youth organisations; local and global multifaith organisations; state-appointed multifaith councils and committees; and multi-actor peacebuilding organisations and networks." While appreciating these insights, I have created my own typology as follows:

Global Interfaith Networks Promoting Dialogue and Tolerance

There are interfaith organisations that endeavour to have a global outreach and focus. Essentially, they have emerged to bring together diverse communities of faith, promote tolerance, dialogue and peace among the religions. To a very large extent, their raison d'etre is to facilitate harmony and co-existence among the different religions of the world. They are playing a major role in toning down the radical religious pluralism that now characterises the world. These include (in no particular order), the World Parliament of Religions, the United Religions Initiative (see the chapter by John in this volume), Religions for Peace, the King Abdullah Bin Abdulaziz International Centre for Interreligious and Intercultural Dialogue (Hereinafter referred to as KAICIID) (see the chapter by Isheanesu S. Gusha in this volume) and others. One of the key areas of engagement that we might readily associate with these global interfaith networks is peacebuilding.

Global Interfaith Networks Focusing on Specific Themes

Some global interfaith networks have emerged to address specific developmental issues. Consequently, the bulk of their activities are located within the particular area of interest. For example, the Women's Interfaith Network concentrates on promoting women's participation in peacebuilding in different parts of the world. Similarly, the Global Network for Children focuses on children's wellbeing throughout the world, as does the Arigatou International. On its part, the Interfaith Rainfall Initiative mobilises faith communities in diverse settings to invest in protecting the environment and responding to climate change. The Global Interfaith Network to End Slavery concentrates on the quest to end human trafficking and modern-day slavery. We have already made reference to INERELA and its focus on addressing HIV and AIDS in different settings across the world.

Global Ecumenical, Denominational and Religion-Specific Organisations

As note earlier, it would be misleading to imagine that only self-declared interfaith networks are involved in activities designed to achieve development. There are some organisations that emerge from a combination of different denominations, particularly from within Christianity (ecumenical) and others from a specific religion (such as Islam) that are doing development work. For example, while it is steeped within the Protestant tradition, the WCC engages in a lot of interfaith work. This is covered in its struggles against racism, peacebuilding, gender injustice, promoting health, pressing for human rights, economic justice, climate justice, migration, and other concerns (for earlier concerns, see for example, Brunn 2001). The WCC's commitment to social justice and diakonia has facilitated such an investment in development work (Belopopsky 2002. See also Chitando 2010). The WCC has a very strong interfaith orientation and promotes collaborative responses to emerging challenges. This thrust also characterises interventions by the Catholic Relief Services and Islamic Relief Worldwide. These two organisations are more actively involved in humanitarian programming and development work.

Regional Interfaith Networks Addressing Particular Concerns

Some interfaith networks operate within specific regions and focus on particular concerns. Here, a region might be defined as an entire continent, sub-continent or a more or less well defined geographical area. Networks addressing pressing issues such as HIV and AIDS, climate change, women's issues and others have often adopted a regional outlook. For example, the Asian Interfaith Network on AIDS, PROCMURA (Programme for Christian-Muslim Relations in Africa) (see the chapter by Iminza and Mombo in this volume) and the Southern African Faith Communities' Environmental Institute (SAFCEI) (see the chapter by Gusha and Gusha in this volume) operate within particular regions. Women's Interfaith Network of the Middle East and North Africa (WIN MENA) works to promote trust and peacebuilding in the MENA region. The African Council of Religious Leaders (ACRL), working for sustainable peace and development throughout the African continent, is another example of a regional entity.

National and Local Interfaith Networks Addressing Broader or Specific Concerns

Recognising the need to amplify national and local realities, there are national and local interfaith networks throughout the world. Some of them seek to promote local action on global issues, while others are preoccupied with addressing developmental issues at the national or local levels. For example, the United States has the National Disaster Interfaith Network (NDIN) which has a proven track record in interfaith urban emergency management.

In most instances, national and local actors are better placed to understand the dynamics and provide more effective responses than international actors who might not have a full appreciation of the complexities at play (see for example, Trotta and Wilkinson 2019). More critically, national and local interfaith networks tend to have greater flexibility to respond to emerging issues than global interfaith networks. For example, national and local interfaith networks were able to respond to the COVID-19 pandemic at very short notice in many settings. Given the devastation caused by the pandemic in some parts of the world, going forward the need for religious leaders to provide hope will become greater (see Hiromo and Blake 2017), alongside transformative reading of sacred texts (Sinn et al. 2017) and oral traditions.

Interfaith Networks and Development: Summarising the Challenges

From the foregoing sections, it is clear that interfaith networks are actively contributing towards the quest to meet the targets of the UN SDGs by 2030. However, there is need to draw attention to some of the major challenges characterizing the operations of the different types of interfaith networks and their development work. It will not be possible to provide a detailed critique in this introductory chapter. Indeed, contributors to this volume have sought to debate this theme in their respective chapters. Here, only some of the major challenges shall be highlighted, alongside making some recommendations.

The Dominance of Global North Christian Actors

Although interfaith networks operate in different parts of the world and new ones are emerging outside the Global North, it remains true that most of the interfaith networks are dominated by Christian actors from the Global North. This is a product of the specific history of interfaith networks, as well as the better financial resources that the Global North have over the global South. The dominance of actors from the Christian tradition tends to marginalize actors from indigenous communities that have suffered at the hands of Christianity. For example, most interfaith initiatives in Africa and North America struggle to include indigenous peace makers and knowledge systems that come from indigenous communities. Therefore, it is vital for interfaith networks to become more inclusive in approach.

Duplication of Activities and Limited Coordination

The increase in the number of interfaith networks undertaking development work is in many senses a welcome development. This has enabled interfaith networks to invest in addressing a wide array of issues and challenges that prevent communities from enjoying health and wellbeing. However, the presence of many players in the same space, sometimes undertaking similar projects, often leads to the challenge of duplication. Furthermore, some interfaith networks do not coordinate their activities effectively, resulting in less than optimal efficiency in the delivery of developmental projects. In other instances, there is an emerging pattern where interfaith networks congregate in one particular country (perhaps due to a more enabling political outlook), while some neighbouring countries would be crying out for development assistance. Better coordination and sharing of plans will result in more effective development by interfaith networks.

The Marginalisation of Women and Youth

Due to the fact that most religions are dominated by men in the formal structures, many interfaith networks end up having more men in leadership positions. This has led to the marginalization of women and youth. However, the reality is that for effective development to happen, it is vital for the capabilities of women and youth to be acknowledged and embraced. Consequently, interfaith networks need to become more intentional about according space to women and young in order to enhance their effectiveness.

Limited Funding

Although some interfaith networks, particularly those with a global outlook, are well funded, this is not the case with many of the emerging ones operating at regional or local levels. Many interfaith networks struggle to meet the expectations of those they seek to serve due to financial constraints. It is important for development actors to make financial contributions towards interfaith network in order to strengthen them in their activities.

CHAPTERS IN THIS VOLUME

The chapters in this volume have been organized into thematically coordinated sections. Chapters in the first section provide theoretical reflections and examples of global/continental interfaith networks engaging in developmental work. Following this Introduction, in Chap. 2, Sokfa John analyses the United Religions Initiative (URI) in West Africa and in Chap. 3, Ahmed Ragab, Emma Rachmawati, Grace Kaiso and Matthias Brucker reflect on contribution of the Faith to Action Network to development with a special focus on Africa. In Chap. 4, Isheanesu S. Gusha reviews the work of King Abdullah Bin Abdulaziz International Centre for Interreligious and Intercultural Dialogue (KAICIID). Florence Iminza and Esther Mombo bring the section to a close in Chap. 5. They focus on the work of the Programme for Christian-Muslim Relations in Africa (PROCMURA) in peacebuilding.

The section that follows focuses on interfaith networks and gender. In Chap. 6, Kathleen McGarvey probes the Women's Interfaith Council in

Northern Nigeria, while in Chap. 7 Klaudia Wilk-Mhagama focuses on the interfaith movement and gender in Tanzania. Fungai Chirongoma reviews the work of the South African Family and Faith Institute (SAFFI) in addressing sexual and gender-based violence in a multi-faith setting in Chap. 8. The challenge of sexual diversity and the tension it breeds is palpable. In Chap. 9, Tshenolo Jennifer Madigele addresses this theme with particular reference to Botswana.

After the section on interfaith networks and gender, the volume's next section presents case studies from selected countries. In Chap. 10, Andrew David Omona details the activities of the Inter-Religious Council of Uganda, while in Chap. 11, Nelly Mwale reviews the impact of the Zambia Interfaith Networking Group (ZINGO). Julio Machele and Mário Jorge Carlos focus on interfaith engagements in Mozambique in Chap. 12 and Samuel Awuah-Nyamekye debates the state of the interfaith movement in Ghana in Chap. 13.

The concluding section provides insights into some of the major themes in studying interfaith networks and development globally. In Chap. 14 Ezekiel A. Babagario analyses the International Centre for Interfaith, Peace and Harmony (ICIPH) in Northern Nigeria. Tapiwa H. Gusha and Isheanesu S. Gusha present the case of the Southern African Faith Communities' Environmental Institute (SAFCEI) in Chap. 15. In Chap. 16, Nomatter Sande brings the volume to a close with his discussion of interfaith communities in the African Diaspora.

Conclusion

Interfaith networks of diverse sizes, with divergent interests and operating in variegated settings, are contributing towards the meeting the targets of the SDGs in Africa. Bringing together actors from different religions and cultures, and sometimes operating across different continents, these interfaith networks are playing a significant role in mobilizing communities and individuals towards profound social transformation. By adopting a broader perspective and covering interfaith networks or initiatives in different parts of Africa, the volume analyses the contribution of interfaith networks to development.

References

Admirand, Peter. 2019. Humbling the Discourse: Why Interfaith Dialogue, Religious Pluralism, Liberation Theology, and Secular Humanism Are Needed for a Robust Public Square. *Religions* 10(450), https://doi.org/10.3390/rel10080450

Adogame, Afe, Olufunke Adeboye and Corey L. Williams. Eds. 2020. *Fighting in God's Name: Religion and Conflict in Local-Global Perspectives.* Lanham, MD: Lexington Books.

Al Qurtuby, Sumanto. 2014. Religious Women for Peace and Reconciliation in Contemporary Indonesia. *International Journal on World Peace* 31(1): 27–58.

Armstrong, Karen. 2015. *Fields of Blood: Religion and the History of Violence.* New York: Anchor Books.

Atiemo, Abamfo. 2003. Zetaheal Mission in Ghana: Christians and Muslims Worshipping Together? *Exchange* 32(1): 15–36.

Bamat, T. et al. Eds. 2017. *Interreligious Action for Peace: Studies in Muslim-Christian Cooperation.* Baltimore, MD: Catholic Relief Services.

Behera, Marina N. 2011. *Interfaith Relations after One Hundred Years: Christian Mission among Other Faiths.* Oxford: Regnum.

Belopopsky, Alexander. Ed. 2002. *From Inter-Church Aid to Jubilee: A brief history of ecumenical diakonia in the World Council of Churches.* Geneva: World Council of Churches Diakonia & Solidarity Documentation.

Biddington, Terry. 2013. Towards a Theological Reading of Multifaith Spaces. *International Journal of Public Theology* 7(3): 315–328.

Blevins, John. 2020. *Christianity's Role in Global Health and Development Policy: To Transfer the Empire of the World.* New York: Routledge.

Bompani, Barbara. 2019. Religion and Development: Tracing the Trajectories of an Evolving Sub-Discipline. *Progress in Development Studies* 19(3): 171–185.

Brunn, Stanley D. 2001. The World Council of Churches as a Global Actor: Ecumenical Space as Geographical Space. *Geographica Slovenica* 34(1): 65–78.

Byamugisha, Gideon B. 2019. *Labors of Love: The Official Biography of Gideon B. Byamugisha.* Kampala: Wilsdom Publishers.

Carbonnier, Gilles et al. Eds. 2013. *International Development Policy: Religion and Development.* New York: Palgrave Macmillan.

Cheetham, David, Douglas Pratt and David Thomas. Eds. 2013. *Understanding Interreligious Relations.* Oxford: Oxford University Press.

Chia, Edmund Kee-Fook. Ed. 2016. *Interfaith Dialogue: Global Perspectives.* New York: Palgrave.

Chitando, Ezra. 2010. Sacred Struggles: The World Council of Churches and the HIV Epidemic in Africa. In Barbara Bompani & Maria Frahm-Arp, eds., *Development and Politics from Below: Exploring Religious Space in the African State*, 218–239. New York: Palgrave Macmillan.

Chitando, Ezra, Masiiwa R. Gunda and Lovemore Togarasei. Eds. 2020. *Religion and Development in Africa*. Bamberg: University of Bamberg Press.

Chitonge, Horman. 2015. *Economic Growth and Development in Africa: Understanding trends and prospects*. London: Routledge.

Christian Aid. 2014. *Ten Years On: A decade of interfaith work promoting good governance and sustainable peace in Kaduna State, Nigeria*. Abuja: Christian Aid Nigeria.

Clarke, Gerard and Michael Jennings. 2008. Introduction, in Gerard Clarke and Michael Jennings, eds., *Development, Civil Society and Faith-Based Organizations Bridging the Sacred and the Secular*. London: Palgrave Macmillan, 1–16.

Cohn-Sherbok, Dan. Ed. 1992. *World Religions and Human Liberation*. Maryknoll, NY: Orbis Books.

Cornille, Catherine. 2013. *The Wiley-Blackwell Companion to Inter-Religious Dialogue*. Eugene: Wipf and Stock.

De La Torre, Miguel A. Ed. 2008. *The Hope for Liberation in the World's Religions*. Waco: Baylor University Press.

Deneulin, Séverine and Carole Rakodi. 2011. Revisiting Religion: Development Studies Thirty Years On. *World Development* 39(4): 45–54.

Fahy, John and Jeffrey Haynes. 2018. Introduction: Interfaith on the World Stage. *The Review of Faith & International Affairs* 16(3): 1–8.

Fahy, John and Jan-Jonathan Bock. Eds. 2019. *The Interfaith Movement: Mobilising Religious Diversity in the 21st Century*. London: Routledge.

Featherstone, Andy. 2015. *Keeping the Faith: The Role of Faith Leaders in the Ebola Response*. London: Christian Aid.

Feener, R. Michael and Philip Fountain. 2018. Religion in the Age of Development. *Religions* 9(382), https://doi.org/10.3390/rel9120382.

Fountain, Philip, Robin Bush and R. Michael Feener. Eds. 2015. *Religion and the Politics of Development*. Basingstoke: Palgrave Macmillan.

Glaab, Katharina. 2017. A Climate for Justice? Faith-based Advocacy on Climate Change at the United Nations. *Globalizations* 14(7): 1110–1124.

Green, M. Christine. Ed. 2019. *Law, Religion and Human Flourishing in Africa*. Stellenbosch: SUN MeDIA.

Halafoff, Anna. 2013. *The Multifaith Movement, Global Risks and Cosmopolitan Solutions*. New York: Springer.

Hasan, Rumy. 2017. *Religion and Development in the Global South*. New York: Palgrave Macmillan.

Heist, Dan and Ram A. Cnaan. 2016. Faith-Based International Development Work: A Review. *Religions* 7(3), 19; https://doi.org/10.3390/rel7030019.

Hiromo, Tatsushi and Michelle E. Blake. 2017. The Role of Religious Leaders in the Restoration of Hope Following Natural Disasters. *SAGE Open* April–June: 1–15.

24   E. CHITANDO

Irvin-Erickson, Douglas and Peter C. Phan. Eds. 2016. *Violence, Religion, Peacemaking*. New York: Palgrave Macmillan.

Khan, H. (2015). Interfaith Contributions to a Just Society. *European Judaism: A Journal for the New Europe* 48(2): 46–53. http://www.jstor.org/stable/43740772.

Knitter, Paul. 2013. Inter-Religious Dialogue and Social Action. In Catherine Cornille, ed., *The Wiley-Blackwell Companion to Inter-Religious Dialogue*. Eugene: Wipf and Stock, 133–148.

Kraft, Kathryn and Olivia J. Wilkinson. Eds. 2020. *International Development and Local Faith Actors: Ideological and Cultural Encounters*. London: Routledge.

Küng, Hans. 1998. *A Global Ethic for Global Politics and Economics*. Trans. John Bowden. New York: Oxford University Press.

Kusuma, Jamuldin H. and Sulistiyono Susilo. 2020. Intercultural and Religious Sensitivity among Young Indonesian Interfaith Groups. *Religions* 11(26); https://doi.org/10.3390/rel11010026.

Lochhead, David. 1988. *The Dialogical Imperative: A Christian Reflection on Interfaith Encounter*. London: SCM Press Ltd.

Lunn, Jenny. 2009. The Role of Religion, Spirituality and Faith in Development: A Critical Theory Approach. *Third World Quarterly* 30(5): 937–951.

Maguire, Daniel C. Ed. 2003. *Sacred Rights: The Case for Contraception and Abortion in World Religions*. Oxford: Oxford University Press.

Marshall, Katherine and Marisa Van Saanen. 2007. *Development and Faith: Where Mind, Heart, and Soul Work Together*. Washington, DC: World Bank.

Marshall, Katherine et al. 2011. *Women in Religious Peacebuilding*. Washington, DC: United States Institute of Peace.

Metz, Thaddeus. 2017. Replacing Development: An Afro-Communal Approach to Global Justice. *Philosophical Papers* 46(1): 111–137.

News24. 2021. Dean, Tahuira. Praying for Patients: Video goes viral of interfaith prayer outside hospital in Cape Town. 10 January. https://www.news24.com/news24/southafrica/news/praying-for-patients-video-goes-viral-of-interfaith-prayer-outside-hospital-in-cape-town-20210110, accessed 12 January 2021.

Nussbaum, C. Martha. 2011. *Creating Capabilities: The Human Development Approach*. London: Harvard University Press.

Ojo, Matthews A. and Folaranmi T. Lateju. 2010. Christian-Muslim Conflicts and Interfaith Bridge-Building Efforts in Nigeria. *The Review of Faith in International Affairs* 8(1): 31–38.

Olarinmoye, Omobolaji O. 2012. Faith-Based Organizations and Development: Prospects and Constraints. *Transformation* 29: 1–14.

Omotosho, Mashood. 2014. Managing Religious Conflicts in Nigeria: The Inter-Religious Mediation Peace Strategy. *Africa Development* 39(2): 133–151.

Orton, Andrew. 2016. Interfaith dialogue: seven key questions for theory, policy and practice. *Religion, State & Society* 44(4): 349–365.

Pereira, Charmaine and Jibrin Ibrahim. 2010. On the Bodies of Women: the common ground between Islam and Christianity in Nigeria. *Third World Quarterly* 31(6): 921–937.

Prozesky, Martin. 1984. *Religion and Ultimate Well Being: An Explanatory Theory*. New York: St Martin's Press.

Rautenbach, Ignatius, Guillermo Kerber and Christoph Stückelberger. Eds. 2014. *Religions for Climate Justice. International Interfaith Statements 2008–2014*. Geneva: Globethics.net.

Religions 2019 and 2020. Special Issue, Multifaith Spaces in Global Perspectives 10(9), 11(3) and 11(9).

Saggiomo, Valeria. 2012. Islamic NGOs in Africa and their Notion of Development: The Case of Somalia. *Storicamente* 8, art. 16, 12 pages.

Sapkota, Mahendra and Mahesh Tharu. 2016. Development as a 'Contested Discourse': An Overview. *Nepalese Journal of Development and Rural Studies* 13(1): 13–28.

Seiple, Chris. 2016. What Faith Can do for Global Systemic Challenges. In World Economic Forum, ed., *The Role of Faith in Systemic Global Challenges*. Geneva: World Economic Forum, 5–6.

Sen, Armatya. 1999. *Development as Freedom*. New York: Oxford University Press.

Shannahan, Chris and Laura Payne. 2016. *Faith-based Interventions in Peace, Conflict and Violence: A Scoping Study*. Washington, DC: Joint Learning Initiative on Faith & Local Communities.

Sharma, Arvind and Kathrine K. Young. Eds. 2007. *Fundamentalism and Women in World Religions*. London: T & T Clark.

Shoko, Tabona. 2007. *Karanga Indigenous Religion: Health and Well-being*. Aldershot: Ashgate.

Sinn, Simone, Dina El Omari and Anne Hege Grunn. Eds. 2017. *Transformative Reading of Sacred Scriptures: Christians and Muslims in Dialogue*. Geneva: Lutheran World Federation.

Soares, Jair, Jr and Rogério H. Quintella. 2008. Development: An Analysis of Concepts, Measurement and Indicators. *Brazilian Administrative Review (BAR) Curitiba* 5(2): 104–124.

Spies, Eva and Paula Schrode. 2021. Religious Engineering: Exploring Projects of Transformation from a Relational Perspective. *Religion* 51(1): 1–18, https://doi.org/10.1080/0048721X.2020.1792053

Swart, Ignatius and Elsabe Nell. 2016. Religion and Development: The Rise of a Bibliography. *HTS Teologiese Studies/Theological Studies*, https://doi.org/10.4102/hts.v72i4.3862

Tarusarira, J. (2020). Religion and the Critique of Human Security. In Joram Tarusarira and Ezra Chitando (Eds.), *Themes in Religion and Human Security in Africa*. London: Routledge, 14–26.

Tarusarira, Joram and Ezra Chitando. Eds. 2020. *Themes in Religion and Human Security in Africa*. London: Routledge.

Ter Haar, Gerrie. Ed. 2011. *Religion and Development: Ways of Transforming the World*. London: Hurst and Company.

Ter Haar, Gerrie and James J. Busuttil. Eds. 2005. *Bridge or Barrier? Religion, Violence and Visions for Peace*. Leiden: Brill.

The UN Inter-Agency Task Force on Engaging Faith-Based Actors for Sustainable Development/UN Task Force on Religion and Development. 2018. *Engaging Religion and Faith-based Actors on Agenda 2030/The SDGs 2017: Annual Report*. New York: The UN Inter-Agency Task Force on Engaging Faith-Based Actors for Sustainable Development/UN Task Force on Religion and Development.

Todd, Nathan R. et al. 2017. Interfaith Groups as Mediating Structures for Political Action: A Multilevel Analysis. *American Journal of Community Psychology*, **59**(1–2): 106–119. https://doi.org/10.1002/ajcp.12121.

Tomalin, Emma. Ed. 2015. *The Routledge Handbook of Religion and Global Development*. London: Routledge.

Tomalin, Emma, Jörg Haustein and Shabaana Kidy. 2019. Religion and the Sustainable Development Goals. *The Review of Faith & International Affairs* 17(2): 102–118.

Trotta, S. and O. Wilkinson. 2019. *Partnering with Local Faith Actors to Support Peaceful and Inclusive Societies*. Washington DC; Bonn: Joint Learning Initiative on Faith and Local Communities; International Partnership on Religion and Sustainable Development (PaRD).

UNAIDS. 2019. *A Common Vision: Faith Based Partnerships to Sustain Progress Against HIV*. Geneva: UNAIDS.

UNFPA. 2009. *Global Forum of Faith-based Organisations for Population and Development*. New York: UNFPA.

UNICEF. 2012. *Partnering with Religious Communities for Children*. New York: UNICEF.

United States Institute of Peace (USIP). 2004. *What Works? Evaluating Interfaith Dialogue Programs*. Special Report 123. Washington, DC: USIP.

Wallis, Roy. 1984. *The Elementary Forms of the New Religious Life*. London: Routledge and Keegan and Paul.

Williams, Corey L. 2019. Chrislam, Accommodation and the Politics of Religious *Bricolage* in Nigeria. *Studies in World Christianity* 25(1): 5–28.

Winkler, Tanja. 2008. When God and Poverty Collide: Exploring the Myths of Faith-sponsored Community Development. *Urban Studies* 45(10): 2099–2116.

World Faiths Development Dialogue (WFDD). 2017. *Interfaith Journeys: An Exploration of History, Ideas, and Future Directions*. Washington, DC: WFDD.

World Faiths Development Dialogue (WFDD). 2018. *Faith and Development in Focus: Nigeria*. Washington, DC: WFDD.

CHAPTER 2

Exploring Interfaith Networks in the Context of Development: Key Considerations

Sokfa F. John

INTRODUCTION: SOCIAL NETWORKS, RELIGION AND DEVELOPMENT

Religions and religious organization have long featured in development debates and practice (Deneulin 2013; Carbonnier 2016; Swart and Nell 2016; Deneulin and Zampini-Davies 2017; Amanze et al. 2019). While the positive role and value of religion in development is increasingly acknowledged, scholars, practitioners, institutions and governments have been widely criticized for the ways they have understood and applied religion and development, both as concepts and as practice. For example, Jones and Petersen (2011) argued that religion has been approached instrumentally, focusing on how it can be *used* for better development practice, which is further demonstrated in a narrow focus on faith-based organizations. They also note that some approaches have utilized problematic conceptions of both religion and development, with donors and development agencies being the major driving force for defining and

---

S. F. John (✉)
University of KwaZulu-Natal, Durban, South Africa

© The Author(s), under exclusive license to Springer Nature
Switzerland AG 2022
E. Chitando, I. S. Gusha (eds.), *Interfaith Networks and Development*, Sustainable Development Goals Series,
https://doi.org/10.1007/978-3-030-89807-6_2

27

utilizing religion for development (Jones and Petersen 2011). Atiemo (2017) decried the lack of attention to religion by policy-makers and development practitioners, despite available information on the relevance of religion to African society and politics. Atiemo (2017) argues that while the little attention given to religion has focused on public religious personalities and institutions, spiritual capital (beliefs and ritual) could add immense value to social capital and needs more policy and development attention.

Religious communities and networks are among the easiest ways through which developmental processes can reach and include people at the grassroots, the marginalized and those in rural and peri-urban areas. The Sustainable Development Goal of achieving greater equality by 2030 (Goal 10) can be a more inclusive process by taking advantage of religious networks and communities to accommodate the perspectives and realities of the grassroots in the process. This is because such people often belong to religious communities. Local religious centres and leaders are among the most accessible institutions in many such communities. In many places, religious communities and organizations serve as the bridges between the people and their political leaders, and as the media through which the voices of the poor, marginalized and unjustly treated reach appropriate authorities (Rakodi 2016; Root et al. 2017). Religion is an important symbol within, and around which people mobilize and collaborate for social change and transformation. Religious values shape the attitude and practice of adherents involved in the development and the pursuit of equality.

By their nature, interfaith networks have immense potential to impact and transform development and reduce inequalities within and between societies and nations. Todd et al. (2015), for example, in their affiliation social network analysis of interfaith groups, demonstrate that interfaith groups contribute to the empowerment of communities and link members to resources within and beyond the community to promote change. They note that interfaith networks could be seen as a part of the social fabric of communities as well as partners and sources of resources of change. In this chapter development is broadly understood as defined by the United Nations in terms of multidimensional activities and processes aimed at achieving a higher quality of life for everyone; and as concretized in the United Nation's 2030 agenda for sustainable development (United Nations 2015; Kurtas n.d.). Religious networks in the context of the Sustainable Development Goals (SDGs), may be viewed as platforms that could immensely empower members and ultimately advance the social, political, and economic inclusion of all people regardless of their religion, race, status, gender, sex and other differences (SDG 10.2). The influence of such networks on the social and political spheres can enable them to push for policies and adequate representation of marginalized voices in order to achieve greater equality and inclusion (SDGs 10.4 & 10.6). By their nature, networks tend to link and reveal overlaps of actors, issues, interests and goals, as will be visible in this chapter. Thus, the issues that will be considered in this chapter will be relevant to several SDGs.

This chapter applies Exploratory Social Network Analysis (ESNA) to study the United Religions Initiative (URI), a large network uniting over a thousand organizations around the world for development and social impact based on collaboration among adherents of diverse faiths. The Chapter utilized the rich publicly available information and documents on the URI Website, including the URI Charter and data on global membership. Focusing on the URI network in West Africa and the fourteen URI action areas, I highlight some key dynamics of social and interfaith networks to consider when reflecting on the interface between interfaith networks and development, and how these networks could inform development practice and produce greater equality. The exploration of the network also reveals important insights on the advantages, challenges and opportunities that interfaith networks could offer sustainable development processes.

The United Religions Initiative (URI)

The URI defines itself as "a global grassroots interfaith network that cultivates peace and justice by engaging people to bridge religious and cultural differences to work together for the good of their communities and the world" (https://uri.org/). The idea of the network was inspired when the Episcopal Bishop, William E. Swing, was invited by the United Nations in 1993 to host an interfaith service for its 50th anniversary. Between 1993 and 2000 the URI was created as a global good organization based on shared spiritual values. The URI Charter was written during this time. It outlines the vision, purpose, principles and structure of the organization, as well as the rights and responsibilities of members and guidelines for membership and action. According to the Charter, the purpose of the URI "is to promote enduring, daily interfaith cooperation, to end religiously motivated violence and to create cultures of peace, justice and healing for the Earth and all living beings" (URI n.d.-a). The URI strategy is to implement its mission through Cooperation Circles. These are grassroots groups that bring people of different faiths together to collaborate on community action. To join the URI as an organization or create a new Cooperation Circle, the organization requests that there be a minimum of seven members belonging to at least three different religions or spiritual expressions. At the time of writing, the URI website indicated that it had 1052 Cooperation Circles. A regional search on the website indicated that 233 of these Cooperation Circles were in Africa, 393 in Asia, 60 in Europe, 58 in Latin America and the Caribbean, 88 in the Middle East and North Africa, 91 in North America, 54 in South East Asia and the Pacific, and 75 were Multiregional.

While there are resource and other forms of support and interaction among Cooperation Circles, they each make their own decisions about how they organize, how they are governed, priority action areas and strategy. All the activities and projects of Cooperation Circles serve one or more of the URI's fourteen action areas. These include Arts, Community Building, Education, Environment, Health and Social Services, Human Rights, Indigenous Peoples, Interfaith and Intercultural Dialogue, Media, Peacebuilding and Conflict Transformation, Policy Advocacy, Poverty Alleviation and Economic Opportunity, Women, and Youth (URI n.d.-b). The URI is highly visible due to its broad network of affiliation and Cooperation Circles as well as the consultative status it has with the United Nations Economic and Social Council (ECOSOC) and several partnerships across UN agencies. The URI website is rich with frequently updated information and media about the activities of its Cooperation Circles around the world. The Circles of Light page on the URI website displays a planned event featuring a documentary episode on the work of URI around the world and a keynote speech by a co-founder of one of the Cooperation Circles in Uganda which helps women who were previously kidnapped and used as sex slaves. This indicates some level of organized interaction in the network. Also, the URI celebrates the International Day of Peace every year, and reports can be found on the website on how the Cooperation Circles in the global community have marked this day since 2009 through diverse peace education and promotion activities.

Web content shows that in Africa, Cooperation Circles are actively engaging many issues at policy and grassroots levels. These issues include peacebuilding, healthcare, education, environment, youth empowerment, HIV and AIDS, human trafficking, hate speech and violent extremism.

URI Africa region has a close working relationship with the Economic, Social and Cultural Council, and the Citizens and Diaspora Directorate of the African Union. It also has signed Memoranda of Understanding with several African Union departments and units. According to the URI Africa website, leaders in "sustainable peace, development, environmental protection, democracy, reconciliation, inter-religious and inter-cultural harmony, and peaceful co-existence", have been recognized with the URI's African Peace Award since 2007.

MODELLING THE URI NETWORK IN WEST AFRICA

Since the URI is a large network with hundreds of members, I focused on the URI ties in West Africa for more meaningful exploration. The use of the URI network, in this case, is primarily for illustrative purposes. The objective was not to make conclusions, generalizations or test any hypothesis about the URI. Therefore, I have utilized a combination of simple exploratory network analysis and calculations of frequency to explore the relations between Cooperation Circles and action areas in West Africa based on data produced from the URI website content. West African countries with Cooperation Circles include Burkina Faso, Cote d'Ivoire, Gambia, Liberia, Nigeria, Sierra Leone and Togo.

Network analysis involves a visual representation of real-world ties using a graph, which consists of nodes or vertices (points) and edges (lines), as well as additional information (attributes) on the nodes and edges (Zweig 2016; Serrat 2017). The lines or edges on the graph indicate *relations* between nodes (actors or events) which is a mathematical relation calculated to reflect the *relationship* in the real world (Zweig 2016). However, the *relations* do not have to correlate to the real-world *relationships* and can sometimes depict relationships that are not considered to be meaningful in the real-world (Zweig 2016). Thus, while the relations represented in this chapter aimed to reflect some characteristics of the real-world relationships of the URI, they do not necessarily reflect all of these real-world relationships or dynamics such as distance or proximity.

Affiliation network analysis was used because it is concerned with the membership of organizations, participation in events or multiple belonging to groups, which is consistent with the aim of this study (De Nooy et al. 2018). Social network analysis makes it possible to map and measure interaction and to uncover relationship principles with implication for social transformation, action and behaviour. The assumption in social network analysis is that the ties—interpersonal, inter-organizational and otherwise—matter, and are channels through which behaviour, information, goods and attitudes are transmitted (De Nooy et al. 2018). The goal of social network analysis is, thus, to identify and interpret the patterns in these social ties. The exploratory analysis assumes that the patterns of ties and structure of the interfaith network, as with other social networks, are, at least, meaningful to members. Thus, exploring these meaningful patterns can reveal important lessons in the context of development goals.

Publicly available data about the names of Cooperation Circles, their location, religious and spiritual traditions, number of members and their action areas were scraped both manually and with the help of a Google Chrome browser extension, Web Scraper. I retained the exact labels of categories used on the site for religious traditions and spirituality and action areas to avoid distorting the connections implied by the URI and its members. The network graph was created in Gephi 0.9.2, an open-source network analysis software. The network is based on affiliations represented in terms of the relations between Cooperation Circles (actors) and action areas (events). Thus, because it is an affiliation network, as opposed to other types of networks, the ties among Cooperation Circles are not represented or explored.

Network Description

Figure 2.1 shows the affiliation network of the URI in West Africa. It should be noted from the onset that network graphs are appealing because one can generally make sense of them and interpret them through visual inspection. However, to the extent that it is important, precise details and calculations are necessary (De Nooy et al. 2018). As stated earlier, my exploratory approach and illustrative use of the URI network does not require much precision in interpretation. However, I draw on other details from the data to explain the relations and nodes in the network whenever this is helpful.

The network (Fig. 2.1) shows the relations between Cooperation Circles and action areas. The nodes represent both the Cooperation Circles and the action areas. The nodes are labelled using IDs instead of names to avoid overcrowding the network and make the relations more visible. Thus, nodes 1–50 represent each of the fifty Cooperation Circles in West Africa and nodes 51–64 represent the action areas of the

2 EXPLORING INTERFAITH NETWORKS IN THE CONTEXT... 33

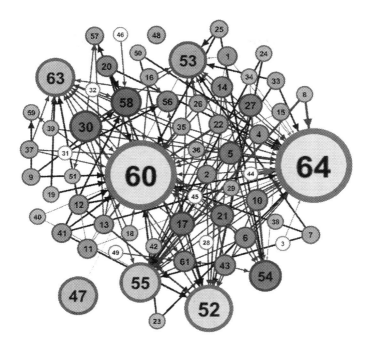

Fig. 2.1 Affiliation network of URI Cooperation Circles and Action Areas in West Africa. (By the author)

URI. Hence, Arts is 51; Community Building–52; Education–53; Environment–54; Health and Social Services–55; Human rights–56; Indigenous People–57; Interfaith and Intercultural Dialogue–58; Media–59; Peacebuilding and Conflict Transformation–60; Policy Advocacy–61; Poverty Alleviation and Economic Opportunities–62; Women–63, and Youth–64.

In the above network, because the relations type is *directed* and the direction is only from Cooperation Circle nodes to action area nodes, the arrowheads of the edges (lines) are only pointed at action areas. The relations are *directed* because my aim is to show how Cooperation Circles are connected only by the issues they address and not by other types of relations. The weight of the edges is also important as it can be observed that some lines are thicker than others on the graph. The weight was computed using the number of religions involved in each case of affiliation. Thus, the thicker the lines, the more the number of religious or spiritual traditions involved in the Cooperation Circles working on the specific action area the line is directed to. For example, Node 25 at the top side of the network represents Mulapnen Capacity Global Services (MCGS), a Cooperation Circle based in Nigeria. The thickness of the edge from this node to Node 53 (Education) indicates that people from more than one religious tradition (four: Islam, Indigenous, Earth-Based, Christianity) are collaborating based on shared spiritual values to address issues relating to education through the MCGS. Compare this to the edge connecting the African Christian Youth Development Fund in Nigeria (Node 8) to Youth (Node 64). There is only one edge from Node 8 and it goes to 64, which shows that this Cooperation Circle is only involved in one action area, which is youth development. Additionally, the line is comparatively thin. It is much thinner than the previous example, indicating that members from fewer religious traditions are involved, in this case, Christianity and Islam.

The edges in the above network generally show that an average of three religions is associated with the URI action areas in the West African sub-region. People from a total of eleven religious, spiritual and value traditions are collaborating in the sub-region to address issues related to the URI action areas. These are Christianity, Islam, Indigenous Religions, Buddhism, Baha'i, Cultural, Hinduism, Atheists, Earth-Based, Judaism, and Spirituality. Spirituality was used to refer to new religious movements, and there was no indication of whether "Cultural" and "Earth-based" referred to what may be generally regarded as indigenous religions.

The most involved religions are Christianity, Islam and Indigenous Religions. As indicated in Fig. 2.2, Christianity has a stronger presence than the other two, except in Ghana and Togo where they are equally involved and in places like Burkina Faso where there is equal involvement of Islam and Christianity. However, this does not reveal much as these places have very few Cooperation Circles. Burkina Faso, for example, only has one. Nigeria appears to have more involvement in the three religions. However, this is because 70% (n = 35) of the 50 Cooperation Circles in West Africa are in Nigeria.

Thus, the strengths of religious participation correspond to the number of Cooperation Circles providing the platform for interfaith collaboration for local action. The figures are also fairly consistent with the distribution of religions in the sub-region, with Islam, Christianity and Indigenous traditions considered the dominant and, to different degrees, more

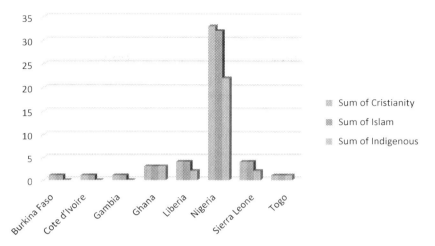

Fig. 2.2 Religions associated with more than 8 Cooperation Circle in each country

publicly active religions, while smaller religions are relatively unknown to many. The majority of people in Africa identify as either Muslims or Christians, and only about 3% identify as belonging to indigenous traditions, and even fewer as belong to other religious traditions (Pew Research Centre 2010). However, it is well established that indigenous religions enjoy high participation by people who publicly identify as Christians or Muslims (Chiorazzi 2015).

The size of the network nodes in Fig. 2.1 are also important as they reflect degrees. The action area node sizes indicate the degrees to which relevant issues are addressed by the total number of Cooperation Circles in West Africa. Thus, a visual inspection shows clearly that youth (Node 64) is the most addressed area in the sub-region followed respectively by Peacebuilding and Conflict Transformation (Node 60), Education (52) and Health and Social Services (55). Areas such as Arts (51), Media (59) and Indigenous People (57) receive comparatively very little attention. Interestingly, no Cooperation Circle is working on Poverty Alleviation and Economic Opportunities (62). This is a limitation in terms of the role that the URI in West Africa plays in reducing economic inequalities.

However, it is difficult to make any major conclusions about this because the types of projects and programmes that the Cooperation

Circles implement often overlap in the real world. For example, the work being done in the area of youth (64) in places with a history of violent conflicts and extremism, are likely to include economic empowerment and strategies to reduce poverty among the youth to reduce their availability for and the appeal of violent groups. This is because poverty and unemployment among young people are factors in social conflicts and violence in the sub-region (Surajo and Karim 2016; Tlou 2016; Musa et al. 2017; Adekoya and Razak 2018). Thus, youth empowerment work in the context of peace and security has implications for achieving greater social, economic and political equality and vice versa.

The node size of Cooperation Circles (1–50) shows the extent to which a Cooperation Circle is involved in the URI action areas, measured by the number of action areas. For example, Node 47, Women's International Leagues for Peace and Freedom, Sierra Leone, at the bottom of the network, is the biggest Cooperation Circle node. While the connecting edges are hardly visible because they do not carry much weight as only one religion (Christianity) is involved, the size indicates that this organization has the most diversified action areas (eleven out of 14). However, a visualization of the network according to a total number of Cooperation Circles in a country will place Nigeria as the most diversified because it has 70% of the Cooperation Circles in West Africa involved in 13 of the 14 action areas. Also, the behaviour of the nodes and edges, to a large extent, may correspond to some of the most pressing issues in each country as perceived by the Cooperation Circles or presented in public discourse.

Several other patterns can be identified and interpreted through a closer look at the network. This is an indication of the rich potential of social networks in understanding society, relationships, attitudes, behaviours and their implication for issues that matter to communities. The patterns in this representation of the URI network and their areas of action and interest do not necessarily give a true or full picture of what is obtainable in the real world. It cannot be used to make conclusions about the accuracy of the action areas in reflecting the exact work of Cooperation Circles or whether these Cooperation Circles are active in their communities. Nonetheless, the interfaith network graph offers us a global analytical perspective for thinking about interfaith networks, their strengths, weaknesses, and the opportunities they present for sustainable developmental practice and theory.

Considerations for Interfaith Collaboration in the Context of Development

Based on this representation of the URI West Africa network, I now highlight key factors to consider in understanding the structure, role and contributions of interfaith networks, and in exploring their potential for sustainable development with reference reducing inequalities.

Spiritual and Value Foundation

Interfaith networks are similar to other social networks and can be analysed using metrics applied to other social networks. Yet, at the heart of interfaith networks is the fact that they rest on diverse religious beliefs, practices and assumptions. People of different religions, which in some contexts have antagonistic relationships, are linked by common interests, goals, activities, beliefs or situations beyond their differences and sometimes collaborating towards a common goal. Religions are often implicated in violent conflicts and several other social problems, including the aggravation of inequalities, partly because they can elicit strong commitments and serve as powerful platforms for mobilizing people (Brubaker 2015; Beyers 2018). Many people feel strongly about their religious beliefs and practices, and these tend to shape their values and behaviours in almost every other aspects of their lives. Thus, the ability to connect across religious and spiritual traditions for support or common purpose; or to explore existing connections for common good is a potentially powerful force for impact. This is one of the strengths of the URI network, illustrated in the weight of the edges (Fig. 2.1) and the bars in Fig. 2.2. It enables actors to contribute in different ways using different strategies and at grassroots and higher levels of social structure and relations. The URI Charter outlines principles, values, responsibilities, action areas and mission that actors from different spiritual and value orientations could identify with and commit to as core to their unique spiritual tradition and allowing them to connect to others without undermining their unique religious values.

Network Size

The size and connectivity of the nodes in a network determine the value of the network (De Nooy et al. 2018). Actors often have limited capacity and resources for developing and sustaining ties within a network. This makes the size of the network crucial to social structure and relations (Serrat 2017). The size is usually determined by the number of nodes. The URI West Africa network is relatively big with 64 nodes including 50 actors and 14 events, and the URI global network is much larger. The size reveals the number of possible connections in the network, factors that determine connection choices in light of limited resources, and the extent to which actors can be directly or indirectly connected to each other (De Nooy et al. 2018; Knoke and Yang 2019). The smaller a network the more likely there are to be direct connections between actors or between actors and events. Affiliation networks also make it possible for actors who are not connected to connect through events. In the URI affiliation network (Fig. 2.1), the ties between actors (Cooperation Circles) was not mapped or explored, although there are indications on the URI website that some actors support each other and collaborate based on their proximity or through formal global events. The events (action areas), however, link Cooperation Circles through shared interests and objectives. These can further serve as channels for creating clusters and promoting other types of support and collaboration among Cooperation Circles with shared action areas. Otherwise, the URI is a large network with limited chances of direct quantitative connections between actors. The size of the network and nature of connections can be insightful on the actual connections and the opportunities for more connections and collaboration.

Connectedness

The connectedness of a network offers many opportunities to understand and take advantage of social relationships and structure for sustainable development. One might look at, for example, which actors are sources of connections and which ones are sinks. The latter are those that receive connections but do not return them (De Nooy et al. 2018). They may be sources for other actors or events but sinks for others. Much can be known about how actors perceive each other or how some actors and events are perceived by other actors. They can also offer insight into the dominant worldviews in the network. Since the inter-actor ties were not examined in the URI West Africa network, much cannot be said here about how actors perceive each other. However, much can be inferred about which events (action areas) are considered important, priority, or urgent in specific countries and the sub-region as a whole. Other factors, such as capacity and resources, which shape and constrain priorities or choices of action areas can be explored. Any of these factors or contextual issues could, for example, explain why Node 64 (Youth) and Node 60 (Peacebuilding and Conflict Resolution) are the most connected events in Nigeria and West Africa. Yet, a closer look at the action areas shows that they overlap in many ways. Thus, understanding the nature of connectedness can enable deliberate re-channelling of network advantages and resources to address overlooked developmental issues or priority areas that are more likely to have trickled down effect on other areas.

In addition to indicating similarities, shared interests, activities or goals, the number and type of connections that actors or events have can be grounds for differentiation and stratification both analytically and in practice (Hanneman and Riddle n.d.). Just as actors can collaborate on action areas, they can form clusters and withhold support based on how different they perceive other actors or action areas to be. Thus, while ultimately, the actors and events in a network are indirectly linked to each other, significant divisions and conflicts can exist within a network. Being connected does not automatically render certain differences, prejudices and conflicts of interests irrelevant. This is important for interfaith networks such as the URI in places like Nigeria where religion can be strongly bound to ethnicity, politics, socio-economic inequalities and competitive advantage in several spheres of life, and therefore, often implicated in violent conflicts, extremism, corruption and crime (Jega 2000; Osaghae and Suberu 2005; John 2018). In such contexts, actors need to take deliberate steps to avoid accentuating differences linked to religious identity or practice and promote healthy communication and dialogue. Additionally, while URI West Africa network reveals a stronger interconnectedness among Muslims, Indigenous practitioners and Christians, who are more likely to collaborate for action, it also reveals opportunities to collaborate beyond these three traditions. There were indications that Atheists, Buddhists, Baha'i, Hindus and new religious movements, are involved in some Cooperation Circles. These religions and orientations appear to be often ignored as they are less visible in West Africa, have fewer numbers and lesser public influence. Deliberate attempts to promote connection across other religions in the region, no matter how insignificant they appear, will create learning opportunities that could transform interactions among the major faith traditions and their role in society. Such efforts will also make the network exemplary in terms of attempts to reduce social, political and economic inequalities. Ultimately, the idea that human beings can cooperate beyond their differences to achieve common goals underlie such interfaith networks like the URI. These values are better communicated when enshrined in the structure and formation of the network itself with every faith orientation and religion feeling welcomed, included and accepted.

Thus, the number and type of ties of a network is a very important metric. It also shows the embeddedness and level of integration of the actors and events in the network and could indicate cohesion solidarity, complexity, social organization, power and influence of actors and the potential of the network to inform and constrain behaviour and outcome (De Nooy et al. 2018; Knoke and Yang 2019).

Multiplicity of Affiliations

Affiliations are an expression of institutional arrangement and affiliation networks reveal a lot about society because society is shaped by institutions (De Nooy et al. 2018). And because religion as an institution is an important source of engagement with and knowledge about society (Beckford 2019; Rakodi 2019), interfaith networks of affiliation such as the URI network, could contain many important lessons about the different societies in which they are located. Actors often have multiple affiliations at the same time, making them the point of intersection of several organizations and social circles (De Nooy et al. 2018). The URI West Africa network graph only represents the affiliations of actors to events. The actors are organizations in this case. While the organizations are affiliated to many action areas, they are—through their work, missions or formal membership—also affiliated to other events and organizations outside those listed in the URI network. Some of the Cooperation Circles are organizations that were not primarily established for interfaith collaboration but to address specific needs in their communities, which places them in different sets of networks. The religious diversity of their membership allowed them to join the URI network and enjoy the opportunities it affords. At the global, regional, national and local levels, the URI network and actors are connected to other institutions and events including through the United Nations, the African Union, private corporations, civil society organizations and governments, which themselves belong to other networks. The individual members of each of the URI network also belong to several other networks at the individual level. The total reported number of individuals belonging to the different Cooperation Circles in West

Africa is 4863. If the affiliation of each member outside the URI is taken into account, the network will be massive with endless opportunities.

While the number of actors within a network or within the broader extended network does not tell us which actors and individuals interact or communicate, it is plausible to assume that the chance that they will interact is significant (De Nooy et al. 2018). This is partly because affiliations can indicate not only multiple memberships of different organizations, but also similarities of people, interests, social circles, shared social platforms and status. Additionally, the more the number of members of organizations or events share, the closer these organizations are socially (De Nooy et al. 2018). For example, since most of the URI West Africa members are Christians, Muslims and Indigenous religious adherents, the URI West Africa can be said to be a part of the dominant religious domain in West Africa with implication for the place and influence of this religious sphere in the political, cultural and economic structures and life of West Africa and constituent individual countries in varying degrees. The same could be said of the URI. The fact that URI members in West Africa are mostly found among these three religions could mean that these religions dominate the policy and praxis influence of the URI in West Africa. Chances are that more of the underlying values and preferences that shape the contributions of the URI to different spheres of governance, civil society and grassroots work can be traced to these religions than to any other. While this indicates the enormous potential for positive influence, it also reveals the potential for exclusion and for power and influence to reside among a few members of a few religions. It also increases the chances that specific developments or outcomes could represent the visions of a few religious traditions based on the subjective understanding of the members involved in the process.

Brokerage

Social relations and networks are also channels for diffusion of information, goods and services (De Nooy et al. 2018). Thus, the social network can be informative on how information, goods, behaviour and attitude spread or diffuse within a network or system. The nature of the network could determine the pace at which the diffusion takes place, and the size and connectivity could determine the extent of spread of diffusion this informs. This perspective on social networks is widely used to understand online social media networks (Bourigault et al. 2016; Jalali et al. 2016).

42   S. F. JOHN

The International Day of Peace celebration of the URI could partially illustrate brokerage. URI Cooperation Circles around the world organize different events to mark this day, which are shared using images, videos and text summaries on the URI website. In a way, the UN's vision of peace which informed its decision to set out a day for peace is being diffused through the URI network. The URI is a decentralized network, therefore, a brokerage may not operate as in centralized networks, but through affiliations of Cooperation Circles, and individual members both within and beyond the URI, much good can be diffused. Interfaith networks offer immense potential for spreading relevant messages to the most marginal of society. Their links to churches, mosques and various local religious centres and communities which are often closer to the people is an asset.

Centrality and Centralization

Centrality and centralization are among the most common ways of analysing social networks. Centralization addresses the extent of integration of the nodes in a network. Thus, a highly centralized network would have clear boundaries between the centre and periphery, making the centre necessary for diffusion (De Nooy et al. 2018). Centrality is about the position of specific nodes or actors within a network and the implication of such positioning (Zweig 2016). It tells us which actors are more important within a network. Having many connections has several advantages including access to information, resources and support, as well as usefulness for the diffusion of social goods and information. It indicates the extent of an actor's social capital or sociability (Hanneman and Riddle n.d.). Thus, in considering interfaith networks for development, it is important to look at how centralized a network is, and the centrality of individual actors and the challenges and opportunities they bring. A decentralized network can allow for a more diversified and contextual approach to solutions but can make the diffusion of specific goods or information more challenging than a centralized network. For example, the URI can respond to needs in a locally relevant way because Cooperation Circles make these decisions and operate independently. But coordinating all members of the network towards a specific action may be very challenging. Because the URI West Africa network graph is represented by affiliation, we cannot tell which actors are central relative to other actors. However, as shown earlier, some events are more central to others because of the number of edges directed at them, giving them higher degrees of importance than others. But this has to be interpreted contextually. Also, if the graph were to show a degree of affiliation based on country, Nigeria would be the most central because it has the highest number of Cooperation Circles and the most connection to action areas. Countries like Cote d'Ivoire and Togo would be least central. Centrality raise critical questions about power, marginality, inclusion and equality. Interfaith networks need to constantly reflect on these with regards to the relationships among actors as well as among issues and the links between issues and actors. It also raises questions about prioritization, how central issues are determined, and which issues resources limited resources should be directed.

Centrality does not only offer power and advantage. Central actors may experience more pressure to deliver, more workload and are more likely to be used by others. This can be a source of profit but also stress. In the case of the URI West Africa affiliation network, the central action areas may indicate the most pressing or urgent issues as perceived by actors. They could also indicate the areas that actors believe that when addressed, would impact positively on other action areas. However, several ties alone do not always indicate centrality (De Nooy et al. 2018). An actor may have many or strong connections with actors that also have similar ties among themselves. Such ties may constitute an asset but in some cases are not as useful as fewer or weaker ties with actors that have no connection to each other (De Nooy et al. 2018). These weaker ties open the network up for new and diverse information and opportunities, rather than the same being recycled within a network where all actors have ties with each other. Also, actors with ties that are not all connected among themselves can play mediation roles when the need arises.

Conclusion

Some other metrics and variables would yield more insight into the URI network and other interfaith networks. I have focused here on a few to analyse the URI network to illustrate the many advantages, challenges and opportunities of approaching sustainable development through interfaith networks. I have avoided making specific conclusions about the URI in the real world because this would require further additional empirical work either on available data or involving members directly. However, the self-reported activities and the extensive connection of the URI network makes it plausible to conclude that it contributes in very important ways to development in different communities across the world. But more importantly, the URI network offers a model of developmental participation in a broad range of issues in many locations and contexts and from the local to a global level. The network also offers a model for finding agendas and practice through which to bridge divisions and promote collaboration. The limited participation of religions beyond Christianity, Islam and Indigenous religions in West Africa potentially challenge the ability of the network to make contributions that accommodate members of all religions. This is, perhaps, partly balanced by the fact that interfaith collaboration of the network, in principle, is based on values that are shared across religions. However, interfaith networks must pursue greater representation and inclusion internally, as well as greater equality among the communities and nations represented in its networks. This way, its wider objectives will be pursued with a sound understanding of inclusion and equality, and the need to see these manifested in other spheres of life. Finally, although there are far more URI Cooperation Circles in Africa than in Europe and America, the organization has maintained its headquarters in the United States. This could be for practical logistical purposes, and also of no practical significance as it is a decentralized organization. However, it calls for a critical reflection on questions of power and equality within the URI, and the implication of these for its objectives. It also indicates that much more about the URI could be explored for important lessons on interfaith networks.

Acknowledgments The author acknowledges the National Research Foundation for its support through the SARChI in Sustainable Local Livelihoods.

REFERENCES

Adekoya, A.F. and Razak, N.A.A. 2018. Unemployment and Violence: ARDL Endogeneity Approach. *Ensayos-Revista de Economía* 37(2): 155–175.

Amanze, J.N. et al. (eds.). 2019. *Religion and Development in Southern and Central Africa: Vol 1.* Mzuzu: Mzuni Press.

Atiemo, A.O. 2017. In Need of a New Lens: An African Christian Scholar's Religious Critique of Western European Attitudes toward Religion and Development in Africa. *Religion and Theology* 24(3–4): 250–273. https://doi.org/10.1163/15743012-02403005.

Beckford, J.A. 2019. *Religion and Advanced Industrial Society.* London: Routledge.

Beyers, J. 2018. Religion and violence: Shutup Shylock! *HTS Teologiese Studies/ Theological Studies* 74(3), p. 6. https://doi.org/10.4102/hts.v74i3.5165.

Bourigault, S. et al. 2016. Representation learning for information diffusion through social networks: an embedded cascade model. In *Proceedings of the Ninth ACM international conference on Web Search and Data Mining*, San Francisco, CA, February 22–25: 573–582.

Brubaker, R. 2015. Religious dimensions of political conflict and violence. *Sociological Theory* 33(1): 1–19.

Carbonnier, G. 2016. *International Development Policy: Religion and Development.* Basingstoke: Palgrave.

Chiorazzi, A. 2015. The spirituality of Africa. *Harvard Gazette* 6 October. Available at: https://news.harvard.edu/gazette/story/2015/10/the-spirituality-of-africa/ [Accessed: 17 May 2020].

De Nooy, W. et al. 2018. *Exploratory social network analysis with Pajek: Revised and expanded edition for updated software.* Cambridge: Cambridge University Press.

Deneulin, S. 2013. *Religion in development: Rewriting the secular script.* London: Zed Books Ltd.

Deneulin, S. and Zampini-Davies, A. 2017. Engaging development and religion: Methodological groundings. *World Development* 99: 110–121.

Hanneman, R.A. and Riddle, M. n.d. Introduction to Social Network Methods: Chapter 7: Basic Properties of Networks and Actors. Available at: https://faculty.ucr.edu/~hanneman/nettext/C7_Connection.html#nets [Accessed: 17 May 2020].

Jalali, M.S. et al. 2016. Information diffusion through social networks: The case of an online petition. *Expert Systems with Applications* 44: 187–197.

Jega, A. 2000. *Identity Transformation and Identity Politics Under Structural Adjustment in Nigeria.* Uppsala: Nordic Africa Institute.

John, S.F. 2018. Genocide, Oppression, Ambivalence: Online Narratives of Identity and Religion in Postcolonial Nigeria. *Open Library of Humanities* 4(2). Available at: http://olh.openlibhums.org/articles/10.16995/olh.284/ [Accessed: 25 September 2018].

Jones, B. and Petersen, M. J. 2011. Instrumental, narrow, normative? Reviewing recent work on religion and development. *Third World Quarterly* 32(7): 1291–1306.

Knoke, D. and Yang, S. 2019. *Social network analysis.* SAGE Publications, Incorporated.

Kurtas, S. n.d. Research Guides: UN Documentation: Development: Introduction. Available at: http://research.un.org/en/docs/dev/intro [Accessed: 17 May 2020].

Musa, A. et al. 2017. Youth Unemployment and Violent Mobilization in Kebbi State. *International Journal of Social and Administrative Sciences* 2(1): 1–7.

46 S. F. JOHN

Osaghae, E.E. and Suberu, R.T. 2005. *A history of identities, violence and stability in Nigeria*. Centre for Research on Inequality, Human Security and Ethnicity, University of Oxford.

Pew Research Centre. 2010. Pew-Templeton Global Religious Futures Project. Available at: http://www.globalreligiousfutures.org/regions/sub-saharan-africa [Accessed: 17 May 2020].

Rakodi, C. 2016. *Religion, Religious Organisations and Development: Scrutinising religious perceptions and organisations*. London: Routledge.

Rakodi, C. 2019. *Religion and Society in Sub-Saharan Africa and Southern Asia*. London: Routledge.

Root, R. et al. 2017. "We Smoke the Same Pipe": Religion and Community Home-Based Care for PLWH in Rural Swaziland. *Medical Anthropology* 36(3): 231–245. https://doi.org/10.1080/01459740.2016.1256885.

Serrat, O. 2017. Social Network Analysis. In: Serrat, O. ed. *Knowledge Solutions: Tools, Methods, and Approaches to Drive Organizational Performance*. Singapore: Springer: 39–43. Available at: https://doi.org/10.1007/978-981-10-0983-9_9 [Accessed: 17 May 2020].

Surajo, A.Z. and Karim, A.Z. 2016. Youth unemployment and poverty in Nigeria: A threat to sustainable growth and development. *International Journal of Scientific Research and Management* 4(12): 4919–4928.

Swart, I. and Nell, E. 2016. Religion and development: The rise of a bibliography. *HTS Theological Studies* 72(4): 1–27. https://doi.org/10.4102/hts.v72i4.3862.

Tlou, T. 2016. Addressing Socio-Economic Challenges to Curb Youth Participation in Terrorism in Africa. *Young African Leaders Journal of Development* 1, article 13. https://doi.org/10.32727/24.2018.13. Available at: https://digitalcommons.kennesaw.edu/yaljod/vol1/iss1/13.

Todd, N.R. et al. 2015. Applying affiliation social network analysis to understand interfaith groups. *Psychosocial Intervention* 24(3), pp. 147–154.

United Nations. 2015. Sustainable Development Goals: Sustainable Development Knowledge Platform. Available at: https://sustainabledevelopment.un.org/?menu=1300 [Accessed: 17 May 2020].

URI. n.d.-a. Charter | URI. Available at: https://uri.org/what-we-do/charter [Accessed: 17 May 2020].

URI. n.d.-b. What We Do | URI. Available at: https://uri.org/what-we-do#action_areas [Accessed: 17 May 2020].

Zweig, K.A. 2016. *Network analysis literacy. A practical approach to the analysis of networks*. Cham: Springer Nature Switzerland AG.

CHAPTER 3

Faith to Action Network: A Permanent Balancing Act

Ahmed Ragab, Emma Rachmawati, Grace Kaiso, and Matthias Brucker

INTRODUCTION: TENSIONS BETWEEN SUSTAINABLE DEVELOPMENT GOALS, HUMAN RIGHTS AND FAITH TEACHINGS AND VALUES?

Faith organisations contribute substantially to realising the Sustainable Development Goals (hereinafter referred to as the SDGs). Deeply rooted in the communities they serve (Mbiti 1999), faith organisations reach large numbers of people with messages on health, gender equality and peace that resonate with local beliefs and culture and provide social

---

A. Ragab
International Islamic Centre for Population Studies and Research, Al-Azhar University, Cairo, Egypt
e-mail: ahmed_ragab@azhar.edu

E. Rachmawati
University of Muhammadiyah, Magelang, Java, Indonesia
e-mail: emma_rachmawati@uhamka.ac.id

© The Author(s), under exclusive license to Springer Nature Switzerland AG 2022
E. Chitando, I. S. Gusha (eds.), *Interfaith Networks and Development*, Sustainable Development Goals Series,
https://doi.org/10.1007/978-3-030-89807-6_3

47

services through sustained networks of support. A World Bank study suggests that their contributions to health services in sub-Saharan Africa range between 30% to 40% (Olivier and Wodon 2012). This is why many governments and development stakeholders have realised that engaging faith organisations is an important pathway to achieving development goals. However, many faith organisations grapple with tensions between understandings of the SDGs, human rights and their faith teachings and values. It is these tensions which prompted the United Nations Special Rapporteur on Freedom of Religion and Belief (2018: 11) to state that, "freedom of religion or belief can never be used to justify violations of the rights of women and girls, and that it can no longer be taboo to demand that women's rights take priority over intolerant beliefs used to justify gender discrimination."

Faith organisations' understanding of development is often different from that of governments and secular organisations because it includes material, social, and spiritual dimensions (James 2009; Tadros 2010; Jajkowicz 2014). Therefore, the nature of a faith organisation's development agenda is often difficult to determine. For example, many faith organisations support different aspects of sexual and reproductive health and rights included in SDG 3 (Ensure healthy lives and promote well-being for all at all ages). They have developed nuanced positions, teachings and opinions on what is permitted and what is not. However, perceptions abound that faith organisations are fully opposed to or do not support sexual and reproductive health and rights (Jajkowicz 2014; Marshall 2015; Wilkinson et al. 2019). Looking at gender equality as articulated in SDG 5 (Achieve gender equality and empower all women and girls), Tadros (2010) notes that often a single organisation takes different standpoints on various gender issues. Faith organisations give women access to social capital and networks, through a range of spiritual and social activities, while at the same time delineating how they can

---

G. Kaiso
Anglican Alliance, London, UK
e-mail: gracekaiso@faithtoactionetwork.org

M. Brucker (✉)
Faith to Action Network, Nairobi, Kenya
e-mail: matthiasbrucker@faithtoactionetwork.org

exercise their agency within often patriarchal frameworks. As regards SDG 16 (Promote peaceful and inclusive societies…), social hostilities involving religion have increased in the past decade (Pew Research Center 2019). Yet, "as a powerful constituent of cultural norms," faith is deeply implicated in individual and social conceptions of peace, respect and tolerance, because it addresses some of the most profound existential issues of human life, such as freedom/inevitability, fear/security, right/wrong and sacred/profane (Said and Funk 2002: 37–38). Such critical challenges ought to be addressed, "not because there will ever be a total agreement but so that common values can emerge in authentic ways and areas of difference can be better understood and managed" (Marshall 2017: 56).

This chapter explores the role of the Faith to Action Network in addressing these tensions by creating spaces and capacity for faith organisations to articulate themselves while engaging constructively in development processes.

The Faith to Action Network

During a range of interfaith consultations on "faith and family planning" in 2011, representatives from 250 faith organisations concluded that they needed a global platform to engage in contested areas. Instead of ignoring or closing their eyes on the topics they felt uncomfortable with, they wanted to confront them through brave debates, mutual learning, increased collaboration, while partnering constructively with governments and other stakeholders. This platform needed to be owned and managed by the faith community on its terms, to set its agenda, define its processes and language. The participants in the consultations mandated six institutions to make the "Faith to Action Network" operational. These six founding institutions are the African Council of Religious Leaders—Religions for Peace (ACRL-RfP), Catholic Organization for Relief and Development Aid (Cordaid), Christian Connections for International Health (CCIH), Council of Anglican Provinces of Africa (CAPA), International Islamic Centre for Population Studies and Research, Al Azhar University (IICPSR) and Persyarikatan Muhammadiyah.

In joining the network, members committed to leveraging their institutions and networks to provide services and education, and influence government and donor policies and funding. The founding principles emphasized respect of each other's diverse faiths and needs while emphasizing the importance of human rights and social justice.[1] Membership was also motivated by their shared conviction that change was possible across religious boundaries, and more importantly, that they could make it happen. Over the years, Faith to Action Network has evolved into a global interfaith network of more than 110 Baha'i, Buddhist, Christian, Confucian, Hindu and Muslim faith organisations in 27 countries on four continents. It has also refined its mission to mobilise faith organisations' support for family health and wellbeing. Its current strategic focus is on issues that faith actors are grappling with, including sexual and reproductive health and family planning as stipulated by SDG 3; gender equality and women's rights as stipulated by SDG 5; as well as peaceful coexistence as stipulated by SDG 16. Its strategies are to engage in policy-making processes, strengthen faith organisations' capacity to contribute to development processes, communicate development and human rights content, promote interfaith experience sharing, learning and exchanges, undertake research and demonstration projects and offer small grants for interfaith work.

THE MASK OF RELIGION HAS BEEN REMOVED

Faith to Action Network's contribution to addressing tensions between faith teachings and practices and human rights and the SDGs merits closer analysis. First, it is a hub for faith organisations that want to make their voice heard but these same organisations often feel isolated from national or global development processes. Faith to Action Network members come in all forms and sizes: They are centralised, decentralised, formal, informal, networked, grassroots, elitist, medical, social and spiritual. They include 1000-year-old universities (such as Al Azhar University), and local youth organisations (for example, Kenya Muslim Youth Alliance). Others are national and regional umbrella networks of faith institutions (for example, All Africa Conference of Churches; Ethiopian Inter-Faith Forum for Development; and Supreme Council for the Confucian Religion in Indonesia), and also local interfaith networks of different faith groups (such as the Western Ugandan FBO Forum). These institutions find it challenging to advocate or speak out on the tensions between their faith teachings, human rights and SDGs. However, they all have a mutual interest in finding solutions to shared problems and articulating a

[1] Interfaith Declaration to improve family health and wellbeing of June 29th 2011.

compassionate voice. Their representatives include women and men, youth, ordained clergy and lay leaders of different faiths, different origins and different professions.

Grape and Karam (2016: 6) have pointed out that "religious women and advocates of the human rights' agenda are rarely heard in global dialogues and negotiations, and when they are present, their voices and perspectives are often on the margins." Faith to Action Network has provided a platform on which women and youth can articulate their perspectives and preferences, even in cases where they don't hold most senior positions in faith hierarchies. In 2019, for example, Faith to Action Network's convention celebrated its members by awarding prizes for outstanding achievements. After presenting their work, participants voted according to different categories. Many women and young people were honoured for their efforts. Among these was Ms. Farida Abdulabasit from the Kenya Muslim Youth Alliance who was recognised for transforming mosques into safe spaces for women and girls. Her organisation's work has offered platforms to youth and women to express their perspectives and address grievances.

Second, the network encourages and supports norms entrepreneurship at all levels. As "norm entrepreneurs," faith actors are well-suited to leading the change of social norms. Passionate individuals, who are well connected or highly central to a faith organisation, or who have high status, can play a key role in catalysing normative change (Ragab et al. 2018). The network seeks to integrate sexual and reproductive health and rights, women's rights and gender justice, peaceful coexistence into theology and pastoral care, faith organisations' institutional policies and practice, faith-run schools, universities and health facilities. For example, the network has worked with the Organisation of African Instituted Churches to develop guidance documents on gender justice. At the All Africa Conference of Churches' General Assembly in 2018, it supported the women's pre-conference develop a communiqué that articulated their vision: "as women from Africa (…), we recommend to: (…) interpret the Bible in liberating ways for all, being careful of the temptation/tendency to use patriarchal values that undermine the dignity of women, in the interpretation of gender-biased biblical texts".

Third, the network has increased faith organisations' participation in decision-making processes, from local to global, and has nurtured dialogue between religious and non-religious organisations effectively. Faith to Action Network members see "value in the international nature of the network, in the connectivity to a variety of organisations and actors addressing the same issues" (Veldkamp et al. 2016: 19). Very often, policymakers are biased by their own cultural and faith backgrounds. A review of proceedings of the East African Legislative Assembly shows the pervasive presence of faith and religion in parliamentary debates. For example, the Assembly's 165th sitting[2] started with a prayer, and continued to debate family law. Parliamentarians constantly referred to their private faiths. One parliamentarian stated; "I would have quoted for him the relevant verse of the Koran and this is on Suratu Nisa". Others admit being informed by obscure faith expert groups outside parliament. Enabling faith organisations to participate in such decision-making processes helps clarify faith-based arguments. Rather than leaving the interpretation of faith texts to unknown individuals or even private opinions, the network enables access to authoritative and credible faith voices.

Thus, Faith to Action Network has accompanied policy-making processes through faith-based delegations, meetings and press conferences. Since 2017, it has organised an interfaith delegation to the Commission on Population and Development in collaboration with the Church of Sweden and ACT alliance. Its presence is increasingly felt, by participating in national delegations, in panel discussions and also submitting written and oral statements. The network has taken a leadership role in informing members of the East African Legislative Assembly in faith and sexual and reproductive health and rights. In Uganda and Kenya, it has spearheaded the development of sub-national costed family planning implementation plans. Kenyan government representatives were proud about the network's contribution to policy-making and even to implementation of policies at the grass-root level. Thus, "The integrity of religious leaders make their contributions undoubted and their influence comes in handy in making the population go with the policies of the government" (Veldkamp et al. 2016: 18). Claiming space at the table has also allowed faith organisations to be involved in policymaking from an early stage. Rather than being invited at the tail end of a process, they have been engaged throughout various processes. This has created opportunities to offer their views. This meaningful participation has increased faith organisations' acceptance and ownership of policies. In turn, it has improved the likelihood that they will support the implementation of these policies. For example, in 2017,

[2] The Official Report of the Proceedings of the East African Legislative Assembly / 165th sitting—third assembly: fifth meeting—fifth session / Wednesday, 8 March 2017.

together with the All African Conference of Churches, the network organised the African Union faith consultations on the new African Union Gender Strategy. Veldkamp et al. (2016: 18) identify Faith to Action Network

> as a major rallying point for international policy-making processes related to sexual and reproductive health and rights, because it monitors and influences international sexual and reproductive health and rights policies. Its members 'have gained a better understanding of global and local issues.'

Fourth, the network has enhanced faith organisations' access to information, skills, resources and social capital. It has contributed towards addressing many intangible barriers to participation in development efforts. Language is one of the major barriers. A Kenyan faith leader advises, "Language becomes totally provocative, even violent to some people. We must be very sensitive about how we are using language. The presentation matters, the packaging matters, the content matters and even how we deliver it matters" (Jajkowicz 2014). Faith to Action Network has made Sustainable Development Goals and human rights language accessible to faith organisations. It has analysed information, presented and explained by drawing on faith scriptures, sources and teachings, and complemented with evidence and testimonials. Methodological guidance developed in 2019 emphasizes:

> Without shying away from controversial topics, it draws on faith scriptures and teachings, medical knowledge and socio-economic insights to jointly reflect and increase faith actors' understanding and support for family planning and reproductive health. This helps clarify myths and misconceptions. (Ragab et al. 2020: 4)

In 2020, Faith to Action Network and ACT Ubumbano facilitated the development of three interfaith briefs. These briefs were developed by 14 Southern African faith organisations on "gender-based violence", "teenage pregnancy" and "sexual and reproductive health and rights." Another barrier to participation in development efforts is the person communicating the information, especially when the person's background becomes more important than the message. Such background includes gender, race, socio-economic power and religion among others. Together with its members, Faith to Action Network has organised exchanges where local faith organisations gain access to global or transnational faith authorities. A case in point is the Learning Caravan championed by Al Azhar University. A multidisciplinary team of scholars from Al Azhar University travels, as in a caravan, to different areas to deliberate with faith leaders on reproductive health, family planning and women's rights. By involving respected scholars from Al Azhar University, the Caravan makes it possible to address deep-rooted misconceptions about, and resistance to, specific issues, and motivates Muslim faith leaders and communities to become champions. The Caravan has been implemented in over 14 countries worldwide (Van Eerdewijk et al. 2018).

A third barrier relates to the conditions of participation in development processes. Many existing capacity development mechanisms have focused on a small range of development professionals and advocates. Local faith leaders do not have access to these mechanisms. For example, they are not invited to advocacy workshops and conferences because they do not fit the selection criteria for several reasons: their perspectives might not fully match Northern bureaucrats' vision of development; they might be unable to develop a conference abstract, and they do not articulate their thoughts in what power brokers consider as rational empirical terms. To address these challenges, Faith to Action Network has given them multiple channels to access information and skills, including global interfaith conferences during the International Conferences on Family Planning in Indonesia (2016) or Rwanda (2018), Faith to Action Network's conventions (2018 and 2019), regional dialogues on the African continent such as the Keep Girls in School Conference (2019) in Nigeria, Southern African Development Community interfaith dialogues (2019), and numerous national and subnational meetings in Burundi, DRC, Egypt, Ethiopia, Eswatini, Ghana, Kenya, Malawi, South Africa, Uganda, South Sudan, South Africa, Tanzania, Zambia and Zimbabwe. Members confirm that activities were organised "for the members and by the members" (Veldkamp et al. 2016: 12). Hall (2020) confirms the relevance of this work.

Another barrier (fourth) to participation concerns the methods of engagement. As it were, secular and faith stakeholders articulate their theories of change on achieving the SDGs very differently. For faith organisations, the "definition of 'development' includes a spiritual dimension (consistent with their theological beliefs about the spiritual nature of human beings)" (James 2009: 15). Their main reference frameworks are sacred text and sources, as well as faith practices such as prayer and worship. The Network and its members have addressed this challenge by trying different methods. In 2018, for example, it organised interfaith celebrations on family planning and reproductive health. The first step of the celebrations required participants to move through three different stations where they prayed for remembrance for those who "have lost their lives through childbirth or conflict". The second step required them to pray about challenges, such as "cultures that encourage early marriage" or "government policies in which girls do not go back to school if pregnant". The last step required them to pray for and celebrate "religious leaders who openly support access to sexual and reproductive health services" and "youth who can make informed choices that enable them to gain their full potential." Such responses to the challenge have empowered the Network members. For example, Burundian faith organisations acknowledge that their participation in several Faith to Action Network training has improved their contacts with journalists and civil servants. Equipped with new knowledge and skills, they have organised follow-up workshops in Burundi for decision-makers and religious leaders to develop a shared guide on sexual and reproductive health (Veldkamp et al. 2016). Moreover, membership in the Faith to Action Network has increased organisations' social capital. According to Veldkamp et al. (2016), members see value in social networking and learning. In their words,

> Membership puts them on the market for speaking engagements, panel group discussions, dialogue and other related activities. Some interviewees gained huge recognition by policymakers, received invitations from religious leaders, church groups and communities or were approached to share their knowledge about specific issues, as the language of birth spacing. (Veldkamp et al. 2016: 21)

Indeed, many who joined the network during its early days have made remarkable career trajectories, rising in ranks within their organisations.

Fifth, Faith to Action Network has triggered and contributed to interfaith action and coordination. Its "dialogical approach" (Knitter 2013), "goes beyond theoretical theological debates and engages participants in pragmatic problem-solving" (Ragab et al. 2020: 4). It focuses on collaborative action as a response to injustice, even as they continue to disagree on what is just. This approach offers safe spaces for interfaith dialogues. Thus, "Discussions are non-judgmental, compassionate, solidary" (Ragab et al. 2020: 4). In faith circles, there are many misconceptions and a simple lack of understanding of different world views, including religious traditions (Marshall 2017). Organised without the glare of publicity, the Caravan methodology encourages faith actors to raise frank questions and engage in brave debates (Ragab et al. 2020). Typically, these activities are accompanied by a consensus document or a declaration and followed up by interfaith action plans. Faith organisations have thus negotiated an *interfaith consensus on family health and wellbeing* (2011), a *joint commitment in support of child spacing* of 63 Kenyan imams (2016), or an *interfaith statement on family planning and reproductive health* in Sud Kivu (2019). These declarations are signed and published through press conferences, meetings with external stakeholders and disseminated in places of worship.

Faith to Action Network supports interfaith action by providing small grants and financial support. As the Network's secretariat does not have any funds of its own, it supports interfaith actions from project grants and contracts. The secretariat has made deliberate efforts to integrate sub-granting mechanisms into all its programmes so that its members gain access to financial resources for interfaith actions. For example, since 2018, together with Council of Anglican Provinces of Africa and the African Council of Religious Leaders—Religions for Peace, it has managed a multi-country programme to enhancing the understanding, tolerance and respect for cultural and religious diversity among young women and men at risk of radicalisation. Its sub-granting scheme finances youth programmes, sometimes called "dialogue of every day" (Marshall 2017: 43), which increase young people's knowledge of their own and other people's faith and culture. Coupled with an improvement of attitudes, emotional response and empathy towards others, the Network's interventions have helped young people overcome faith-, culture- and gender-based stereotypes and negative perceptions towards others.

Faith to Action Network has imparted skills and practices of inclusive interfaith and intercultural activities and built common ground among people holding different worldviews. This has helped young people believe in their role as agents and facilitators of interfaith/cultural dialogue and their ability to constructively and peacefully participate in public life (Shauri 2019; Katungi 2019). Amongst others, the grants have supported the Interreligious Council of Burundi to engage faith leaders as mediators between young people of different political, ethnic and religious backgrounds in Muyinga, Rumonge, Bujumbura Rural and Bujumbura Mairie provinces. It has supported the Anglican Diocese of Egypt to organise interfaith youth programmes in Gusour Cultural Centre in Cairo, Old Cairo, and Ezbet El-Nakhl and El-Salam City Community Centres in Cairo. Young women and men of different faith backgrounds come together for pantomime, drumming and other joint activities. With Kenya Muslim Youth Alliance, it has organised interfaith and intergenerational dialogues and activities in Mombasa and Kilifi.

According to Halafoff (2013: 4), there are thousands of interfaith initiatives, "from small local grassroots efforts to national-level conflict resolution and transnational organizations that span the globe". Marshall (2017) points out that these initiatives remain mostly separate and largely uncoordinated. Through establishing the Faith to Action Network, its members have attempted to better coordinate their actions. Members in Rwanda, Ghana, and Burundi say that the Faith to Action Network responds to "the urgent need to create unity between different religious leaders and groups in their countries" (Veldkamp et al. 2016: 11). In Kenya, faith leaders and organisations have realised that other faith leaders face similar challenges. They appreciate that Faith to Action Network has eased cooperation, by removing religion as an obstacle and made it a resource for solutions. Thus, "the mask of religion has been removed" (Veldkamp et al. 2016: 19).

ALTERNATIVE PATHS TO ENGAGE IN THE SDGS

Faith organisations' societal and political influence, their reach and trust amongst large swathes of the world's population, and their vast networks of hospitals, schools and other platforms, are untapped potential in reaching the SDGs. The Lutheran World Federation speaks of sleeping giants that must be woken up.[3] During the Faith to Action Network 2018 convention, Rev. Canon Grace Kaiso, the network's chairperson and General Secretary of Council of Anglican Provinces of Africa reminded participants:

> You enjoy legitimacy, respect and influence; please use this immense potential to bring behavioural and attitudinal change in the society, your contribution to development and implementation of value-based policies at local, regional and global levels is very much needed.

[3] https://wakingthegiant.lutheranworld.org/.

With its focus on contested areas, Faith to Action Network makes important contributions to achieving the SDGs 3, 5 and 16. Guided by respect and sensitivity, the network offers its members alternative paths to engage on sexual and reproductive health and rights, women's rights and gender justice and peaceful coexistence. It offers faith organisations a platform to understand, engage and take action. These paths are more adapted to faith organisations' worldviews. Its members emphasise that Faith to Action Network responds to the urgent need "to stimulate interfaith dialogue and collaboration on sexual and reproductive health and rights topics, including the promotion of maternal health and the fight against HIV/AIDS" (Veldkamp et al. 2016: 11). The network is a space for expression as well as transparent dialogue on divergent views which has led to common engagement (Veldkamp et al. 2016). Faith to Action Network's solution-oriented approach translates this in tangible improvements for communities across the world. Only the tip of the iceberg has been documented, utilising empirical methods. Much remains undocumented. Meanwhile, the following are some examples of these achievements.

Jointly, Faith to Action Network members have contributed to numerous policy changes. A rough review of these processes between 2015 and 2019, counts 62 policies, budget and administrative changes in the areas of sexual and reproductive health, one in HIV/AIDS, three in health more broadly and two in adolescent health. Members have participated in four policy changes on gender-based violence and six on women's rights and gender justice more broadly. For example, the Uganda Joint Christian Council organised a national women's prayer day and handed a petition to the speaker of parliament, issued a pastoral letter and concluded the day with a press conference on women's rights. Rights defined at one level are often denied because of norms operating at another level. Changes in social norms, attitudes and practices are key to transforming the lives of women and girls, men and boys. Faith to Action Network members have leveraged their influence to adapt and reform their policies, teachings and practices. Thus, 35 changes have been reported in the areas of sexual and reproductive health and rights, one in gender-based violence, one in health, nine in women's rights and gender justice, three in the area of peacebuilding. Further, 29 additional changes are emerging. The Muslim Family Counselling Services has implemented a campaign to fight female genital mutilation and child marriages in Ghana. The Evangelical Association of Malawi has developed and adopted a sexual and reproductive health and rights policy, and currently disseminates it to its 70 member churches. The Ibrahimia Media Center organised a workshop to respond to domestic violence, and launched the Arabic version of a toolkit titled "ending domestic violence—a pack for churches". During its General Assembly, the All Africa Conference of Churches developed a new strategy prioritising women's rights and reproductive health, and inter-faith understanding. The Apostolic Women Empowerment Trust has engaged over 45 Apostolic groupings in Zimbabwe and sensitised them on the importance of developing teachings and policies that address gender-based violence and teenage pregnancy. It has created safe spaces where women and adolescent girls can talk about sexual reproductive health. In its Muslim women leaders' workshop, the Fatima Zahra Women's Organisation introduced Fatima Zahra (AS), the daughter of the holy prophet of Islam as a role model of Muslim women, and justified gender equality based on religious sources. It trained 55 participants from Manicaland Province, Mutare, Midlands Province, Shurugwi and Gweru, Matabeleland Province, Bulawayo, Chitungwiza, Kadoma and local areas in Harare. In Uganda, the Rgt. Rev. Stanley Ntagali, Archbishop of the Anglican Province of Uganda, wrote a pastoral letter urging clergy to include messages on child spacing and ending teenage pregnancy into their sermons.

Through Faith to Action Network's large-scale family planning pro-gramme, the Supreme Council of Kenya Muslims, Anglican Development Services Mount Kenya East, Christian Health Association of Kenya and the Organisation of African Instituted Churches have expanded women's access to health services in Kenya's most marginalized counties. In one year, they have strengthened 72 faith-based facilities to deliver these life-saving services, conducted 500 outreaches, trained 180 health workers, trained 212 community health volunteers, 36 community-based distribu-tors and 248 faith leaders. These stakeholders work hand in hand to share medical information and faith teachings on family planning with women and men. Faith leaders conducted sermons and khutbahs on health timing and spacing of pregnancies and participated in community outreaches. The Ethiopian Graduate School of Theology's Masters' course has become a growing academic discipline by increasing the number of graduates and enabling health and gender experts to work across disciplinary boundaries. In addition, 121 graduates have been trained since it integrated family planning into its curriculum. Recently, it revised its curriculum, now with courses in "Faith, Gender, Health and Development in Africa";

"Psychosocial Issues in Gender and Health"; "Philosophy of Gender and Sexuality"; "Fundamentals of Gender and Reproductive Health" and a Practicum. Further, 1108 Ethiopian Orthodox, Catholic, Muslim, Seventh-day Adventists and Protestant faith leaders have graduated from its faith and community leaders training package. At the community level, 1538 women and children have accessed improved preventive health services while enhancing the capacity of a women health development army.

Formed in 2012 by the Roman Catholic Church, Church of Uganda, several mosques and other faith organisations, the Western Uganda FBO Network (WUFBON) has 82 faith-based member organisations. Its advocacy to the Kyenjojo district leadership has greatly improved access to family planning services in Western Uganda. Between 2015 and 2017, the district's total number of family planning clients increased by about 50% from 14,987 to 22,016 (HMIS data).

Through its youth programme to increase interfaith and intercultural understanding, Faith to Action Network reached 9489 youths with interfaith messages of respect, understanding and tolerance in six African countries in 2019. An analysis of resulting behavioural changes in Kenya's multi-faith coastal counties showed that young people's awareness of similarities between each-others faith had increased from 33.3% to 50.7%. Young people who felt that their grievances were not addressed reduced from 36% at baseline to 21.2%. The share of those who believed that their cultural differences don't allow peaceful coexistence dropped from 22.2% to 3% only (Shauri 2019). In Burundi, a very senior faith leader reported with amazement that after the Inter-Religious Council's awareness creation, he was welcomed by community members of an opposing political party. Not only did he set foot into an opposition stronghold, where he never would have dared venture before, but he also stayed there for many hours, engaging in dialogues and conversations with young people from different political parties who engaged him without hostility.

Walking a Thin Line

Faith to Action Network is walking a thin line in many ways. It is a permanent balancing act between a secular world view of SDGs and human rights, and faith world views. During its recent interfaith dialogues in Southern Africa, a participant requested Christian faith leaders to edit a Bible quote because it was not inclusive enough. A participating Bishop explained that sacred scriptures could not be amended arbitrarily. Instead, they engaged in a dialogue and jointly selected a text that both felt happy with: "There is no longer Jew or Greek, there is no longer slave or free, there is no longer male or female; for all are one in Christ Jesus" (Galatians 3: 28). The resulting consensus document caused uproar and Faith to Action Network and ACT Ubumbano received letters and messages from all corners. One critique found that it was using binary language; another critique said that it was going too far. A way of bridging differences is to focus on seeking practical solutions. This can be illustrated by quotes from Johannesburg dialogues, which involved faith participants from all backgrounds, men, women, conservative, progressive etc.: "Instead of punishments, girls who fall pregnant need love, solidarity and compassion", "The church must be more understanding and supportive to girls who get pregnant. For example, it is known that to pursue education many poor girls engage in transactional sex." "We are talking about practical things that are happening. While we encourage abstinence, if this is not possible, they should use condoms." And "as women, we need to move away from a point of view where men are always right".

Faith to Action Network navigates different views on how change ought to be achieved. Within network membership, the authors identify both 'activist' institutions and 'incremental change' institutions. Activists find it important to take clear positions and force closed doors. Their sit-ins, marches and manifestoes cause an uproar. They are revolutionaries who do not fear the sacredness of religious doctrine. Defenders of a cautious approach, want to engage in an incremental approach. While they see themselves as schmoozing decision-makers, trying to gain small concessions, others perceive them as co-opted by power-holders, perpetuating unjust systemic structures. For Faith to Action Network's Chief Executive Officer Peter Munene, "this is a long journey. In this journey some might fall off, others will do leaps and others will do small steps, while others will not move at all. Everybody is welcome."[4] What is important is to understand that the faith environment is extremely dynamic. What seemed true a few years ago, does not necessarily reflect today's situation. An assessment of faith groups in one country does not hold for a faith group of the same religion in a different country. Many studies point out that one needs nuanced understandings (Wilkinson et al. 2019). The authors of this chapter emphasize that it is about negotiating practical solutions without a race to the lowest common denominator.

---

[4] Peter Munene face to face interview.

This balancing act is also about navigating different interests and needs while staying relevant and truthful to its founding act. Internally, there are faith organisations' perspectives with their expectations. However, faith organisations have not yet fully lived up to their original aim of developing a platform fully owned and driven by themselves. Only very few have paid membership fees, and a handful has made larger financial contributions. The network is mainly bankrolled by Northern donor institutions who include foreign governments and philanthropies with their own set of interests and policies. The network secretariat needs to avoid falling into the trap of being utilised as a conduit to reaching faith organisations. The sole suspicion of utilising members to rubberstamp Northern blueprint policies would destroy trust within and of the network. Thankfully, trust and credibility have emerged over time. The enduring success of this network is the result of many enthusiasts who have contributed their brick to the edifice. Of course, the edifice has many gaps. It is indeed difficult to ensure equal participation to hugely diverse members. Some of them are well resourced, well skilled. Others remain institutionally weak.

Conclusion: Starting from Where There's Agreement

There is a lot of disagreement among faith actors on issues articulated within the SDGs. There is also a lot of disagreement between faith actors and non-faith actors. Faith to Action Network believes that too much attention is given to those voices that propagate disagreement, and insufficient space is given to voices that seek agreement and constructive engagement. Faith to Action Network would like to turn around the question posed at the beginning by the United Nations Rapporteur on Freedom of Religion and Belief. It is not a question of faith OR human rights OR SDGs. Rather it is about faith AND human rights AND SDGs. This is where the network is positioned. Starting from where there is an agreement, it seeks to tiptoe into unchartered grounds, amplifying and elevating constructive voices, walking a thin line between different interests. This is a permanent balancing act that helps ensure "that perceived differences do not impede or detract from wider, constructive religious engagement" (Marshall 2017).

REFERENCES

Grape, M. & Karam, A. 2016. *Women, Faith, and Human Rights: at the Intersection of SRHR and Population Dynamics.* New York: UNFPA.

Halafoff, Anna. 2013. *The Multifaith Movement, Global Risks and Cosmopolitan Solutions.* New York: Springer.

Hall, Mary. 2020. *ROM Report. State of the African Woman Campaign.* Brussels: European Commission.

Jajkowicz, Dominik. 2014. *Advancing sexual and reproductive health and rights through faith-based approaches: A mapping study.* Nairobi: Faith to Action Network.

James, Rick. 2009. *Praxis Paper 22: What is Distinctive About FBOs? How European FBOs define and operationalise their faith.* Oxford: Intrac.

Katungi, Brian N. 2019. *Baseline and endline report on cultural diversity, norms and drivers of intolerance in Yumbe District, Uganda.* Nairobi: Faith to Action Network.

Knitter, Paul. 2013. "Inter-Religious Dialogue and Social Action". In Catherine Cornille (ed.), *The Wiley-Blackwell Companion to Inter-Religious Dialogue.* Chichester, West Sussex: Wiley-Blackwell.

Marshall, Katherine. 2015. *Religious engagement in family planning policies. Experience in six Muslim-majority countries.* Washington, DC: World Faiths Development Dialogue.

Marshall, Katherine. 2017. Foreword. In World Faiths Development Dialogue, *Interfaith Journeys, An exploration of history, ideas, and future directions.* Washington, DC: World Faiths Development Dialogue.

Mbiti, John. 1999. *African Religions and Philosophy.* Oxford: Heinemann.

Olivier, Jill & Wodon, Quentin. 2012. "Market share of faith-inspired health care providers in Africa: comparing facilities and multipurpose integrated household survey data", In Olivier, Jill & Wodon, Quentin (Eds.), *The role of faith-inspired health care providers in Sub-Saharan Africa and Public-private partnerships. Strengthening the evidence for faith-inspired health engagement in Africa, Volume 1.* Washington, DC: The World Bank.

Pew Research Center. 15 July 2019. *A Closer Look at How Religious Restrictions Have Risen Around the World,* Washington DC: Pew Research Center.

Ragab, Ahmed (et al.). 2018. *Norm entrepreneurs—faith actors' role in family planning, panel discussion at the International Conference on Family Planning.* Nairobi: Faith to Action Network.

Ragab, Ahmed (et al.). 2020. *Interfaith caravan on family planning and reproductive health. Facilitators' guide.* Nairobi: Faith to Action Network.

Said, Abdul Aziz & Funk, Nathan C. 2002. The Role of Faith in Cross-Cultural Conflict Resolution. *Peace and Conflict Studies* 9(1): 37–50.

Shauri, Halimu Suleiman. 2019. *Kenya Muslim Youth Alliance baseline and end-line reports for Mombasa and Kilifi counties, Kenya*. Nairobi: Faith to Action Network.

Tadros, Mariz. 2010. *Faith-Based Organizations and Service Delivery. Some Gender Conundrums*. Geneva: United Nations Research Institute for Social Development.

United Nations. 28 February 2018. *Report of the Special Rapporteur on freedom of religion or belief (Focus: State-Religion Relationships and their Impact on Freedom of Religion or Belief)*. Geneva: Office of the High Commissioner for Human Rights.

Van Eerdewijk, Anouka (et al.). 2018. *The State of African Women report*. The Hague: KIT, Royal Tropical Institute

Veldkamp, Tine (et al.). 2016. *Faith to Action. End of project evaluation. Final Report*. Hague: The Coalition Factory.

Wilkinson, Olivia (et al.). 2019. *Faith Actor Partnerships in Adolescent Sexual and Reproductive Health: A Scoping Study*. Washington DC; Bonn: Joint Learning Initiative on Faith and Local Communities (JLI); International Partnership on Religion and Development (PaRD).

CHAPTER 4

KAICIID: An Emerging Significant Player in Global Interfaith and Development Initiatives

Ishanesu Sextus Gusha

INTRODUCTION

The subject of peace building at international level had taken increasing urgency since the September 11, 2001 bombings in the United States of America by religious fundamentalists. The event triggered a new approach to peace building by the United Nations (UN) and the role of religion in peace building or promoting violence could no longer be underestimated. Religion is now considered a major stakeholder in peace building, dialogue facilitation and conflict transformation. It is clear that the Sustainable Development Goals (SDGs) that are being promoted by the UN can only be met when there is peace in the world. This chapter will also explore how the SDG 10, "Reduce inequality within and among countries" is being promoted by the Inter Religious Dialogue (IRD) programmes of King Abdullah Bin Abdulaziz International Centre for Interreligious and

I. S. Gusha (✉)
Anglican Diocese in Europe, Palma de Mallorca, Spain

© The Author(s), under exclusive license to Springer Nature Switzerland AG 2022
E. Chitando, I. S. Gusha (eds.), *Interfaith Networks and Development*, Sustainable Development Goals Series,
https://doi.org/10.1007/978-3-030-89807-6_4

Intercultural Dialogue (KAICIID). It is within this context that the world witnessed the rise of interfaith/interreligious dialogue organisations in a bid to promote peace, harmony, and social cohesion. KAICIID is one such rising giant among international interfaith/interreligious/intercultural dialogue organisations that cannot be ignored in a meaningful discussion on the role of such organisations in peace building initiatives at global level.

Background to KAICIID

What is KAICIID? "KAICIID is an intergovernmental organization whose mandate is to promote the use of dialogue globally to prevent and resolve conflict to enhance understanding and cooperation. Over a seven-year-long negotiation and development process, KAICIID's mandate and structure were designed to foster dialogue among people of different faiths and cultures that bridges animosities, reduces fear and instils mutual respect" (*https://www.kaiciid.org/who-we-are*). The question then is, which governments comprise KAICIID? The following governments make up the KAICIID: Austria, Saudi Arabia and Spain. These three nations constitute the 'Council of Parties' responsible for overseeing the work of the Dialogue Centre. The Holy See (Vatican) is the founding observer. The Dialogue Centre is situated in Vienna, Austria at Schottenring 21, 1010 Vienna. According to Abu-Nimer and Anas Alabbadi, "the International Dialogue Centre seeks to bring religious leaders and political decision-makers together to develop and implement multilateral social cohesion building and coexistence initiatives. KAICIID supports experts, trainees and organisations working in this area through capacity building programs, workshops, training and partnerships" (Abu-Nimer and Alabbadi 2017: 1). The Dialogue Centre was inaugurated on 26th November 2012 (Rizvi 2019: 6). In a unique way, KAICIID is governed by governmental representatives and religious leaders from five different religions, namely; Judaism, Christianity, Islam, Hinduism and Buddhism. These are the world's biggest religions and this makes KAICIID one of the strongest interreligious organizations in the world.

The governance of KAICIID is as follows; Council of Parties (Austria, Kingdom of Saudi Arabia, Spain and Holy See). What is the role of this Council?

4 KAICIID: AN EMERGING SIGNIFICANT PLAYER IN GLOBAL INTERFAITH... 67

The Council of Parties adopts the Centre's financial regulations, work programme and annual budget. The Council of Parties also, on the basis of proposals of the Board of Directors, nominates the members of major religions and faith-based and cultural institutions to the Advisory Forum. It will approve international agreements and will approve the establishment of cooperative relationships with public or private entities that can contribute to the Centre's work. The Council of Parties will decide on the admission of new parties and observers to the Agreement. (*https://www.kaiciid.org/governance*)

Below the Council of Parties are the Board of Directors who are drawn from the five major religions mentioned above. At the time of writing, they were nine members who constituted the Board of Directors. These are prominent representatives of the five major world religions. Their duty is to design and supervise the Centre's programmes. Next in the line of the hierarchy is the Advisory Forum. The Advisory Forum is made up of one hundred members drawn from world religions, religious organisations and cultural institutions. The role of the Advisory Forum is:

To support the activities of the Board and advise on their programs. The Advisory Forum will provide content to the Centre's activities by providing a broader global perspective from all regions of the world. Its members will also form working groups, as directed by the Board of Directors, to address certain themes and issues. Its members, who shall be appointed for a renewable term of four years, will meet at least once a year. Members of the Advisory Forum shall serve in their individual capacities but take independent decisions as far as possible by consensus or, if not achieved, by a two thirds majority. (*https://www.kaiciid.org/governance*)

The secretariat is important in the day to day running of the organisation's business and is headed by the Secretary General who happened to be Faisal Bin Abdulrahman Bin Muaammar at the time of writing. He works with the Deputy Secretary General who is Alvaro Albacete and the Director General-Fahad Abualnasr. In their headquarters in Vienna are the following portfolios with office bearers from different nationalities; programmes, executive management, communications and organizational support services. Upon arrival at their headquarters in Vienna, one meets an embodiment of a multi-cultural, multi-religious and multi-national organization. Upon entering that headquarters, one experiences practical interreligious and intercultural dialogue in a unique fashion. The governance organogram of KAICIID on its own is a clear demonstration of serious commitment to sustainable interreligious/intercultural dialogue. Where there is serious commitment, resources follow and this is the reason why KAICIID is in partnership with big and prominent organisations such as; Mindanao Peace building Institute, Conference of European Rabbis, Coexister, Institute of Peace and Conflict Resolution, Office of the UN Special Adviser on the Prevention of Genocide and the World Council of Churches. These are just some of the fourteen partners they are working with. In summary, they have signed memoranda of understanding with twelve organisations and are in partnership with fourteen reputable organisations. Since the organisation's inception in 2012, they have also worked closely with twenty-five reputable organisations from the different parts of the world.

KAICIID AS A RISING GIANT IN THE GLOBAL INTERFAITH NETWORK

KAICIID has proved to be a rising giant in the globe in the areas of interreligious/intercultural dialogue. KAICIID is now counted among the three biggest interfaith organisations in the world. Since its inception, KAICIID has held international conferences in different parts of the world. For example, Manue Lopez (2013) reports that in 2013 alone, KAICIID managed to organize regional conferences in countries such as Austria, Ethiopia, India and Argentina. As a rising giant, KAICIID has worked in partnership with international organisations such the United Nations, the African Union, European Union, UNICEF, UNESCO, World Scouts Foundation, and the Islamic Educational, Scientific and Cultural Organization. According to the *2018 KAICIID Annual Report*, KAICIID budgeted 11.4 million Euros to cover the programmes and activities of the Centre (KAICIID Report 2018: 51). In 2017, their budget was even higher, with 13.9 million Euros. This demonstrates the organization's commitment to interfaith dialogue and peace building. The 2018 budget allocation was as follows; 20% (Organizational Support Service), 9% (Communications Department), 30% (Executive Management), and 41% (Programmes Department).

The staff complement of the organization also testifies to a rising global giant. According to Heather Wokusch, "KAICIID roughly employs 60 employees and 50% are women" (*Wokusch: Metropole* n.d.). Their staff complement is made up of employees from the following countries; Armenia, Austria, Bangladesh, Bosnia and Herzegovina, Brazil, Bulgaria, Croatia, North Macedonia, Germany, Greece, Hungary, India, Italy, Jordan, Kyrgyzstan, Mauritania, Mexico, Norway, Romania, Saudi Arabia, Slovenia, Spain, Sri Lanka, United States of America, the United Kingdom, Venezuela, and Yemen. This is a wide geographical representation of the staff body. This is a fulfilment of SDG 10.2, namely, "empowering and promoting the social, economic and political inclusion of all irrespective of age, sex, disability, race, ethnicity, origin, religion or economic or other status" (SDG 10.2) Please note that this staff complement was according to 2018 report, but when the author visited their headquarters in 2019, they were already staff from Africa. 30% of the staff was from the host country, Austria, 4% from Spain, 8% Saudi Arabia, and 58% from the rest of the world. (KAICIID Annual Report 2018: 51). Importantly, KAICIID also partners with the African Union in providing interreligious and inter-cultural education (African Union Report 2013). This is where its presence and contribution in Africa is heavily felt. By spring of 2019, KAICIID had trained 276 fellows, 36% female and 64% male. The distribution of fellows is was follows; 64% were affiliated with academic/research institutions, 81% were affiliated with religious/confessional institutions, 40% were religious leaders. The fellows were from 59 countries, 9 religions and the average age was 40 years.

KAICIID INITIATIVES

This section is exploring the initiatives that are being carried by KAICIID all over the world and among them are; applying Interreligious Dialogue for peace and reconciliation in four designated conflict situations (The Arab Region-Iraq/Syria, the Central African Republic, Myanmar and Nigeria); capacity building efforts that are meant to equip religious leaders for peace building in their communities. The last initiative is where the International Fellows Programme falls. Thirdly, advocacy on behalf of Interreligious Dialogue with international organisations, policymakers and other stakeholders. Lastly, providing a virtual platform with resources for the field of dialogue worldwide. This virtual platform is provided through the Dialogue Knowledge Hub. These are the areas to be explored further in this section.

Interreligious Dialogue for Peace and Reconciliation

Interreligious Dialogue is done at different levels which are; first, interreligious dialogue for Theological Reflection. This means dealing with certain theological themes from an interfaith perspective. Second, there is interreligious dialogue for Life-encountering. This is interreligious dialogue through life experiences such as weddings, funerals and marriages. Third, there is interreligious dialogue for Action. This implies agreeing on a common platform for a certain cause. Dialogue is for the purpose of action. Fourth, we have interreligious dialogue for Common Action. This is for doing work together in the community. KAICIID operates at all these four levels. Interreligious dialogue for peace and reconciliation falls under the categories of dialogue for action. Kimball (2011) argues that religion is frequently considered as a factor in international conflicts and dialogue processes. Iren Franda also echoes the same sentiments as she argues that "interfaith dialogue in polarized societies can be a source of peace instead of war and violence" (Franda 2016: 21). The importance of interfaith dialogue to peace building initiatives is something that the world cannot afford to ignore. Abu-Nimer, Khoury, and Welty conclude that:

> Interfaith dialogue contributes toward conflict resolution because its concept of reconciliation involves processes of confession, repentance, mercy and forgiveness. Bringing religion into the dialogue allows the participants to engage in the processes, with their religious identity as their primary point of reference (Abu-Nimer et al. 2007: 10)

To what extent is KAICIID involved in interreligious dialogue for peace and reconciliation? Four projects, namely, the Arab region, Central African Republic, Myanmar and Nigeria will be discussed. It is important to note that two of the four projects are from Africa, which demonstrates the commitment of the organization to African affairs. Africa is also included on SDG 10.b as a developing continent that deserves special treatment in developmental projects. KAICIID has been seen prioritising Africa in its initiatives as a way of empowering developing countries in the world.

The Arab Region (Syria and Iraq)

The conflict in Syria is a complex one and the major question has been around how it began. Hafeez Ullah Khan and Waseem Khan narrate that:

> In March 2011, anti-government protests erupted in Syria. These protests were inspired by similar protests across the Middle East as a result of the Arab Spring. The Assad regime responded aggressively against the peaceful protests and aggravated the situation. He unleashed the security and intelligence services to break up rallies and demonstrations, often with live fire, and to arrest dissidents. However, events took a ghastly turn. By the end of 2011, armed warfare began between the government forces and the opposition rebels. In the war, the government- essentially the Alawite-ruling elite and the state machinery—are pitted against an alliance of the opposition rebels—mainly Sunnis. However, the complexity of the war has intensified due to the interference of global and regional powers as well as Islamic Jihadists in the imbroglio. (Khan and Khan 2017: 591)

In the Arab region, KAICIID initiated a programme called 'United against violence in the name of religion' and the programme is specially focussing on the conflict in Syria and Iraq. Under this programme, in February 2014, KAICIID organized a conference which was attended by leading representatives from different religious communities to support peaceful coexistence. It was at the conference that a historic interreligious platform was launched and supported by Christian and Muslim leaders to advocate for the rights and inclusion of all communities in the Arab world. Thus, "The Platform is the first interreligious dialogue platform of its kind. Planned activities of the platform include training clergy of all religions to combat hate speech, implementing initiatives which empower youth and women, and working with local and national authorities on policy which promotes social cohesion and equal rights" (*https://www.kaiciid.org/what-we-do/united-against-violence-name-religion*). In many communities, youth and women are amongst the people at the bottom of the social stratum. The bulk of unemployment falls with these two groups of people hence the need to deliberately focus on them as recipients of empowerment initiatives. Therefore, by paying special attention to these groups, KAICIID is in alignment with SDG 10.2. In 2015 an important conference was organized in Amman to develop new strategies for using social media as a tool to promote dialogue between people of different regions and cultures. The conference was attended by 120 participants

72   I. S. GUSHA

from religious communities, civil society and interreligious organisations. The outcome of the conference was the production of a training manual which was later used in Jordan, Egypt, Iraq, Tunisia, and Lebanon. "The training manual informs users about dialogue tools, the value of social media in promoting dialogue and social cohesion, and how to use social media to implement dialogue" (*www.kaicidd.org*). Further trainings were also done in 2015 where conference participants were also trained to become trainers and the outcome was the training of a further 400 people.

THE CENTRAL AFRICAN REPUBLIC

The Central African Republic (CAR) gained independence from France in 1960. The sad scenario is that the country has witnessed 10 military coup attempts between 2005 and 2015, which have aggravated political and economic development of the CAR. The conflict has resulted in the displacement of hundreds of thousands of people and the death of thousands of people. Abdurrahim Sıradağ argues that "although the violence in the CAR partially polarized Muslims and Christians, the driver of the conflict in the CAR is more a struggle for power among political elite" (Sıradağ 2016: 86). However, one cannot ignore the fact that religion is mentioned as another contributor to the conflict. At the time of writing, more than 460,000 people from CAR were refugees in neighbouring countries and over 436,000 were internally displaced.

A closer analysis of the conflict reveals that intra-religious and interreligious division affects the stability of the country. According to a KAICIID report, "due to the magnitude of this displacement, the country risks becoming divided between a Muslim north and a Christian south. According to various sources, Christians represent 80% of the population (55% protestant, 25% Catholic) and Muslims approximately 15%" (*https:// www.kaiciid.org/what-we-do/our-work-central-african-republic*). Inequality among people of different religions is another area of concern in CAR hence KAICIID is working on elimination such inequalities that have been identified as the sources of conflict. SDG 10.2 aims at reducing such inequalities especially on religious identities and KAICIID is playing a crucial role in the realisation of such a sustainable goal. This is where KAICIID is seen making an important contribution in dialogue facilitation and conflict resolution.

How is KAICIID intervening in the CAR conflict? KAICIID is pushing for the establishment of operational and sustainable mechanisms to strengthen the capacity of the religious leaders (with an initial focus on the Muslim community) to prevent violence and engage in interreligious dialogue for reconciliation. To achieve that aim,

> KAICIID aims to foster an environment in which religious actors work together to build trust to promote social cohesion and peace through:
> 1. Establishing inclusive mechanisms that strengthen the capacity of the CAR religious community leaders to successfully engage with each other, including an early warning mechanism to monitor, mitigate & prevent interreligious violence in the conflict areas.
> 2. Developing the capacity of religious actors to conduct interreligious initiatives. This includes training Muslim leaders for future intergroup cooperation with Christian leaders.
> 3. Implementing pilot initiatives in targeted conflict areas in partnership with members of the existing Interfaith Platform.
> 4. Providing technical and financial support to the Interfaith Platform to coordinate the activities of its members. A needs assessment study was conducted to map issues as well as identify gaps that need to be addressed in future. (*https://www.kaiciid.org/what-we-do/our-work-central-african-republic*)

This work is being done with the blessings of the African Union who are partners to KAICIID. On the other hand, the United Nations and African Union are dealing with the crisis from the political front. It is hoped that through this holistic approach to the conflict, a sustainable solution will be established.

MYANMAR

Myanmar is one of the countries that has been experiencing conflict which is religiously motivated for a long time. According to Farhana Morshed, "the Government of Myanmar is facing serious challenges to resolve between the conflicting demands and aspirations of the Rakhine Buddhist and the Muslim communities" (Morshed 2018: 3). The country went through 50 years of dictatorship which ended with the general elections of 2010. There has been political exclusion of other stakeholders in the country for fifty years. This contravenes SDG 10.2 on the subject of promoting equality among people on economic and political issues regardless of their identity. The results of the elections were also contest as the losing parties claimed that they were rigged. KAICIID has played a significant role in mitigating these challenges of polarization in the country. Since 2011, the country has been affected by waves of conflict. Factors behind the conflict range from political, economic, social, and religious. The nature of the conflict is so complex and this section is interested mainly on the religious reasons. The religious demography of Myanmar illustrates that it is a multi-confessional society. According to the 2014 census, "87.9% of the population is Buddhist, 6.2% Christian and 4.3% Muslim. Christians, mainly Baptists and Roman Catholics, have a strong presence in Chin (85%), Kayah (46%) and Kachin (34%), and to lesser extent in Shan and Kayin States" (Stokke et al. 2018: 29). The constitution of the country provides for the freedom of worship. However, from 2011, they has been a wave of anti-Muslim rhetoric and violence and this has been expressed in the public space, thereby degenerating into violence. Religious institutions have been hijacked by political parties in a bid to further political goals. It is within this background that we find KAICIID getting involved, particularly with the aim of breaking religious polarization.

KAICIID is supporting inclusive dialogue in Myanmar through promoting interreligious dialogue, coexistence and reconciliation between the followers of the main religious traditions in the country. The KAICID initiatives are impacting through:

> Supporting and strengthening an inclusive and sustainable national interfaith dialogue platform—the Peaceful Myanmar Initiative. Training of religious and community leaders on interreligious dialogue in pilot regions, with a focus on using social media as a space for dialogue. Supporting local peacebuilding initiatives through a small grants scheme, awareness raising campaigns and interfaith forums. Initiating pilot activities through local partners also in Rakhine State. (*https://www.kaiciid.org/what-we-do/supporting-inclusive-dialogue-myanmar*)

The initiatives have made some milestone achievements in the following ways, first, the establishment of a new network for peace & interreligious dialogue in Myanmar (PMI) in 2016. Second, was the official opening of an Interreligious Dialogue Training Centre, led by the PMI. Third, was the organization of an interfaith harmony expo on the International Day of Peace in Yangon. Fourth, was the training of 443 religious leaders and civil society activists on promoting peace and interfaith harmony in Myanmar. Fifth, the development and publishing of an Interfaith Study Guide on Peace and Dialogue, which is used by PMI

Peace Educators in Myanmar. Sixth, they conducted a needs assessment study to map out the current Interreligious Dialogue landscape and key stakeholders and issued recommendations for further interaction. Seventh, they launched three large scale PMI led interfaith dialogue events in Myanmar, including the Myanmar Interreligious Dialogue Forum, in Yangon, which brought together religious leaders from all States and Divisions of the country. Lastly, they launched PMI social media pages to promote peace & interfaith work in Myanmar with over 14,000 followers.

NIGERIA

Nigeria is one of the biggest countries in Africa and well known for her riches in oil reserves. However, the country has been known for serious violent clashes over the years. Ray Ikechukwu Jacob attributes much of the conflict to ethnicity which dates back to the pre-colonial era (Jacob 2012). Ethnicity has been identified by SDG 10.2 as another common source of inequalities among communities. Besides ethnicity, religion is another major source of conflict in Nigeria and sometimes it is difficult to separate the two. "Nigeria has three major religious identities: Christian, Islam and traditional religions" (Omorogbe and Omohan 2005: 557; Osaghae and Suberu 2005: 11). In Nigeria, both religious and ethnic causal agents have always acted together in the perpetuation of social conflicts. Haldun Canci and Opeyemi A. Odukoya argue that the major cause of the conflicts has been the state's use of religion and ethnicity in political discourse or action (Canci and Odukoya 2016). Conflicts in Nigeria have claimed thousands of people, with the most causalities caused by the extremist group known as Boko Haram. The Muslim-Christian clashes coupled with ethnicity in Jos from 2001 claimed over 10,000 of live. This is the context that necessitated the involvement of KAICID.

KAICIID's involvement in Nigeria is through the Interreligious Dialogue for peace and reconciliation. The work of KAICIID in Nigeria is simply summarized as follows:

> KAICIID sees the considerable potential of functioning dialogue platforms which leaders from different religious traditions can use to address these and other emerging issues. These platforms can serve to combat growing intolerance and mistrust. The Centre has solidified its role as a dialogue facilitator in Nigeria and laid the foundations for sustainable interreligious dialogue through the establishment of dialogue spaces, capacity building, and support of local

initiatives. In order to foster collaboration, and provide resources and support for local initiatives, the Centre works through a three pillar approach. (*https://www.kaiciid.org/what-we-do/peace-and-reconciliation-through-interreligious-dialogue-nigeria*)

The three pillar approach constitutes; the interfaith dialogue forum for peace, support for local initiatives and strategic partnerships. In terms of achievements in Nigeria, KAICIID has managed to organise visits to communities in Kaduna State, Plateau State, Taraba State, Benue State, and Zamfara State affected by tensions between farming and pastoralists groups; host high level intra-faith round table meetings; hold a workshop for women which raised awareness on hate speech and incitement to violence, and equipped participants with tools to foster peace, and training for 120 Nigerian youth.

CAPACITY BUILDING

KAICIID is heavily involved in capacity building of different interreligious/ interfaith and intercultural organisations. However, before exploring ways in which KAICIID is involved in capacity building, one needs to the first of all define the term itself. Beesley and Shebby (2010) define capacity building as a process for strengthening the management and governance of an organization or individual so that he/she/it can effectively achieve set objectives and fulfil mission. Capacity building includes training of the personnel, financing incapacitated organizations and strengthening the governance of organizations. In terms of capacity building, KAICIID runs two fellows' programmes, the international and regional fellows' programmes.

FELLOWS PROGRAMME

The KAICIID International Fellows' Programme (hereinafter referred to as KIP) is "a one-year training programme designed to connect and cultivate a network of leaders who are committed to fostering peace in their communities" (*www.kaicidd.org*). At the time of writing, four KIFPs had been successfully completed. These are thorough programmes meant to equip fellows with the dialogue skills need to tackle real issues affecting the world.

The aim is to facilitate dialogue encounters by giving these teachers the tools, experience, networks and knowledge to pursue interreligious dialogue and further be able to prepare their own students to become facilitators and leaders in interreligious dialogue. In addition to interreligious dialogue training, the fellows will also learn how to train their own students in conflict transformation so as to be active peacemakers in their respective communities. (*www.kaiciid.org*)

The training programme is structured in the following ways; first, is the empowerment of institutions by providing capacity-building to select teachers. The capacitated teachers are then expected to educate their students about interreligious dialogue, equip their students with the necessary skills to become active facilitators and leaders in interreligious dialogue, train their students in conflict transformation so as to be active peacemakers in their respective communities. Second, the trainings then provide the opportunity to network these institutions and their selected teachers into an active transnational community of interreligious dialogue peacemakers and peacebuilders. Third, during the one-year training, the participants have the opportunity to develop to implement small-scale local and/or international initiatives within their institution or beyond. KAICIID provides them with small grants amounting to 2000 euros. These small grants are meant to improve the income growth of those at the bottom of the population. This is in line with the SDG 10.1 which speaks to the "progressively achieving and sustaining of the income growth of the bottom 40 percent of the population." They are also expected to participate in and organize dialogue sessions, lectures, field visits and conferences. During the year fellows are also expected to complete a one-year online training programme on IRD. After the one-year programme, the fellows become part of the KAICIID Fellows Network. This is the same pedagogy that is employed on regional fellows. Three one week trainings are held in year in different venues (countries), but the third training session is always held in Vienna, Austria and it is followed by the colourful graduation ceremony. The network works on following up on the fellows' progress, and invest in their long-term sustainability as resource persons in the field of interreligious dialogue and conflict transformation. As of December 2019, a total number of 300 fellows had graduated at KAICIID through their capacity building programme. These fellows are from the following programmes; KIFP 2015, KIFP 2016, KIFP 2017, KIFP 2018, Southeast Asia 2016, Arab World 2017, Africa 2018, Europe 2019, and

Arab 2019. The twenty African fellows came from the Central African Republic, Ethiopia, Ghana, Kenya, Nigeria, South Africa, Tanzania, Chad, Uganda and Zimbabwe. To date, KAICIID has trained more than thirty fellows from Africa and this is a significant contribution towards IRD in Africa. Further, the Fellows are engaged in development work across the continent.

SUCCESS

KAICIID has registered great successes in their IRD story. The Fellows who have graduated have managed to train more people in their communities. Yes, directly, KAICIID has capacitated three hundred fellows but indirectly, they have trained thousands of people globally. This is a clear success story that cannot be veiled. Besides capacitating individual fellows and communities, KAICIID has also managed to capacitate more than two hundred interreligious organisations, churches, confessional institutes, seminaries, and other religious bodies. KAICIID has also done exceptionally well in promoting local initiatives of IRD institutes through the micro grant programme. They have allowed the creativity of individuals and institutions without bottlenecking them. They have seen other players in the field as partners and not competitors. That is a big success story. They are not out to build their own kingdom but to engage and transform the world. To date, they have scored so much successes and credit goes to the dedicated staff and visionary leadership under the Secretary General.

CHALLENGES

KAICIID's story cannot be completed without highlighting the challenges they faced in the past eight years. The biggest challenge has been calls by the Austrian parliament to close down the institute in Vienna. In June 2019, Austria's government unveiled plans to shut a Saudi-funded centre for religious dialogue in Vienna after parliament urged it to try to prevent the possible execution of a teenager in Saudi Arabia over acts committed when he was a minor. They have been accused of being funded by a government that is grossly violating human rights. The motion was backed by the Social Democrats, the far-right Freedom Party and the liberal Neos. The news evoked responses from people all over the world and these people included past fellows and other IRD institutes all over the world. The plans to close the centre, however, failed to materialize. This was one of the biggest challenges that the organisation has faced, especially in a polarized world where there is lack of trust and good will. Another challenge relates to the need for KAICIID to adopt a long-term strategy when embarking on development projects.

CONCLUSION

The transformation of the world is very possible with dedicated organizations such as KAICIID. The chapter has established that KAICIID is truly a rising giant in global IRD initiatives and their contribution to global peace, security and development is noteworthy. Other global interfaith networks could learn great lessons from the governance and organisational structure of KAICIID for them to score great successes in their initiatives. It is from the initiatives of KAICIID that African institutions in particular need to learn that it is from partnerships rather than competition that great outcomes are achieved. The chapter also makes it clear that global interfaith initiatives, such as those championed by KAICIID, are key to achieving Sustainable Development Goals, especially Goal Number 10 on reducing inequality within and among countries. In line with SDG 10, much attention has been given to less privileged communities in Africa and Asia. Discriminatory policies that are impoverishing some of the communities in Asian and African countries have been challenged and in some other cases repealed. KAICIID is therefore a valuable case study that demonstrates the key role that interfaith organisations are playing in promoting sustainable development in Africa and beyond.

REFERENCES

Abu-Nimer, Mohammed and Anas Alabbadi. 2017. *Interreligious Dialogue Resource Guide. KAICIID International Fellows Programme. Practitioners of Interreligious Dialogue*. Vienna: KAICIID.

Abu-Nimer, Mohammed, Amal I. Khoury and Emily Welty. 2007. *Unity in Diversity—Interfaith Dialogue in the Middle East*. Washington, DC: United States Institute of Peace Press.

African Union Report. 2013. Addis Ababa: African Union.

Beesley, A. D. and S. Shebby. 2010. "Evaluating capacity building in education: The North Central Comprehensive Center." Paper presented at the Annual meeting of the American Educational Research Association, Denver, Colorado, May.

Canci, Haldun and Opeyemi A. Odukoya. 2016. Ethnic and religious crises in Nigeria: A specific analysis upon identities, 1999–2013. *African Journal of Conflict Resolution* 16(1): 87–110.

Franda, Irene 2016. "Interfaith Dialogue and Religious Peacebuilding in the Middle East." *Master's Thesis.* Uppsala: Uppsala University.

Jacob, Ray I. 2012. A Historical Survey of Ethnic Conflict in Nigeria. *Asian Social Science* 8(4): 13–29.

Khan, Hafeez Ullah and Waseem Khan 2017. Syria: History, The Civil War and Peace Prospects. *Journal of Political Studies* 24(2): 587–601.

KAICIID 2018 Annual Report. Vienna: KAICIID Centre. https://www.kaiciid.org. (Accessed 10 March 2020).

Kimball, C. 2011. *When Religion Becomes Lethal: The Explosive Mix of Politics and Religion in Judaism, Christianity, and Islam.* California: Jossey-Bass.

Lopez, Manue. 2013. KAICIID Interfaith Global Forum in Vienna Concludes. *Periodistas. periodistas-es.com/kaiciid-interfaith-global-forum-vienna-concludes-23194.* (Accessed 28 March 2020).

Morshed, Farhana. 2018. The Role of Religion in Conflict and Peace Building-The Context of Rakhine State in Myanmar. *Master Thesis.* Uppsala: Uppsala University.

Omorogbe, S.K. and M.E. Omohan. 2005. Causes and management of ethno-religious conflicts: The Nigeria experience. In: Alhaji M. Yakubu, R.T. Adegboye, C.N. Ubah and B. Dogo, Eds. *Crisis and conflict management in Nigeria since 1980. Vol. II.* Kaduna: Nigerian Defense Academy.

Osaghae, Eghosa E. and Rotimi T. Suberu. 2005. "A history of identities, violence, and stability in Nigeria." *CRISE working paper No. 6.* Oxford: Centre for Research on Inequality, Human Security and Ethnicity.

Rizvi, Syed A. A. 2019. *Promoting Interfaith Dialogue in Classroom Teaching: A Resource Guide for Teachers and Teacher Educators.* Islamabad: Orient Printer & Publisher.

Sıradağ, Abdurrahim. 2016. Explaining the Conflict in Central African Republic: Causes and Dynamics. *Epiphany: Journal of Transdisciplinary Studies* 9(3), 86–103.

Stokke, Kristian, Roman Vakulchuk and Indra Overland. 2018. "Myanmar: A Political Economy Analysis." *Report Commissioned by the Norwegian Ministry of Foreign Affairs 2018.* Oslo: Norwegian Institute of International Affairs.

Wokusch, Heather. n.d. "Closing KAICIID, Silencing Dialogue", *Metropole.* Assessed Online; *metropole.at/guest-commentary-closing-kaiciid-silencing--dialogue.* (Accessed 28/03/2020).

CHAPTER 5

The Programme for Christian-Muslim Relations in Africa (PROCMURA) Work in Building Peaceful and Inclusive Societies

Florence Iminza and Esther Mombo

INTRODUCTION

The role of faiths in development is becoming more visible as faith is one of the unifying factors in the community. The documentation of this role is yet to be given the visibility that it requires. This chapter discusses the role that PROCMURA has played in development of peaceful and inclusive societies, as envisaged by the overarching aim of the Sustainable Development Goals (SDGs). The Programme for Christian-Muslim Relations in Africa (hereinafter referred to as PROCMURA) is a Pan-African Christian organization that stretches a hand of friendship to the Muslim communities in sub-Saharan Africa. PROCMURA is one of the

F. Iminza
Programme for Christian-Muslim Relations in Africa (PROCMURA),
Nairobi, Kenya

E. Mombo (✉)
St. Paul's University, Limuru, Kenya

© The Author(s), under exclusive license to Springer Nature Switzerland AG 2022
E. Chitando, I. S. Gusha (eds.), *Interfaith Networks and Development*, Sustainable Development Goals Series,
https://doi.org/10.1007/978-3-030-89807-6_5

Christian organizations in Africa that is dedicated to building positive relationships between Christians and Muslims across the entire continent.

Although strictly speaking it is neither a multi-faith organization nor an interfaith one, but an organization whose membership is rooted in the Churches (PROCMURA Constitution and By Laws 2003), it carries out work that can rightly be categorised as interfaith. It works towards constructing Christian and Muslim relations for peace and peaceful coexistence. Its focus is only on Christians and Muslims who have the largest numerical strength in Africa and therefore are the major religious actors in the continent. It was founded in 1959 by the missionary churches in Europe, North America, and Africa. It covers countries in sub-Saharan Africa that are predominantly Christian and Muslim in population. These include countries in East, Central, Southern and West Africa; Francophone and Anglophone regions. It has its central office in Nairobi, Kenya whereas its regional offices for Anglophone countries are in Nigeria and Togo (Francophone).

To date, PROCMURA's presence is felt in 20 countries, while 10 others are at contact-persons-experience levels that are being explored for substantive interfaith work. PROCMURA works with and through National Councils (NCCs), membership churches, ecumenical movements and interfaith networks. It collaborates with government and non-governmental organizations, Faith Based Organizations (FBOs), Civil Society Organizations (CSOs), Community Based Organizations (CBOs), and Regional bodies whose goals and aspirations are in part or in whole consistent with PROCMURA's. It consults with the African Union (AU) and diplomatic agencies on matters of peace, security and interfaith relations. Alliances with the World Council of Churches (WCC) and other similar global religious organizations such as multilateral and bilateral institutions are very important to PROCMURA given the global nature and interest in the issues of inter-faith.

As a pan-African Christian organization, PROCMURA upholds the pursuit for a just and peaceful society for all. It affirms freedom of religion where everyone is free to practice their faith and co-exist with other faiths peacefully. It believes in the equality of all people, that as an FBO, truth and love are of paramount values for peaceful co-existence. It acknowledges mutual respect, good neighbourliness, and tolerance as critical components in the search for a peaceful, compassionate, and just world and strives to serve as a resource pool for the churches to interpret the gospel faithfully in an interfaith environment of Christians and Muslims (PROCMURA Handbook 2019).

A Brief History and Interfaith Work

PROCMURA was founded at a time when most of the African nations were agitating for political independence from colonialism (PROCMURA Handbook 2019). This was in 1959. Most states were seeking for cooperation and collaboration across diverse ethno, religious and linguistic divides, to rid Africa of the colonial grip and that independent states would consist of Muslims, Christians and African Religionists. It is against this backdrop that the churches called for a moratorium; for missionary churches to allow the African churches to self-propagate, self-govern, self-support, and self-sustain. As a result, the seed of PROCMURA was sown.

Interfaith Work

PROCMURA's work among Christians and Muslims in Africa is predicated in the mission of its Founders who envisioned a continent where Christianity and Islam, though rivals and competing in their ideological world view, would have to seek ways to coexist peacefully. The mission agenda and universal appeal of Christianity and Islam has led to the pitting of Muslims and Christians against each other as competitors; to win souls; and as rivals in trying to supersede each other. Informed by this reality, and as affirmed years later, by various theologians working for peace among religions such as Lamb (1985) and Knitter (1995, 2002), there has been an urgent quest to nurture tolerance between Christians and Muslims, as well as among the different religions. It is anticipated that will create a peaceful environment that will lead to overcoming inequalities as articulated by SDG 10.

Firstly, there is the drive to promote among the Churches in Africa faithful and responsible Christian witness in an interfaith environment of Christians and Muslims that promotes and not unduly jeopardizes the spirit of good neighbourliness. There is also the need to help the African churches and Christians in understanding Islam and Muslims so that they can relate with Muslims from an informed perspectives and secondly, to have constructive engagements with Muslims for peaceful coexistence and development. The first mandate in PROCMURA circles, usually referred to as the *intra faith work*, helps PROCMURA put its own house in order.

It is deemed the core business of the organization as it helps dispense ignorance of the religious other—*the Muslims*, and stereotyping that would otherwise be a fertile ground for breeding misunderstanding and conflicts. Sometimes violent conflicts have been witnessed in some countries as a result of misunderstanding over what would appear simple issues. Such controversies revolve around animal slaughter, Christian and Muslim public debates (*Mihadhara*), Crusades, and more recently, ethno-religious conflicts (Ngwobia 2019) and radicalization and violent extremism (*see, PROCMURA Programme Reports at www.procmura-prica.org*).

The second part of PROCMURA's mandate is to promote Christian constructive engagement with Muslims, so that together, members of the two communities can work towards the promotion of peace and peaceful coexistence, and embark on joint actions on issues that militate against the development of society. Thus, there is the drive to reach out to the Muslim communities for constructive engagements, in conversations and dialogue around issues that concern humanity as a whole. This is categorized within PROCMURA, as *interfaith work*. Christians and Muslims, men, women and youth have not only been able to sit down around tables to consult on issues of conflict prevention, peace building and reconciliation among other issues, but also carried out joint community activities (diapraxis) in a bid to solve problems of life. These practical activities make a significant contribution towards meeting the Sustainable Development Goals (SDGs).

PROCMURA has made major strides in forging Christian-Muslim relations in the African continent and coalescing communities of faith together on matters of conflict prevention and peace-building. This is expressed in the SDG number 16 on promoting peaceful and inclusive societies for sustainable development. The achievements and strengths of PROCMURA are hinged on the development of human resource within the churches that understand Islam and Christian-Muslim relations. The pool of experts on Islam and Christian-Muslim relations (Islamicists) produced by PROCMURA and the increasing capacity of Church leaders and women knowledgeable on issues of Islam and Christian-Muslim relations, as well as the inclusion of Islamic studies at theological colleges, are evidence of PROCMURA's contribution to issues of Christian-Muslim relations in Africa and interfaith network (Mbillah 2013). Many of these have been made possible by asserting objectives such as: To effect and facilitate research and education; To assist the churches in a given country or region within a country to create Area Committees that are main channels of implementation of projects at the grassroots (country levels); To serve as representatives of churches cooperating with the Programme in their respective areas; To subscribe to, assist, subsidize, and cooperate with any Organization or Institution whose objectives are in whole or in part similar to those of PROCMURA, and to subscribe to any funds, charitable or otherwise, which may be deemed likely to promote the interest of the Organization; To serve as a continental point of contact and reference to the Churches and para—church communities in Africa and beyond, and without prejudice to its autonomy and what it stands for, promote collaboration and coordination on matters relating faithful Christian witness and Christian constructive engagements with Muslims for peace and peaceful coexistence (*PROCMURA Handbook*, 2019). Substantive areas of interfaith work in PROCMURA are seen in the following areas:

Awareness Creation on Christian-Muslim Relations and Vanguards of Peace Youth Programmes

In view of the relative lack of knowledge, especially among Christians, on Islam, awareness creation is the basic foundation of information sharing about the two religions that make it possible for members to begin to appreciate key areas of the others faith. Through awareness creation, youth, women and church leaders, including lay people, access basic information that is expected to enhance their decision-making of faithful witness and collaboration for peace and peaceful co-existence.

Christian-Muslim relations in Africa, like elsewhere in the world, constitute complex business as it has the field has at its core issues of politics, economics, culture, religion and social issues. These core issues are not always understood and appreciated as a wholesome package, which everyone engaged in the vocation needs to take on board. To fully understand this, PROCMURA embarks on awareness creation involving the leaders of the churches in Africa, women, youth, lay and ordained members, and eventually the wider society of Christians at the grassroots levels who live and practice their faith in an interfaith environment of Christians and Muslims.

ACHIEVEMENTS

PROCMURA affirms the principle of partnership, collaboration and networking in communities. Being a capacity building and relational organization, PROCMURA believes in the need to network and collaborate with other actors in the same area of work.

Networking

Networking is a process whereby experience and information are shared and organizations complement one another. Presently, PROCMURA networks at regional and continental levels with those actors who share the same values and vision. Thus, PROCMURA networks with international institutions and development partners and with other similar institutions such as the All Africa Conference of Churches (AACC). Collaboration with relevant actors includes participation in workshops and conferences. An opportunity to network and collaborate provides the platform for PROCMURA to influence others to share its vision and also to avoid duplication of effort.

The overall achievement has been networking and collaboration aiming at increasing efficiency and best practices in the institution. Ecumenical and church related organizations which are collaborator include the AACC, Fellowship of Christian Councils and Churches in the Great Lakes and Horn of Africa (FECCLAHA) Organization of African Instituted Churches (OAIC), World Student Christian Federation Africa Region (WSCF), International Movement of Catholic Students (IMCS) International Young Christian Students (IYCS). Inter-faith organizations that have been collaborators or potential collaborators include the African Council of Religious Leaders (ACRL), Interfaith Action for Peace in Africa (IFAPA), World Conference on Religions for Peace (WCRP), Interfaith Youth Peace Initiative (IYPI) and the United Religions Initiative (URI). Two cases are highlighted in relation to PROCMURA's work for peaceful and inclusive societies in turbulent times in two countries, namely, the Republic of South Sudan (RSS) and the Central African Republic (CAR).

Engagement in South Sudan

We need not emphasize how much the Republic of South Sudan (RSS) needs peace. In the period preceding and following the Referendum (which was held in 2011), PROCMURA carried out a series of consultations and conferences in Upper Nile State of Southern Sudan, and in Malakal, replicating them in the Equatorial Region in Juba. The civil war in Sudan left the southern part of the country ravaged and grossly under developed. Teeming tension between Christians and Muslims had become the norm given that the war took on a religio-political face. Yet, the potential was with the younger generation, fresh with experiences of refugee status and a new generation with new ideas, all at the cusp of a new Sudan and a new era. PROCMURA had a responsibility to ensure that peace and development underlie the emotions, notions and goals of a new era. What was unique with PROCMURA's programmes was that it brought Christian and Muslim leaders together to inculcate in them a spirit of positive tolerance as South Sudan was preparing for their historic referendum for self-determination.

On the Christian and Muslim youth, HIV/AIDS was a thematic area that needed attention. Joint consultations had to be made and seen against the background of the vulnerability of the youth, a good number of whom returned to South Sudan following the Comprehensive Peace Agreement (CPA) of 2005. Others had also come in from neighbouring countries to prepare themselves to vote at the referendum. The Sudan Council of Churches (SCC) leadership, and the South Sudan Muslim Council (SSMC) had been and continued to be very instrumental, working hand in hand with PROCMURA (Report_Sudan_Youth_on HIV/AIDS.pdf, www.procmura-prica.org). An opportunity to re-evaluate South Sudan has been that of uncertainty, but the major investment lies in safeguarding the principles of peace, justice and reconciliation. Good governance underlies these principles but the prerequisite here is peace. Building bridges between Christians and Muslims is one of the ways in which peace can be successfully sustained in the country.

Activities in the Central African Republic

The situation in the Central African Republic (CAR) where the Anti-Balaka ("anti-machete" or "anti-sword" in the local Sango language) militia who are largely non-Muslim and therefore labelled Christian are attacking Séléka "(Coalition" in Sango) Rebels labelled Muslim and the actual Muslim communities has caught the world's attention. PROCMURA had been inundated with phone calls and emails seeking to understand whether what was happening in the CAR was a religious war. Some asked bluntly: "Is it a Christian war against Muslims?" As an organisation dedicated to Christian constructive engagement with Muslims for peace and peaceful co-existence, it was always clear that when the Séléka Rebels leader Michel Djotodia (a Muslim by religion) recruited mercenaries from Chad and Sudan (who by religion were also Muslims), to fight alongside with him, the conflict was going to assume a religious label. True to this, François Bozizé, the former president (himself a Christian) of the CAR in his determination to ward off the rebel attack played the religious card when he suggested to the majority Christian population that Muslim forces were coming to take over the country.

In its modest attempt to stop religion being misused in the conflict, PROCMURA in January 2013, rallied Christian and Muslim religious leaders of the French-speaking countries of Central and West Africa to issue an appeal to the two factions (government and rebels) to make peace so as to prevent mayhem in the country. (See the Maroua message of peace in the Central African Republic on; www.procmura-prica.org/en). When the appeal was not heeded, and Michel Djotodia took power by force of arms, the perception of some non-Muslims (especially Christians) was that the Muslims had taken over the country. On the other hand, some of the Muslims' perception were that it was now their time to rule the country. As these sentiments were being expressed openly, Christian and Muslim religious leaders who were deeply concerned about the polarization of society along religious lines invited PROCMURA to intervene. The General Adviser of PROCMURA went to the country and met with Christian and Muslim religious leaders as well as political leaders of the then new government, and laid bare to them the consequences ahead, if they failed to unite and reconcile the country. (See the Bangui Briefing on www.procmura-prica.org/en/ and Bangui Report). These attempts by PROCMURA did not yield the desired results. Religion had been politicised and politics had been religionised, thus creating the mayhem that was feared. The situation in the Central African Republic had important lessons for African political and religious leaders and possibly political and religious leaders elsewhere. The lessons are simple and straight forward as outlined by the then PROCMURA General Adviser, Rev. Dr. Johnson Mbillah, "Do not ever try to politicise religion or religionise politics. If you do, the consequences will be far reaching. Distant and recent history provides such lessons for the present and for posterity" (*PROCMURA Handbook* 2019).

Consequently, consultation and conference methods are used to ensure joint identification of community issues and to enhance participation of Christians and Muslims but not to the exclusion of any other religions. A workshop setting usually, would consist of 20–35 participants to enhance its effectiveness. These are held as regularly as funds would allow for different categories of groups of persons on different thematic areas. It is an opportunity to train on issues and to enhance the knowledge base and sharing of specific issues.

ADDITIONAL DEVELOPMENTAL ACTIVITIES

Alongside the engagements outlined above, PROCMURA has been involved in the following developmental activities:

Communication and Information Sharing

Other related approaches are seminars and conferencing where research findings through occasional papers are presented and discussed and Communication and Information Sharing as an approach to enable PROCMURA Constituencies to be productive and cost effective. PROCMURA has increased its computer accessories and online visibility. However, this becomes a challenge when the Area Advisers (Field Staff) and other stakeholders are considered, since access to computers and internet varies from one individual to the other. More important is the information dissemination to the members, which is in the form of literature, newsletters, books, and other print materials. This is an important approach of creating awareness within the constituency and other relevant institutions such as theological colleges.

Research Training, Facilitation and Accompaniment

The main function of research is to encourage and support action on academic and relevant topics. It is aimed at producing academic papers and documenting research findings through occasional papers, and publishing volumes thereof to help shape and reframe narratives, etc. Training on the other hand, aims at the development of skills and professional competences. PROCMURA Central Office perceives itself as a facilitator and coordinates. Implementation of activities is mainly through Area (country) Committees facilitated by Area Advisers. In this case, the Central

Office personnel plan jointly and facilitate Area Advisers in their work. This role of facilitation and accompaniment feature more prominently as PROCMURA builds capacities of grassroots facilitators and theologians.

Empowerment of Women on Christian-Muslim Relations

Providing adequate information and empowering women on issues of Christian-Muslim relations in Africa is an area which generates a lot of challenges, especially when it comes to women. Women constitute the group that suffers the most when violence erupts and yet are seldom included in peace and reconciliation meetings (Chitando 2020). The African legend, Kofi Annan, noted that there is no more effective tool than the empowerment of women (news.un.org. acc. 05.05.2020). It is therefore urgent and important to have women informed and educated on matters related to Christian-Muslim relations for a better understanding. These is also in line with popularization of the UNSCR 1325 (2000) and 2242 that seek to increase the participation of women in peace-building and conflict prevention and reconciliation. Women are well known to have the ability and openness to interact with one another without considering their religious barriers/differences, and conscious that they are vessels of informal relations. This has informed the processes of conscientisation that have been conducted in such a way that women are informed about matters related to Islam and Christian-Muslim relations. The women are able to discuss issues of particular and common concern to both Christian and Muslim women, for the promotion of a better environment. In addition, the fact of providing women with education on Christian-Muslim relations has spread the PROCMURA message and equipped women to be active in both the governance and programmatic work of faithful Christian witness and peace and peaceful coexistence.

The Empowerment of Youth

PROCMURA prioritises building the capacity of youth to practice their faith peacefully. Recognizing that youth form at least sixty per cent of the populations of many countries in Africa and acknowledging that young people are energetic but with little experience, PROCMURA seeks to build the capacity of the youth so that they can talk about and practice their faith in non- provocative ways. The youth constituency forms the majority of many countries' population in Africa. They bear the brunt of negative effects in society; a situation that they are able to change. The negative effects in the society they contend with on a daily basis range from being both 'executors' and victims of all forms of violence, armed and institutional, to circumstances of being school dropouts because of poverty or sheer youth delinquency. Situations arise where, based on ignorance and illiteracy among them, they get absorbed in spearheading prejudiced religious positions and violence both of which do not augur well for the peaceful environment which is a prerequisite for sustainable development.

The situation described above can be reversed if the dynamic living nature of the youth, their level of understanding and interpretation of issues, and readiness to interact, as well as exchange ideas across diverse ideological leanings is identified, explored, synergized and consciously given a space to contribute to peaceful, positive, socio-economic transformation. One of the areas that can either galvanize or send them separate ways is the use of religion. It has been witnessed throughout the continent that just as inter-faith cooperation has enabled people of faith to generate understanding and tolerance among themselves, religious conflicts have infused, in several communities, the culture of non-cooperation and self-defence, thus bringing in the elements of mistrust and prejudices. PROCMURA is investing towards an environment where through generation of responsible actions by Christian youth and encouraging joint Christian and Muslim youth efforts, a culture of tolerance and constructive engagement for mutual attendance to issues of commonality in society can be arrived at. PROCMURA deems it critical to engage in the construction of harmonious relationships and spawn processes through which issues such as peace building and conflict transformation, radicalization and violent extremism, can get practical and full attention of the youth.

A focus on youth is set within a context of understanding that these are young, dynamic and energetic people who in some cases are idle and unemployed. Therefore, they are susceptible to manipulation by forces of war and conflict. The youth programme aims at making it possible for youth to talk about their faith in non-provocative manner. Youth are becoming peace vanguards and peace ambassadors in Africa, when they understand the norms of religious freedom and tolerance. Capacity building/training is done to establish a corps of trainers at the local, national and international levels. More recently, PROCMURA embarked on launching PROCMURA Youth Chapters in universities and other

CHALLENGES

institutions of learning in a bid to help build religious tolerance and social cohesion amidst the raging mayhem of radicalization and violent extremism.

There is a skewed attempt to foster Christian-Muslim interfaith work in two ways. Firstly, as 'a Christian only' and secondly as 'a male dominated' enterprise. This is implied in an account relayed by Rev. Silas Wanda to the Christian-Muslim dialogue workshop, held from 3rd to 5th December (1985), in Kenya. The report details the initiatives of Christian-Muslim dialogue in Kenya whose main endeavours was to form 'right attitudes among the faithful Christian toward the Muslim brothers in Christian-Muslim predominant areas and an attempt at fostering mutual understanding between Christians and Muslims' respectively. There are no equivalent initiatives from the Muslim side and neither do we have women voices, as observed by Iminza (2018: 26). The skewed attempt is also observable in Christian-Muslim conflicts and interfaith bridge-building efforts in Nigeria (Ojo and Lateju 2010). Although PROMURA has achieved wide African support from Christian denominations, its primarily Christian composition and agenda has not made room for active Muslim participation. Consequently, its activities have largely been restricted to Christian churches and have built few direct bridges for Christian and Muslim interaction and relationship building (Ojo & Lateju 2010: 6). Similarly, there is no Muslim organization equivalent to PROCMURA that works towards building Muslim-Christian relations in Africa. This leads to a lopsided approach to dialogue and interfaith work, as dialogue is deprived of equal partnership on issues of mutual concern.

According to the Rift Valley Institute Meeting Report, on *Violent Extremism, Risk and Resilience*, held in 2017, there are waning relations between Christians and Muslims as reflected by increased radicalization and violent extremism in which religions of Islam and Christianity are implicated. In addition, there are politico-religious and ethnical conflicts that tend to create confrontation between Christians and Muslims. Terrorism and terrorist ideologies that seem to identify with certain religious/political/ideological beliefs have complicated issues. This makes PROCMURA's work in interfaith engagement precarious. There are a myriad of misconceptions of PROCMURA's ideologies. There are high levels of illiteracy and misinformed youth, which result in degrees of stereotyping. As a result youth have been used and misused by the profiteers of violent conflicts. There are those who think of interfaith work as a mean action towards conversions across faiths. Types and modes of approaches of evangelization adopted by other organizations may not augur well with the principle of promoting good relations between Christians and Muslims as propounded by PROCMURA.

Christian and Muslim misunderstood ideologies remain sensitive, causing tension and may result in conflicts. Muslims and Christians in Africa have been known to fight proxy wars. It is common to see the alliances being formed along the protracted Israeli-Palestinian conflict as negative solidarity is wedged back at home. The net effect is to frustrate the quest for open and honest dialogue with the religious other and missing out on the richness brought about by such interfaces (Amaladoss 2017).

On the political front, a tendency to vote for one particular individual in national elections because of the person's religious affiliation seems to be on the ascendancy (Oded 2000). In the same vein, there is enough reason to believe that some political appointments are carried out because of one's religious affiliation. These have been divisive of society and thereby created conflicts. Globalization and forces of urbanization resulting into increased movement of youth to cities and subsequent increase in the number of slum dwellers and destituteness, breakdown of socio-cultural fabric of society is leading to the decline of moral values resulting in vices and issues like corruption, violence etc. This makes it difficult for youth to settle in specific locations and effect long term projects that can effect desirable changes.

Conclusion

In Africa, Christianity and Islam are the two oldest world religions, brought by Christian missionaries and Muslim merchants, respectively, to sub-Saharan Africa. These two religions currently wield the largest numbers of African peoples, who live side by side. There are families where some are Christians, others Muslims and others practitioners of African Traditional Religion(s). In the distant past African spirituality contributed to a tolerant religious environment. Conflicts between Christians and Muslims then could be described as skirmishes as they were less widespread on the continent. In the recent past and at the time of writing, the situation has changed. It has become increasingly clear that politics, economics, and culture, as well as social and religious issues, are part and parcel of a package in Christian- Muslim relations which have sometimes contributed to or stimulated conflicts between Christians and Muslims in some parts of Africa. Yet religion is becoming increasingly definitive of people's identity and a hoard of extremism.

The window of hope is that religious leaders are ready to cooperate in matters of common interest and to promote peace. The existence of regions where PROCMURA is not yet operational means that there is scope for it to expand significantly and promote sustainable development in Africa. PROCMURA recognises the need of such expansion of programmes to include social issues such as putting in place youth sustainability projects such as car wash to help create job opportunities for the youth. Today, interfaith work is closely linked with diplomacy and international relations. This in itself remains part of the unexploited opportunities for PROCMURA in its quest for interfaith work and development (Madelaine 2006; Troy 2008). Hope is also reflected in the growing interest of churches and their availability and willingness to work with PROCMURA, including the interest by universities and seminaries to embrace PROCMURA's principle of faithful Christian witness in an interfaith environment of Christians and Muslims. This has been motivating PROCMURA staff to continue undertaking interfaith work.

Improved ICT facilities in Africa, air waves and FM radio stations to convey messages of peace, especially the handy mobile phones that are making computer technology and information accessible and transforming lives in Africa, has given impetus to PROCMURA's interfaith work in mobilization of groups to action and information dissemination. Overall, PROCMURA represents a unique and strategic organization that is investing in peacebuilding, cultivating healthy Christian-Muslim relations and providing a sound platform for the achievement of the SDGs in Africa.

References

Amaladoss, M. 2017. *Interreligious Encounters: opportunities and Challenges.* New York: Orbis Books.

Chitando, A. (Ed.). 2020. *Women and Peacebuilding in Africa.* London: Routledge.

Iminza, F. 2018. *Women Participation in Christian–Muslim Dialogue in Kakamega and Nairobi Counties, Kenya.* (Unpublished) PhD Thesis, Kenyatta University.

Knitter, P. 2002. *Introducing Theologies of Religion.* New York: Maryknoll, Orbis Books.

Knitter, P. 1995. *One Earth Many Religions: Multifaith Dialogue and Global Responsibility.* Maryknoll, New York: Orbis Books.

Lamb, C. 1985. *Belief in Mixed Society.* London: Lion Publishing plc.

Madelaine, A. 2006. "Faith and Diplomacy," *Review of Faith & International Affairs* 4(2): 3–9.

Mbillah, J. 2013. "The Inclusion of the Study of Islam and Christian-Muslim Relations as an Imperative for Theological Education in Africa." In I. A. Phiri and D. Werner (ed). *Handbook of Theological Education in Africa.* Oxford, UK: Regnum Books International.

Ngwobia, J. M. 2019. 'Causes and Effects of Ethno Religious Conflicts on Women. In *'Nigeria': a Paper Presented at PROCMURA Seasonal School in Jos, Nigeria.* (Unpublished)

Ojo, M. A. and F. T. Lateju. 2010. Christian-Muslim Conflicts and Interfaith Bridge-Building Efforts in Nigeria. *The Review of Faith in International Affairs* 8(1): 31–38.

Oded, A. 2000. *Islam and Politics in Kenya* . London : Lyne Riener Publishers.

PROCMURA Publications. 2003. *PROCMURA Constitution and By Laws.* Nairobi.

PROCMURA Handbook, 2019. *PROCMURA What It Is And What It Stands For.* Nairobi.

Rift Valley Institute, (2017, February). "*Meeting Report on Violent Extremism Risk and Resilience.*" Retrieved 25.03.2020, from http://riftvalley.net/download/file/fid/4519.

Troy, J. 2008. "Faith-Based Diplomacy Under Examination." *The Hague Journal of Diplomacy* 3(3): 209–231.

UN News, www.un.news.org. Accessed 05.05.2020.

PART II

Interfaith Networks and Gender in Africa

CHAPTER 6

Women of Faith Working Together as Mothers of a Culture of Peace: The Women's Interfaith Council in Northern Nigeria

Kathleen McGarvey

INTRODUCTION

Northern Nigeria is a vast region made up of three geo-political zones (North-East, North-Central and North-West), covering a total of nineteen of the thirty-six States of the Federal Republic of Nigeria. For many centuries, Muslims and Christians co-existed peacefully, even though Christians are the minority and Islam has always been associated with political and traditional powers, especially after the Jihad of Usman Dan Fodio in 1804 which led to the foundation of the Sokoto Caliphate. However, in recent decades, the region has witnessed troubled Muslim-Christian relations, which is escalated by the unstable socio-political situation in the country. Women in this region are seriously impoverished and

K. McGarvey (✉)
Missionary Sisters of Our Lady of Apostles (OLA), Lagos, Nigeria

© The Author(s), under exclusive license to Springer Nature Switzerland AG 2022
E. Chitando, I. S. Gusha (eds.), *Interfaith Networks and Development*, Sustainable Development Goals Series,
https://doi.org/10.1007/978-3-030-89807-6_6

99

religious arguments, especially within Islam, have often been used to discriminate against women in the game of identity-politics. This has created and deepened gender inequality, thereby threatening Sustainable Development Goal (SDG) 10 focusing on overcoming inequality. In addition, it is contrary to SDG 5 focusing on the empowerment of all women and girls.

In May 2010, together with women religious leaders and supported by the Sisters of Our Lady of Apostles, we established the Women's Interfaith Council. This initiative has made and continues to make important steps in giving women a voice in the whole difficult task of dialogue and peace-building in Northern Nigeria, particularly in Kaduna State where it is situated. We also established an Interfaith Forum of Muslim and Christian Youth Associations based on the same principles. The women and youth leaders are inspired and motivated by their faith convictions and they all work together on a voluntary basis. This chapter presents a summary of the work of the Women's Interfaith Council and raises some questions which I believe are important to consider in the practice of interreligious dialogue and in the studies of religious pluralism. While the Women's Interfaith Council has an active website, many of the Reports and papers it has produced and which are referred to in this chapter are not yet available online. They can, however, be requested from their office.

Some Background to Interfaith Relations in Nigeria

My experience in Nigeria taught me that most of the conflicts are as a result of political manipulations of religion for economic and political gains. Many Nigerians are very critical of the colonial enterprise and see that so much of the suffering endured today is a legacy inherited from that phase of history. More immediate causes of the conflict and the serious security challenges in the Northern States of Nigeria today are a variety of factors that tend to differ in emphasis from one State to another. These generally include economic issues and narrowing opportunities, resource-related conflicts, unequal access to political power and position among ethnic groups, the feeling of marginalization, and issues around appointments into traditional leadership positions. All these affect relationships between individuals and groups, resulting in deep-seated suspicion and the inability to develop cooperative relationships. Especially in the North, there is an overlap of ethnic identities with religious affiliation. This unfortunately finds expression in growing polarization along religious fault lines, thus creating a mixture of ethno-religious crisis which is grounded in a long history of unequal power distribution.

Religion becomes the instrument of offence and defence; and a tool in the hands of people who utilise it to manipulate the consciousness of the people. This manipulation takes place in many ways, including at the levels of political campaign messaging, political appointments, allocation and citing of projects, sponsorship of Pilgrimages abroad, all of course influencing how people should vote. Furthermore, the weak adherence to the rule of law promotes impunity and the large pool of unskilled, unemployed and indeed unemployable youths are ready tools for violence, drug abuse, criminality and insurgency. Radicalization of the religious space has also been a serious factor and while it is not the only reason for groups such as the infamous Boko Haram, certainly the provocative and inciting preaching by some religious clerics has been instrumental in the rise of today's insurgency in the north.

Women in Nigeria

Women in Nigeria constitute 49.2 percent of the country's estimated population of 193 million (NPC 2017). Despite a slow but significant advancement for women in politics, and although these numbers can fluctuate, women still constitute well below 10 percent of the executive and judiciary at local, state and federal levels. Political processes have tended to highlight the involvement of men in decision-making. However, women have always been present, active and influential even if most often in an invisible and non-institutionalized way. The same can be said about peacebuilding processes. Although a lot has been written on peacekeeping operations, information on gendered perspectives of peacekeeping in Nigeria is rather scanty. Where women are featured in peacekeeping and management of violent conflicts, they are portrayed as merely victims; rarely is their involvement as combatants or peacemakers discussed. In Nigeria, there is a tendency to have all male bodies of leaders (particularly at religious and traditional ethnic levels) who are presumed to be able to speak for the whole community, women included. Therefore, incorporating a gender perspective into peace building efforts involves helping men and women to work together in a participatory way. This involves trying to subtly and diplomatically avoid these situations where one sex dominates the decision-making process and claims to know more about the needs and interests of the other (McGarvey 2009; Yusuf and McGarvey 2015).

WOMEN'S INTERFAITH COUNCIL, NIGERIA

In Kaduna, North West Nigeria, following an initial invitation made in May 2010 by the author to women leaders of women's faith-based groups to come together in a spirit of sincere and active dialogue and seek to confront women's common concerns, the Interfaith Forum of Muslim and Christian Women's Associations was established. The primary concern shared by women in Kaduna is the lack of peace, security and justice in the region. Very much related to this is the fact that women's poverty and lack of voice in their religious community as well as in the larger society present great obstacles to women's assuming their responsibility to be Mothers of a culture of peace. Thus, the Forum, commonly known as the Women's Interfaith Council (WIC), strengthens women's voices by bringing them together to speak as one. The executive council is formed of the state or diocesan leaders of each major women's faith group: Catholic Women's Organization (CWO), Federation of Muslim Women's Associations in Nigeria (FOMWAN), Anglican Mothers' Union, Muslim Sisters Organization, Baptist Missionary Union, Women's fellowship of the Association of Evangelical churches (ECWA and TEKAN), Women's fellowships of the Pentecostal churches and of the Organization of African Instituted Churches, Women in Da'wah, NASFAT women's wing, Ansar ud deen, Unique Muslim Sisters Association, and so on. All major faith groups in the state are represented by their leaders.

Today, WIC is legally registered at national and state level, has a Constitution, a Board of Trustees, an Executive Council, registered member faith organizations, sponsors, and partners. Its vision is "a society where Muslims and Christians live together in peace, where the rights of women are respected and where women and youth are protagonists of peaceful coexistence and development". Events are held on a regular basis, bringing women members of the faith organizations together. Their activities range from formation in conflict analysis and transformation, press statements on some recent moment of tension or violence, radio programmes on issues relating to women and religious coexistence, seminars with political and religious leaders on contemporary issues of conflict and women's concerns, conferences on pertinent issues such as insecurity and women's response, interfaith prayer, celebrations of women's day, solidarity visits as interfaith women religious leaders to the victims of ethnic-religious violence, skills acquisition programmes, sensitization on pertinent issues in local communities and in schools, and so on.

At most of its events, WIC invites prominent political and religious leaders to attend and thus ensures they hear their voice. WIC now networks with government and non-government organizations as well as with civil society organizations involved in the promotion of women's rights, peace and development. Their newsletter is published annually and lists all their partners and the various initiatives they have organized or participated in. This includes for example, in 2017, a Stakeholders' Sensitization on Voters Education using Electronic Voting in Kaduna State Local Government Elections organized by the Kaduna State Independent Electoral Commission (KAD-SIECOM); a Women Entrepreneurship Programme (WEP) Sensitization and Exhibition Programme organized by ABANTU for Development; Documenting Memory and Encouraging InterGroup Engagement in Southern Kaduna: Roundtable Meeting for Women organized by the Kukah Centre; a Sensitization Workshop on Violence against Women and Girls organized by Gender Awareness Trust (GAT) in collaboration with Friends Unite; an International Conference on Love and Tolerance: Countering Violence Extremism through Peace, Education and Love organized by UFUK Dialogue in collaboration with the Institute for Peace and Conflict Resolution (Ministry of Foreign Affairs), UN Women, European Union, Nigeria Stability and Reconciliation Program; a Workshop on Climate Change Knowledge Immersion which was jointly organized by the Federal Ministry of Environment and the World Bank; a courtesy visit to the Commissioner of Women Affairs and Social Development, Kaduna State; a focus group discussion on conflict resolution through inter-religious dialogue organized by the Postgraduate Students of Kaduna State University. This list only demonstrates the scope of engagements which this interfaith organization has enabled women of faith to come together across the perceived religious divide to be empowered and formed, to express their concerns as women, and to ensure their active engagement in the promotion of peace and development in their society.

A seminar was held in Kaduna in 2015, organised by the Kukah Centre (a Public-Policy Think-Tank), with the Women's Interfaith Council, where women of both faiths gathered to share on 'Northern Women, What do you want? (in Hausa: *Matan Arewa: Me Kuke So?*' (Kukah Centre 2015). This seminar was organised as an effort to give women a voice in an environment where men take decisions and where even women leaders in political parties are chosen by men. This was a very good occasion for women to speak openly not only about their dreams but also the obstacles they face in realising them. One of the papers presented was 'The Northern Women's Manifesto and Charter of Demands,' an excellent document prepared in 2010 by the Gender Equality and Women's Empowerment Strategy Group. Here it is stated that

> A key challenge to women's human rights in Nigeria is the interaction and often times conflict of the three parallel systems of laws, namely statutory, religious and customary especially on issues of women's rights, participation and well-being in general. For instance, the re-introduction and expansion of Sharia in the northern states has legitimised and encouraged extremism. This has aggravated a myriad of discriminatory practices against or with implications for women. Examples include withdrawal of freedom of movement provided for by the constitution; imposition of dress codes on women; promotion of child marriage at the expense of girl-child education; violation of women's reproductive rights by criminalising pregnancy outside marriage; intimidation of women's human rights activists; ban on provision of sexuality education and information in schools or by non-governmental organisations, among others. The consequences of these practices or the threat are enormous and constitute colossal barriers to the enjoyment of rights provided for in regional or international treaties that Nigeria has committed itself to over the years.' (GEWESTRAG 2010)

The participants, members of the Women's Interfaith Council, agreed with this reality. As on so many other occasions, in their group sharing following the input, they highlighted the importance of them as women coming together, supporting other women, knowing their rights both in the constitution and in their religions, and contributing to public discussions.

Why Interreligious Dialogue of Women Is Necessary

I am convinced that if we are to eliminate discriminations suffered by women in Africa, where religious identity is valued by a great majority of the population, we must give our full support to any effort that involves bringing women's faith-based groups together in sincere and active dialogue. Working with and through women's well-organized faith-groups will be much more effective than working to confront women's concerns through secular discourse. Change will not be brought about through secular discourse or laws alone. Women's lives at community level are much more affected by religious and customary laws and norms and it is faith based groups working within the framework and terminologies of their faith communities that can best ensure that oppressive customs are somehow eradicated and women's oppression is overcome. The analysis of cultural and religious beliefs, which is necessary if the greatest obstacles to women's promotion are to be removed, will undoubtedly be much more effective if it results from reflections are done within women's faith-based groups. Thus, women can be empowered to truly be catalysts of positive change in their communities. One can more easily reach down through women's faith-based groups to the very local levels. If the leaders of these faith groups see peace-building and positive interreligious relations as a priority, as they are beginning to do in Kaduna through the work of the Women's Interfaith Council, change can truly happen. Below I identify some reasons why interreligious dialogue of women is an imperative and raise some observations which can be learnt for interreligious dialogue and development at global level.

Common Concerns

The first and basic reason why interreligious dialogue of women is imperative is that the sufferings and concerns of women in their shared social, political, cultural and economic context are very often quite similar. These include issues that affect the whole population in Northern Nigeria such as poverty, unemployment, insecurity, bad governance and civil unrest. Also included are issues that affect women alone, such as abuses within marriage, disinheritance and lack of access to resources, reduced decision-making power, and greater responsibility for sexual morality in society. These issues are intensified due to diverse forms of cultural and religious discrimination which women of both faiths experience, just as the poverty in the region is intensified by the conflicts. The Women's Interfaith Council in Kaduna has on numerous occasions highlighted these common concerns. In fact, the very initial gathering of women faith leaders in May 2010 was an invitation to identify concerns and having done so and seen the similarity. The women faith leaders saw the advantages of coming together to face these as one body.

Discourse About Women in Divisive Identity-Politics

As I have stated above, throughout Northern Nigerian history, religious discourse has been an organizing and mobilising force used to establish distinct identities as a means of gaining access to power. Christianity united the many minority tribes in the region, just as Islam served to fortify and justify the quest of the Hausa-Fulani elite to maintain power and control in the region. Often times, particularly among the Muslim leaders, the symbol and visible affirmation of a distinct, superior, pious Islamic identity has been women—seclusion, hijab segregated public space, refusal of suffrage, controlled sexual behaviour. The superiority of Islam is emphasised as a religion that gives women great rights and upholds sexual morality. Only in recent years have women, now educated and with a feminist awareness of oppression and of rights, organized themselves to contribute to and redefine the Islamic discourses on women, doing so in a way that maintains legitimacy with the religious and political authorities. They are not opposing the view that Islamic society is superior, but they are insisting that that superiority be lived rather than only claimed. Christianity has not used religious discourse about women to gain political power in the region. While patriarchy is an overarching issue on women's discourse, particularly within Islam as practiced in Nigeria and especially in the North, within Christianity also it has been and still is used to define distinct identities of men and women. This discourse justifies patriarchal power in the family, the church and in the larger society. Christian women are today seeking to redefine their identity and they too do so in a way that maintains legitimacy with their religious and community leaders.

Particularly well documented is the focus put on women in the initial fervour of shar'ia implementation when this was introduced in twelve of the nineteen northern states in 1999. At that time, international attention was drawn to the cases of Safiya Yakubu Hussaini and Amina Lawal, two separate cases, one in Sokoto in 2000 and the other in Katsina in 2002, both accused of adultery and sentenced to death by stoning (Ibrahim 2004: 183–204). In both instances and due to the use of *fiqh* arguments, the appellants in shar'ia courts were successful. Of course, many other violations and abuses were and still are suffered by women within their homes and communities in the name of religion and the victims do not find such professional support. Challenging this trend will place women more strategically to contribute towards achieving the SDGs in Northern Nigeria.

6 WOMEN OF FAITH WORKING TOGETHER AS MOTHERS OF A CULTURE...

Women's Role as Mothers of a Culture of Peace

In Nigeria, it is generally accepted by people of all ethnic groups and religions that specific gender roles are true to human nature. The dominant religions, Christianity and Islam, have served to sustain the cultural concept of male headship; hence to challenge this is tantamount to rebellion against God and is not acceptable to most. How to promote women and society at large within this hierarchical male-female relationship is basically the thrust of the women's movement in Nigeria today, including that of women's peace-building and interfaith efforts. Most women's groups strive to operate cautiously within traditional gender boundaries, articulating the theory of complementary rather than competitive roles in gender relation (McGarvey 2009: 143–162; Kisekka 1992: 105–121). There is great recognition both in Nigeria and globally of the importance of the family, and hence there is conflict between women's domestic responsibilities and their participation in the wider society.

The insistence in both faith communities on women's primary responsibility as mothers is not one to which women in Nigeria have any objection. They, like many women globally, find greatest fulfilment in their maternal role and struggle to live it as best they can within their diverse socio-economic and cultural situations. The Women's Interfaith Council places emphasis on women's important role as Mothers and see this as the primary way in which they can be instrumental in promoting a culture of peace and development. This is of course indicated by their motto which is 'Women of Faith Working Together as Mothers of a Culture of Peace'. A 'Mothers School for Prevention of Violent Extremism', was organised by WIC in Kaduna in July 2017. This was a three-day training of trainer's event, with the aim of training the women leaders of faith groups who in turn would pass on the training received to the members of their groups. An excellent training was given, ranging from mother's self-awareness, the role of women in community development, the role of women in building the security infrastructure for their communities and society, understanding political violence and radicalization.

The group discussions which followed included very emotional moments as women shared on their direct experience of violent extremism, particularly through their own children being involved in one way or the other. While one is challenged by the general acceptance by the women that the male is the authority in the family and they must obey their husbands, as is recorded in their group feedback, there is also great importance and value in the recognition that they have a very great influence as mothers in the eradication of extremism and in the promotion of positive interfaith relations and social development. It was certainly life-giving for women of both faiths to share on how they understand their role as mothers, and on the limitations they experience in living that role, so that they can better assume their responsibility to be mothers of a nation of peace and wellbeing. It was also an opportunity for them to share on the pains of motherhood and indeed as wives in a patriarchal culture and an insecure environment, with so many economic and social impediments. Their sharing as well as the formation they received empowered them to more confidently assume their capacity to work for change.

Important Role of Women in Peacebuilding

Throughout its many different seminars and discussions, WIC has identified many ways in which women have a particular role in peacebuilding. These include their influence over their children as mothers: monitoring their children's behavioural changes, noticing any indication whereby the youngsters might be influenced by radicalism, ensuring they know the friends and circles their children move in, avoiding hate speech of any kind in the home, awareness and curbing of prejudices, promoting interfaith friendships, and so on. Given that women are still very absent in any political or leadership positions, they also noted the 'soft power' women have and which they must use to build sustainable peace. This includes the psycho-social support of friendship and listening to individuals and neighbours who are potentially threading the path of violent extremism; being negotiators in communities especially with women and youth, where violent extremism has torn relationships apart; using their story-telling skills to narrate the adverse effects of violent conflicts towards creating awareness against further occurrence; and indeed the various ways they can influence the behaviour of men even in and from their own home.

They also of course highlighted that women and men often experience violence and peace differently, and this must be brought to the table where the consequences of violence and the path towards peace are discussed. They raised awareness of the realities and difficulties of women as bread winners when the men have been killed in conflict, the increased precariousness faced by women due to lack of education and skills, the vulnerabilities of women in the homes when villages are attacked and ambushed, the particular difficulties of raising children in internally displaced camps, and other very concrete realities often ignored in discussions where men solely participate.

Of course, women [or men] in Nigeria do not constitute one homogenous group. They are diverse not only in religious adherence but also in their understandings of their religion, as well as in their ethnic, social, economic and other categories of identity. If Nigeria is to develop a gender sensitive approach to peace building and development, the experiences of women, including those of the many diverse categories of women, need to be visible and need to be reflected in the design of relevant strategies. The efforts of women need to be recorded since much of what women do is not given the same media coverage as that done by male religious and political leaders. This is repeatedly emphasised and called for by the Women's Interfaith Council which now ensures a press statement is released after many of the events it holds as well as on any occasion when violence erupts. It also hosts a regular radio programme so that the voices of women and youth are heard.

WIC has also taken it upon itself to carry out advocacy or assessment visits in local government areas, especially where violent conflict has been experienced. They meet with leaders of the community (religious and ethnic), and ensure women and youth are also present and heard at these gatherings, to express their concerns and support the greater involvement of women in the conflict resolution processes. Almost inevitably, poverty, voicelessness, ignorance and lack of skills are identified as factors in any conflict, and the need for skills acquisition and empowerment for women and youth is raised. WIC has in fact received funding from various national and international organizations for several projects which it has provided to women and youth faith group leaders and members who in turn pass on this training to their wider membership. This includes training in managerial and financial management skills, training in confectionary/baking and cosmetics/body essentials, bead making, and such. Having met the leaders at community level beforehand ensures women are supported so that they are permitted to participate in these trainings and become somewhat more financially viable and assertive at local level.

Women and Official Interreligious Dialogue Encounters

As we know, women are rarely admitted to leadership of religious bodies, and in most religions, women did not, until quite recently, have access to theological studies. In Nigeria today, there are women leaders in some

Pentecostal churches, some which women have founded. However, in mainline churches, for example, in the Anglican Province of Nigeria, women's ordination is not accepted. Thus, when interreligious encounters are held at official level, women's absence is noticeable. This applies to interreligious encounters of religious leaders in Nigeria as also at international levels. Not only are women themselves visibly absent at interreligious encounters of religious leaders, but gender issues have been given little treatment in theological interreligious discussions (WCC 2005). In theological circles on religious pluralism, most focus has been on the contribution of religious thought to the suppression or oppression of the other, defining that otherness in terms of religious adherence; little attention has been given to how within religious thought women have also been viewed as the Other. Participants in such theological dialogue are challenged by feminist thought, and by the voice of women speaking from the margins to address the insights they raise, particularly that relating to religious symbols, rituals, teachings and structures and to look at how these contribute to women's oppression (King 1998: 40–55).

In Kaduna State, just as women's poverty and vulnerability is greater than that of men, due in great part to a patriarchal culture, so too women's voices and their concerns are often times excluded from Government programmes of response and of mediation in times of conflict and in efforts at reconciliation and peacebuilding. Similarly, women are excluded from the mainline decision-making levels in religious bodies, both Christian and Muslim, as well as prominent interfaith councils and state-sponsored religious bureaus. When interfaith events are organized, especially when it is by government or by influential circles, it is the male religious and community leaders who are invited. For example, in 2012, after the outbreak of violence in June, a State Committee on Reconciliation was established in Kaduna, consisting of sixty men (as in, male). People objected, so ten more were added, three of whom were women; the others included youth representatives and some other groups that had felt left out. In August 2012, a Committee was established by the Northern Governors Forum for Reconciliation, Security and Healing. It was initially all male with one woman; she objected so she was asked to get five other women to join her; I happened to be one of them and I admit the experience of working on that Committee was challenging but very enriching. And although the women were few, we ended up contributing far more than our fair share! In April 2013, the World Muslim League held its annual meeting in Sokoto, Nigeria—I looked at the list of those present, including the Christians who were invited to speak: all men! This is the norm. If women are invited, it is usually as an afterthought and as a symbolic gesture of 'gender awareness'! Thanks to international pressure, it is very important nowadays to be seen to show some sense of gender awareness. WIC is today invited to be present at state as well as other events and on occasions has been invited to speak—on women's issues. The general notion still seems to be that men can speak on just about anything, but women can speak only on 'women's issues'. Hence, in work with women and for women in peacebuilding, serious obstacles due to patriarchy are still encountered.

There are many studies today on religions from a gender perspective and many books have been edited, with papers given during women's interreligious conferences by women theologians from different traditions (Oduyoye 1995; Bayes and Tohidi 2001; Haddad and Esposito 2001; Ruether 2002; King and Beattie 2004). The universal quest for women's equality inherent in gender debates does not seek an accord of all religious traditions on women's rights or on family and social structures. Interreligious dialogue on gender issues does not aim at establishing a universal declaration of women's rights based on religious teachings. What it does seek is that, as a result of the dialogue, religious teachings become instruments of greater gender equality in the world.

As we have seen in Nigeria, there are women of both faiths who challenge traditional gender thought patterns from within their own traditions, convinced that it is possible to remain faithful to that tradition and at the same time move towards gender equality. The women would insist that yes, men and women are different, and have different roles and responsibilities. Men and women are equal in dignity, but they are not the same. They use the term gender equality to mean the equal right to access to resources and opportunities, including economic participation and decision-making. They are only too aware of unjust gender inequalities experienced in their society, and often times supported by religious interpretations, and they struggle to promote women's rights, interests and issues within their social, cultural, and religious contexts.

The women in Kaduna, many of them actively engaged in the Women's Interfaith Council now for almost ten years, are convinced of their religious tradition because they have experienced the sustaining power of that tradition, having lived it from within. They believe that their religion itself is not the problem; but rather the religions as taught and practiced are called to grow by being examined with a new approach to gender, based on the essential equality of all God's children, male and female, on the ethical, spiritual and social levels: respecting each one's identity and difference, while also respecting fully this fundamental principle (with its diverse nuances) on which their religions agree.

Salvific Dialogue Begins from the Lived Reality of the Poor

It is my sincere belief that the merit or value what we might call 'salvific truth', of any religion must be based on and begin from concrete lived experience. Beginning with a concern for the poor and oppressed, we can all enter into a deeper understanding of God, humanity, and human relations. To discuss how religions as practised and as taught contribute to the fullness of life, the human dignity of all people including women, will lead to much fuller and more beneficial discussions on how salvation is to be understood and how the Gospel, the Islamic message, or any other, is truly universal and salvific for humanity. Such discussions will also lead the way to renewal and transformation of the religions themselves.

In my experience with the WIC, I did not find women of either religion very willing to challenge, or indeed capable of challenging, religious teachings they had been taught by their usually male religious teachers. However, they were very willing to challenge what they would call cultural misinterpretations or lack of adherence to religion. Things such as the denial of political space to women, domestic violence, female illiteracy, child marriage, female genital mutilation, voicelessness, poverty, and of course violence and extremism, were seen by them as cultural misinterpretations or lack of following correct religious teaching. While some women's rights NGOs are actively engaged in Nigeria and struggle within the secular sphere of discourse, faith groups tend to speak of women's rights within a religious framework. For example, FOMWAN leaders refuse to label themselves or their federation as feminist and they are careful to avoid giving any grounds to justify accusations of being anything other than strictly Islamic (McGarvey 2009: 197). In the communiqué from the 1985 meeting at which it was decided to form a national federation of Muslim women's groups, they clearly stated their rejection of western ideas of women's liberation which have no relevance in Muslim communities because Islam grants Muslim women all the rights they need. Some Nigerian Christian women theologians have attempted to offer alternatives to the dominant gender discourse of Christian churches and have called for a deeper inculturation of the inclusive and egalitarian ethos of the Gospel message. They have also proposed some concrete theological-based strategies for such an inculturation. Primary among these are Rose Uchem, Rosemary Edet, Teresa Okure and Dorcas Olu Akintunde; the first three are Catholic Religious from the eastern part of the country while Dorcas was a member of the Christ Apostolic Church based in Ibadan. Their position as lecturers in Catholic seminaries, theological schools and national universities has certainly brought an awareness of gender issues to these establishments and to their students, many of whom study for the priesthood. Thus, a form of feminist theological reflection which analyses cultural factors that are 'innovations in the form in which Christianity and Islam is interpreted and practiced', is gradually entering Nigerian circles.

Despite the lack of theological or scholarly analysis, women of faith, in circles such as the WIC, can challenge practices based on their own experience and this in turn causes them to challenge religious interpretations and teachings. The readiness to enter into sincere dialogue about the limitations of religious teaching and practice when facing as equal partners those whom this teaching has previously excluded and oppressed involves a humble recognition that the path towards truth has not been completed but has yet to be continued. It involves not only seeking the truth but also admitting the truth, being truthful in a spirit of charity and love. The Muslim and Christian women in Kaduna, in their interactions and sharing with one another, in their conflict analysis and their listening to each other's experiences both of their own lives and of the effects of marginalization and of violence, are helped to move away from any tendency to idealize their own faith and the way in which it is practiced and they are adamant and sincere in their call for mutual respect, both of one another and of each other's faith. This has helped their dialogue to be sincere and salvific since it involves humility and meekness from all concerned. Hearing one another, they recognize the sins traditional or 'cultural' religious interpretations have committed against them, and they do not approach the dialogue table with anger and bitterness, seeking only to offend. Rather they come to the dialogue table to share and to listen, to be transformed, and together to construct a better society.

Conclusion

Interreligious dialogue often remains in the realms of academia or at the symbolic level of gatherings of religious leaders, removed from concrete contexts and from the lived reality of the adherents of the religions under discussion. I believe it is vital that dialogue be developed to become a transforming and liberative force in the actual lives of a fractured and suffering community. Based on the example of the Women's Interfaith Council in Kaduna, I have suggested how this dialogue is entered into and lived not just by an elite few but by the numerous women in Northern Nigeria who are organized in their faith-based groups. By challenging some presumptions and practices which they experience in their everyday lives in their societies, and without requiring deep theological preparation, together they move towards a deeper analysis and transformation of the cultural, social and political dynamics which shape the dominant religious discourse. In doing this, they are making a significant contribution to the attainment of the SDGs that seek to address inequality and to promote women's empowerment.

The success story recorded by the Women's Interfaith Council in Kaduna has also highlighted the value of working in collaboration. It is a project jointly owned and nurtured by women across the religious and ethnic divide. Although the initiative and administration rests heavily on the Sisters of Our Lady of Apostles (OLA), all member Organizations rightfully claim ownership and are part of the decision-making process. This ensures that the project is protected by the local community and this guarantees its survival over a long period. Feminist discourse on a global scale, with its awareness of the limitations within religious traditions as well as its insights on and difficulties with the questions of difference, sameness and otherness, can help to situate interreligious dialogue and the theology of religious pluralism in the concrete lives of religious adherents. The struggle of authentic and life-giving human relationships continues. All relationships, of individuals and of religions, can only be understood and developed on a local, personalized level, in the concrete lived experience of human beings, where God speaks and human beings respond, through and with one another. That these relationships will be life-giving for those concerned and will contribute to the common good, can only be understood, from a Christian perspective, in the light of the difficult but basic commandment to love.

REFERENCES

Bayes, J.H. & Tohidi, N. 2001. Eds. *Globalization, Gender and Religion: The Politics of Women's Rights in Catholic and Muslim Contexts*. New York: Palgrave.

GEWESTRAG (Gender Equality & Women's Empowerment Group). 2010. *"Our Five Political Asks: The Northern Women's Manifesto and Charter of Demands"*.

Haddad, Y. Y. & Esposito, J.L. 2001. (Eds). *Daughters of Abraham: Feminist Thought in Judaism, Christianity and Islam*. Florida: University Press of Florida.

Ibrahim, J. (ed). 2004. *Sharia Penal and Family Laws in Nigeria and in the Muslim World: Rights Based Approach*. Zaria: ABU Press.

King, U. 1998. "Feminism: The Missing Dimension in the Dialogue of Religions". In D'Arcy May, J. Ed. *Pluralism and the Religions: The Theological and Political Dimensions*. London: Cassell.

King, U. & Beattie, T. 2004. Eds. *Gender, Religion and Diversity: Cross-Cultural Perspectives*. London/New York: Continuum.

Kisekka, Mere. 1992. *Women's Health Issues in Nigeria*, Zaria: Tamaza, Zaria.

Kukah Centre. 2015. Available online at http://thekukahcentre.org/wp-content/uploads/2018/11/2015-2016-Annual-Report.pdf.

McGarvey, Kathleen. 2009. *Muslim and Christian Women in Dialogue: The Case of Northern Nigeria*. Oxford: Peter Lang Ltd.

NPC. 2017. "National Bureau of Statistics, Statistical Report on Men and Women in Nigeria". Available online at www.nigerianstat.gov.ng.

Oduyoye, Mercy Amba 1995. *Daughters of Anowa: African Women and Patriarchy*. New York: Orbis Books.

Ruether, Radford R. 2002. (ed). *Gender, Ethnicity & Religion: Views from the Other Side*. Minneapolis: Augsburg Fortress.

WCC (World Council of Churches). (7th–9th June 2005). "Critical moment in interreligious dialogue". Geneva.

Women's Interfaith Council. www.womeninterfaithcouncil.org.

Yusuf, Bilkisu & Kathleen McGarvey. 2015. Women, Religion and Peace Building in Nigeria: A Case Study of Kaduna State. In Hayward, Susan and Marshall, Katherine (eds). *Women, Religion, and Peace: Exploring the Invisible*. Washington: USIP publications.

CHAPTER 7

An Interfaith Body for Gender Justice in Tanzania: An Overview

Klaudia Wilk-Mhagama

INTRODUCTION

Since the independence of Tanzania on 09 December 1961, religion became a very sensitive political issue in the country, and politicians were far from including it in social sciences and political discourse. Religion was seen as a factor potentially leading to divisions in the newly independent state. This would explain why the last census regarding religious affiliation took place in Tanzania in 1967. Regardless of the approach of researchers and politicians of this period, there is no doubt that religion at that time played an important role in shaping social and political relations as well as taking an active part in shaping the new image of the Tanzanian people. This became even more evident with the onset of economic and political liberalization in the mid-1980s and gained momentum during political reforms that ultimately led Tanzania to multi-party democracy in 1992.

The universality of religion has started of course to also lead to problems that contribute to stunting development in the country. It could lead

K. Wilk-Mhagama (✉)
Dar es Salaam, Tanzania

© The Author(s), under exclusive license to Springer Nature
Switzerland AG 2022
E. Chitando, I. S. Gusha (eds.), *Interfaith Networks and Development*, Sustainable Development Goals Series,
https://doi.org/10.1007/978-3-030-89807-6_7

117

to social divisions, especially if the religions face competition and fight for social and political influence. The period of economic, social and political liberalization in Tanzania allowed organizations to step out and reveal their frustrations. However, two important things happened in Tanzania, which prevented religious misunderstandings. The first is the insistence on national identity as predominant over all other affiliations—ethnic, religious, and linguistic—and credit this to the lasting legacy of Julius Nyerere's ujamaa policies. The second is the inception of interfaith bodies whose central goal is to support the design and implementation of Tanzania's development initiatives. This is how interfaith-based organisations in Tanzania since the early 1900s have started playing an important role as spiritual guides, service providers in the education and health sectors as well as supporting many new civil initiatives.

There are numerous interfaith organisations operating in Tanzania focusing on different development sectors. Most of FBOs are Christian and Muslim organizations since these are two main religions in the country. Although it is hard to estimate how many FBOs run in Tanzania at present, it is known that faith-based organizations in Tanzania are contributing to development, specifically education, health care and addressing poverty. In this regard, they are championing the achievement of Sustainable Development Goal (SDG) Number 10 focusing on reducing inequality. However, the challenge is, how in Tanzania they can effectively foster democracy without being regarded as "political" and thereby risking the loss of registration since the state may deregister NGOs that seek to enter the political arena, given that democracy is considered a "political" issue (Norwegian Church Aid 2010: 7).

This chapter acknowledges the phenomenon of religion in Tanzania and interfaith bodies focusing mostly on gender in terms of development to shed light on the perspectives that have been far overlooked or obscured. The chapter's main purposes are: (a) to provide a brief overview of the formation of numerous FBOs and interfaith networks in Tanzania (b) to highlight the main development issues in Tanzania in context of gender equality and existing the inter-faith commitment to this development (c) to indicate the main places where interfaith organizations cooperate in and take initiatives to support the gender development in Tanzania.

Tanzania's Religious Landscape

The Tanzanian nation is marked by its plural religious setting. According to the Report from Berkley Centre for Religion, Peace, and World Affairs at Georgetown University, nowadays, Christians are Tanzania's largest religious group, comprising around 56% of the population. Christianity is internally diverse, split between Roman Catholics comprising around 26.5% and Protestants as the largest denominations with 27.7% of the population. Other Christians (including Orthodox, Jehovah's Witness, Mormon, Quaker, Seventh-day Adventist) constitute only 2.8%. The remainder of the population is predominantly Muslim—about 34%—with small groups of Buddhists, Hindus, Jains, Sikhs, and Baha'is. The overwhelming majority of Tanzania's Muslims identify as Sunni, although prominent minority groups exist, among these the Isma'ili and Twelver Shia, as well as Ahmadi and Ibadi communities. African Traditional Religion (ATR) represents a diverse set of beliefs and practices that vary with geographic location (Faith and Development in Focus Tanzania 2019: 33–34).

Analyzing the origins of Islam and Christianity in East Africa, it is worthy to note that Islam emerged in these areas much earlier than Christianity, for nearly eight centuries. Islamic civilization dominated for long on the east coast of Africa. Also, while Christianity spread primarily through a well-organized mission (which provided a range of services to the community, such as education and healthcare), the spread of Islam occurred mainly through traders or part-time preachers who do not engage in large scale conversion work. The ultimate goal of the Christian mission was to get new believers through social activities or education and health assistance. Such organizations opened schools and health centres and then built the churches. Muslims, however, did not have specialist's proclamation of the faith and did not build schools or health centres. Instead, they built mosques, as the daily prayer was a priority for them. At mosques often were madrasa, or religious school, which educated Muslims only in terms of deepening their faith and observance of the rights of Islam. On the other hand, in both cases the local community undoubtedly tried to incorporate some African traditions into the established framework of foreign religions in the foreseeable future, which contributed to the emergence of religion referred to later as "African Islam" and "African Christianity".

During colonization, both German and British colonial rule facilitated the growth of religious activities. When the nationalist movement under Nyerere started to embark on a national integration project, the state encouraged religious organizations to actively participate in the struggle for unity and development (Liviga 2006: 329). The fact is that Christian churches had more developed organizational structures than Islamic ones in Tanzania and thus they were asked to play their part and contribute to developing the country through their strong social resources in the sectors of education and health care, as well as educating Tanzania's citizens (Olsson 2011: 29). Tanzania's two major Christian umbrella organizations, the Catholic Tanzania Episcopal Conference (TEC), founded in 1956, and the Protestant Christian Council of Tanzania (CCT), founded in 1934, soon followed this request (Heilman and Kaiser 2002: 700). From the Muslim community, the East African Muslim Welfare Society (EAMWS) was the one concentrating on building schools and mosques, providing scholarships and spreading literature. Shiite Muslims, especially the Ismaili followers of Aga Khan, have concentrated on establishing schools, hospitals, libraries, building societies as well as engaging in industrial development (Lodhi and Westerlund 1997). After 1986, when Ali Hassan Mwinyi took his presidency, the number of NGOs was rapidly growing. Among religious organizations, there are several "apex bodies" that act as national umbrella bodies for Christian and Muslim religious communities and their institutions, but also which are also directly engaged in various forms of development work. In 1992, the TEC and the CCT formed interfaith organization, the Christian Social Services Commission (CSSC) as an ecumenical body to facilitate the provision of social services by the churches. They manage roughly 40 per cent of the health and education services in the country (Leurs et al. 2011: 31). The two most important Muslim apex bodies are the Bakwata and BarazaKuu. However, Bakwata is less well funded than the TEC or the CCT and therefore only able to work on a smaller scale and exercising less influence on policy. The state has also been called to intervene in inter-religious conflicts, particularly between Muslims and Christians. The huge increase in the number of development NGOs since the mid-1980 can be seen as a response both to the increasing gaps in service provision left by former *ujamaa* system and as a response to new opportunities to access international funding. However, for faith institutions, these political changes had important consequences. Olsson suggests that for institutions like TEC, CCT and Bakwata, which had been closely affiliated to the *ujamaa* regime and its

7 AN INTERFAITH BODY FOR GENDER JUSTICE IN TANZANIA: AN OVERVIEW   121

principles, liberalization faced them with new challenges (Olsson 2011). Nowadays, Tanzania is represented by several major interfaith organizations formed at local[1] and international[2] level.

THE GENDER ISSUE IN TANZANIA

Undoubtedly, referring to the history of the formation of Tanzania as a nation, one should look at the issue of gender equality as quite sensitive and still requiring great work on the part of Tanzania to equalize the chances of women in the country. Of course, after independence, the

---

[1] At the national level, these relationships are embodied by the Inter-Religious Council for Peace Tanzania (IRCPT), Tanzania's premier interfaith organization that has pioneered a holistic response to HIV/AIDS in Tanzania. Its members include major Christian denominations (Catholics, mainline Protestants, and Pentecostals), Muslim organizations (BAKWATA, Ahmaddiya Muslim Jama'at), and other religious traditions (Baha'i, Buddhist, Hindu, Sikh). From 2008 to 2012, IRCPT collaborated with Religions for Peace (RfP) to equip local faith leaders with the tools to address the numerous facets of HIV/AIDS in their communities. IRCPT implements the project through the Tanzania Women Interfaith Network (TWIN) to scale up the religious body's response to HIV/AIDS prevention, OVC care and support, and home-based care and economic development for people living with HIV. See: https://uri.org/who-we-are/cooperation-circle/inter-religious-council-peace-tanzania; The Christian Social Services Commission (CSSC) is also active in this field. As an ecumenical institution, whose founders and only members are TEC and CCT, the organization aims to provide social assistance through Christian churches, with a focus on the education and health sectors. Among many activities run by organization, promotion and development of education, health and other social services sectors are key. (On the Christian Social Services Commission, see: http://www.cssc.or.tz/history). When referring to Muslim representatives, the National Muslim Council of Tanzania (suah. Baraza Kuu la Waislam, BAKWATA) is the biggest organizations established in 1968 to bring together all Muslims from different denominations and backgrounds. This organization is also involved in many educational projects, for example in the field of entrepreneurship or prevention of HIV/AIDS. What is more, the organization also cooperates with aid agencies: on health policy with Norwegian Church Aid, on civic education with UNDP and the US embassy (Tumaini-Mungu 2007).

[2] At the International level the Tanzania is a member of World Conference on Religions and Peace—Tanzania Chapter, WCRP/Tz which is a multi-denominational organization and the largest coalition in the world representing religious communities. Among numerous activities of WCRP/Tz gender discrimination is included (Mhina 2007). Another one is Norwegian Church Aid which in Tanzania is linked to the Christian Council of Tanzania, the Evangelical Lutheran Church of Tanzania, the Tanzania Episcopal Conference and the national Muslim Council of Tanzania. NCA's involvement in empowering FBOs to access critical information and resources to strengthen their advocacy work (Norwegian Church Aid 2010).

government of Tanzania leaned towards women, focusing on their rights in the constitution. The constitution of Tanzania promulgated in 1977, and the amendments that followed, both forbid discriminations based on gender. The country also ratifies key international—and regional human rights documents[3] (Country Gender Profile 2016). Another commitment of the Government of Tanzania is the support for the wider participation of women in the government decision-making, through the formulation of Women and Gender Development Policy (WGDP) for 2010–2020 and the re-enforcement of the quota system for female representatives at the national parliamentarians and local councils (Country Gender Profile 2016). Contrary to the government's commitment to gender equality, many articles and clauses in Tanzania's constitution and laws remain discriminatory against women that places Tanzania in the bottom fifth of countries in the UNDP's 2017 Gender Inequality Index, which measured women's access to health care, education, economic opportunity, and policymaking (Gender Inequality Index 2019). The major sectors that point to explicit discrimination and violations of women's rights focus on labour, agriculture, gender-based violence (GBV) including physical and psychological violence, child marriage and female genital mutilation (FGM).

Despite the crucial role women play in agriculture, their access to productive resources is more limited than that of their male counterparts. While nearly 70% of women work in agriculture, only 20% possessed land in their name, which is very often with much lower quality and size. Even though a law from 1998 gives women equal rights to access, own, and control land, in reality, it is very difficult for women to buy land in the first place (Faith and Development in Focus Tanzania 2019). What is more, women are overrepresented in unpaid employment. This is probably because more women have a second job which is mostly for household well-being as well as domestic tasks such as food preparation, water and

---

[3] Tanzania has ratified such as the Convention on the Elimination of all forms of Discrimination Against Women (CEDAW) from 1979, Nairobi Forward-looking Strategies for the Advancement of Women from 1985; and the SADC Protocol on Gender and Development from 1997. At the domestic policy level there is the 'Vision 2025' that recognizes the importance of gender equality and the empowerment of women, and the National Strategy for Poverty Reduction 1 and 2 (MKUKUTA, 2011–2015) that highlights gender mainstreaming and describes specific strategies on related education and on Gender-based Violence (GBV). Tanzania has ratified also both the 2030 SDG Agenda and the long term 2063 Agenda, as well as regional development plans, such as the Regional Indicative Strategic Development Plan (2005–2020).

fuel collection, and caring for children and the elderly. Already at a young age, girls tend to be more involved than boys in activities such as cooking, fetching water and taking care of younger household members (Osorio et al. 2014: IX).

Another significant problem concerns gender-based violence, GBV. According to the Tanzania Demographic Health Survey (TDHS), 38% of female respondents (between age 15 and 49) experienced physical violence in the past, and 20.3% suffered from sexual violence (Ministry of Health 2017). One of the most characteristic acts of sexual violence is the culturally marked female genital cutting (FGC) which is considered as a rite of passage for young women among numerous ethnic groups concentrated primarily in Tanzania's Central and Northern zones (Faith and Development in Focus Tanzania 2019). Even though the Sexual Offences Special Provision Act 1988 (SOSPA) effective in 1988 strictly forbids FGM from being operated on women under 18 years of age, the FGM is still practiced in a certain part of Tanzania and even the women over 18 years old rarely receive legal protection against it. This is because of the very strong cultural background related to woman's virginity, discouraging sexual promiscuity, and fertility. In particular regions and groups in Tanzania, women who have not undergone the procedure are often stigmatized, discriminated against, and socially excluded from their communities (Faith and Development in Focus Tanzania 2019). Nowadays, up to 14.6% of women in Tanzania have experience with FGM, while the practice is rather specific to certain provinces and regions than being a country-wide phenomenon (Country Gender Profile 2016: 12).

This leads to another very serious problem related to sexual violence against women, namely, child marriage. One in three girls in Tanzania is married by the age of 18. Child marriage is most prevalent in the Western and Lake zones, where close to 60% of girls under 18 are married (Tanzania Girls not Brides). Marriage is viewed as a way of protecting young girls from pre-marital sex and pregnancy that undermine family honour and may decrease the amount of dowry a family may receive. Many Tanzanians regard child marriage as a way of securing financial security for themselves and their daughters. The practice of dowry payment by the groom to the bride's family is a key incentive for many families to marry off their daughters. Girls Human Rights Watch reveals that some girls who were married to their husbands are beaten and raped and they are not allowed to make any decisions in their homes. A large number of girls are abandoned after marriage and left to care for children without any financial support. Many said they also experienced violence and abuse at the hands of their in-laws (Human Rights Watch). Although the Government has committed itself to the SDGs, which include the elimination of child marriage by 2030, data collected for the Demographic and Health Survey conducted in Tanzania (TDHS) 2015/16 show a 5 per cent increase in marriage among adolescent girls in the 15–19 age bracket since the previous survey in 2010 (Tanzania Demographic and Health Survey and Malaria Indicator Survey 2016: 85). Also, former president Magufuli's decision initially pronounced in 2017 raised considerable controversy after endorsing a law dating back to the 1960s allowing state schools to expel young mothers. According to a 2013 report by the Centre for Reproductive Rights over the past decade, more than 55,000 Tanzanian pregnant schoolgirls have been expelled from school (Center for Reproductive Rights). Women's groups said the ban was out of touch with public opinion and breaks international human rights conventions. It also contradicts a promise set out in the ruling party's 2015 election manifesto, which pledged to allow pregnant school girls to continue with their studies (Girls not Brides). Even though numerous FBOs have started to advocate for women's political, social, and economic equality, there is still some way to go in creating up to date gender justice equality policies. In this way, development partners, as well as faith and interfaith organisations started to work together by pulling their resources to ensure that the development of such a policy is in place, it is comprehensive, coherent and implemented both at organizational and programme level. This approach was essential in contributing to a faith movement on gender justice (Abuom 2015).

However, some institutions have frequently partnered with one another in delivering programming that includes one or more of these methods. One of the biggest is the Side by Side Faith Movement for Gender Justice Founded by a coalition of international FBOs in March 2015. Side by Side is a global interfaith movement committed to harnessing the platform of religious institutions to advocate for women's social, political, and economic inclusion. A Tanzanian chapter was launched in late 2017 with the support of local Christian, Muslim, and traditional religious leaders. The movement is targeting Faith leaders since they have the enormous power to influence their communities because they have an ongoing leadership role and influence as opposed to NGO's which come and go. They know their people and their local culture; hence they have authority to question cultural traditions and practices that harm, burden or diminish women and girls dignity. Since religion touches people's hearts, minds and actions, religious have enormous power, influence and crucial voice in the public space (Nillan 2017: 1). On November 2015 a meeting took place the at the All Africa Conference of Churches Centre in Nairobi, where religious leaders representing various religious institutions from Uganda, Kenya, Tanzania, South Sudan, Sudan, Burundi, Rwanda as well as DRC Congo shared vision, commitment and a plan of action for establishing a regional faith movement for gender justice. It was organized jointly by ACT Alliance Africa Regional Office, the All Africa Conference of Churches, Christian Aid, Church of Sweden, FECCLAHA, Fin Church Aid and Norwegian Church Aid. The Conference offered a platform pointing out the most important challenges that characterize the quest for gender equality. In particular, cultural beliefs and practices where highlighted. Other issues focused on the activity of the leaders and religious institutions themselves, indicating insufficient commitment, lack of professional activities and lack of proper knowledge around gender justice issues (Eastern Africa Faith Leaders' Consultation on Gender Justice). One of the main challenges that the Church faces in the effort to create gender parity is the reading, interpretation and application of canonical biblical texts, where numerous texts in the Bible create gender disparity (Mwaniki 2015: 8). Dr Lydia Mwaniki from AACC suggested that the solution to this situation is to deliberate effort to interpret and apply the Bible in liberating ways, to eradicate cultural beliefs and practices that create gender injustice, and promote relationships of partnership and mutual interdependence (Mwaniki 2015: 8–9). Ezra Chitando also reflected on various factors that deepen gender injustice (Chitando 2015: 12–13). Interfaith institutions are working in Tanzania to address the challenges of gender inequality. A good example is the Norwegian Church Aid,[4] which is already created a programme to address gender inequality, including FGM, early marriages and GBV. Thus, the NCA aims to care and support of survivors of GBV as well as advocate for national laws preventing violence against women, which enforce policies ensuring survivors' access to care and legal justice

---

[4] Norwegian Church Aid (NCA)'s comparative advantage in Tanzania is linked to its commitment to partner with different FBOs. NCAs core partners comprise large FBOs such as the Christian Council of Tanzania, the Evangelical Lutheran Church of Tanzania, the Tanzania Episcopal Conference and the national Muslim Council of Tanzania. NCA Tanzania's has succeeded in strengthening the poverty eradication focus among FBOs and to spur their capacity to engage in governance and economic justice issues. NCAs contributed to strengthen the inter-faith movement with joint advocacy initiatives and coordinated work on the ground.

(Norwegian Church Aid 2010: 11). The NCA, for example, supported Village Community Bank (VICOBA) groups to start micro-enterprises and income generating activities at household level, where the majority of the VICOBA members are women, in order to give them opportunities to become more active in economic life and enable them to take care of their families (Norwegian Church Aid 2010: 8).

CONCLUSIONS

Tanzania, as a religiously diverse country, places great emphasis on preserving unity and cooperation for the development of society. Nowadays, Tanzania is dealing with several interfaith organizations that are the common denominator for these needs. On the one hand, they work for dialogue, while on the other, they focus on sectors that seek to develop the community and the country. The vast majority of their activities has been therefore focused on the education and health sector with a lack of awareness of the moral and theological imperative of religious leaders to use their influence to challenge gendered social norms. At present, however, interfaith organizations are starting to be aware of the problem of discrimination and violation of women's rights. Many of them are undertaking activities to help women. Despite the Tanzanian Government's welcoming of organisations that provide service delivery, it still retains some skepticism towards some of the advocacy NGOs. This includes faith and interfaith organizations that are aware of being accused of being "political" which can make them lose their registration as NGO. This means that despite the real commitment of interfaith organizations to work towards gender equality, it is still difficult to point to specific projects working on the gender issue. This applies mainly to national faith and interfaith organizations registered under the NGO Act from 2002. This brings an uncoordinated faith-based response to gender justice across their spheres of influence. Tanzanian interfaith organizations are therefore deciding to actively cooperate with international interfaith bodies that are taking decisive steps in creating more coordinated and effective action to improve the situation of women in Tanzania.

Although women and men are equally entitled to protection under the Tanzanian Constitution, the reality on the ground is that there are serious violations of the right to protection for many. International conventions where the effective ideas for women's equality and the activity are articulated have led to several important conclusions regarding the directions in which denominational and interfaith organizations should operate. In Tanzania at the community level, there is a need to focus on education to discuss some cultural conditions and practices which perpetuate gender injustice and engage communities to reduce women's vulnerability to GBV. At the level of institutions, interfaith and faith organisations are the ones who are most responsible to give an example of teaching men and women to work together starting from mainstreaming gender justice issues in sermons as well as to use of faith-based community groups to respond to GBV. At the national level, the most important is a lobby for the full implementation of gender-related policies based on laws and policies that perpetuate gender injustice and increase the punishment of FGM and GBV perpetrators. The CCT, as the one of the leading Tanzanian FBOs, seeks to coordinate existing religious leaders' forums to address gender injustice, focusing on creating the initiative for Religious Leaders (Muslim & Christians) and creating a social media forum e.g. Facebook and Twitter. At present, however, interfaith organizations in Tanzania still need to develop a clear indication of the structure and plan of their action towards common gender justice goals, as well as building a more comprehensive evidence base for faith actors to appropriately respond to gender injustices in their particular communities. Interfaith groups are collaborating to promote gender justice, Tanzania, therefore contributing to the achievements of the SDGs.

References

Abuom, A. 2015. "Potential Coordination Structures and Spaces for the Faith Movement for Gender Justice". East Africa Regional Consultation for Faith Leaders on gender Justice. Online: http://sidebysidegender.org/wp-content/uploads/2016/01/Spaces-for-the-faith-gender-justice-movement-Agnes-Abuom.pdf

Chitando, E. 2015. "Why Establish a Faith Movement for Gender Justice?". Eastern Africa Faith Leaders' Consultation on Gender Justice. Online: http://sidebysidegender.org/wp-content/uploads/2016/02/East-Africa-Faith-Leaders-Gender-Justice-Workshop-Report.pdf

Centre for Reproductive Rights. "New Report: Tanzania Forces Girls to Undergo Invasive Pregnancy Tests, Expels Pregnant Students". Online: https://www.reproductiverights.org/press-room/new-report-tanzania-forces-girls-to-undergo-invasive-pregnancy-tests-expels-pregnant-stud

Country Gender Profile. 2016. Tanzania Final Report, March, Japan International Cooperation Agency (JICA) Japan Development Service Co., Ltd. (JDS), Equal Measures 2030. Online: https://data.em2030.org/countries/tanzania/

Eastern Africa Faith Leaders' Consultation on Gender Justice. Online: http://sidebysidegender.org/wp-content/uploads/2016/02/East-Africa-Faith-Leaders-Gender-Justice-Workshop-Report.pdf

Faith and Development in Focus Tanzania. 2019. World Faith Development Dialogue Berkley Center for religion Peace & World Affairs. Online: https://berkleycenter.georgetown.edu/publications/faith-and-development-in-focus-tanzania

Gender Inequality Index. 2019. UNDP, Online: http://hdr.undp.org/en/composite/GII

Heilman, B. E. and P. J Kaiser. 2002. Religion, Identity and Politics in Tanzania. *Third World Quarterly* 23(4): 691–709.

Human Rights Watch. Online: https://www.hrw.org/report/2014/10/29/no-way-out/child-marriage-and-human-rights-abuses-tanzania

Inter-Religious Council for Peace Tanzania. Online: https://uri.org/who-we-are/cooperation-circle/inter-religious-council-peace-tanzania

Leurs, R., P. Tumaini-Mungu, and A. Mvungi. 2011. "Mapping the Development Activities of Faith based Organizations in Tanzania", Working Paper 58, Birmingham, UK: Religions and Development Research Programme, University of Birmingham.

Liviga, A. J. 2006. Religion and Governance in Tanzania: The pre-liberalisation period. In R. Mukandala, S. Yahya-Othman, S. S. Mushi and L. Ndumbaro (eds.), *Justice, rights and worship: Religion and politics in Tanzania*. Dar es Salaam: E & D.

A. Y. Lodhi, and D. Westerlund. 1997. "African Islam in Tanzania". Online: http://www.islamtanzania.org/articles/islam2.htm

Mhina, A. Ed. 2007. Religions and development in Tanzania: A preliminary literature review. Working Paper 11. Birmingham: University of Birmingham.

Ministry of Health. 2017. "Tanzania Demographic and Health Survey and Malaria Indicator Survey: 2015–2016." (2017). 367. "Summary of Results: Afrobarometer Round 7 Survey in Tanzania." Questions 78B.

Mwaniki, L. 2015. Eastern Africa Faith Leaders' Consultation on Gender Justice. Online: http://sidebysidegender.org/wp-content/uploads/2016/02/East-Africa-Faith-Leaders-Gender-Justice-Workshop-Report.pdf

Nillan, F. 2017. Online: http://sidebysidegender.org/wp-content/uploads/2018/01/SBS-Tanzania-chapter-launch-Nov-2017.pdf

Norwegian Church Aid. 2010. Country plan 2011–2015 Tanzania. Online: https://www.kirkensnodhjelp.no/contentassets/a11f250a5fc145dbb7bf932c8363c998/01384-4-norwegian-church-aid-strategy-for-tanzania-2011%2D%2D-2015.pdf

Olsson, H. 2011. *The Politics of Interfaith Institutions in Contemporary Tanzania*. Uppsala: Swedish Science Press.

Osorio, M., M. Percic and F. Di Battista. 2014. "Gender Inequalities in Rural Employment in Tanzania Mainland An Overview", Food and Agriculture Organization of the United Nations, Rome.

Tanzania Demographic and Health Survey and Malaria Indicator Survey 2015–2016 Final Report (2016). Online: https://dhsprogram.com/pubs/pdf/FR321/FR321.pdf

Tanzania Girls not brides. Online: https://www.girlsnotbrides.org/child-marriage/tanzania/

The Christian Social Services Commission. Online: http://www.cssc.or.tz/history

Tumaini-Mungu, P. 2007. The development activities of faith-based organizations in Tanzania". In A. Mhina, (ed.), *Religions and development in Tanzania*. Working Paper 11. Birmingham: University of Birmingham.

CHAPTER 8

Interfaith Approaches to Violence against Women and Development: The Case of the South African Faith and Family Institute

Fungai Chirongoma

INTRODUCTION

Violence against women is rife in South Africa. Although there are a number of reasons for the causes of violence against women in South Africa, violence against women is mainly caused by unequal power relations between men and women in the society. Several reforms have been put in place to address such violence. These include; the Domestic Violence Act 116 of 1998 and the Criminal law (Sexual Offences and related matters) Amendment Act 32 of 2007. Despite having these reforms in place, cases of violence continue to increase. While Wael considers 'the law as a powerful tool that can be used to put the society on the right track for the implementation of human rights values' (Wael 2019: 55), it appears laws

F. Chirongoma (✉)
University of Cape Town, Cape Town, South Africa

© The Author(s), under exclusive license to Springer Nature
Switzerland AG 2022
E. Chitando, I. S. Gusha (eds.), *Interfaith Networks and Development*, Sustainable Development Goals Series,
https://doi.org/10.1007/978-3-030-89807-6_8

131

addressing violence against women have not been effective in stemming violence against women in South Africa.

Although laws and policies are important in addressing violence, there is need to consider other strategies in addressing women's violence. Elizabeth Petersen, the founder of the South Africa Faith and Family Institute (SAFFI), a multifaith organization based in Cape Town that addresses violence against women from a faith perspective, contends that laws are not an effective strategy in a society where religion determines gender power relations (Petersen 2016). It is against this background that Petersen established SAFFI to address violence against women from a faith perspective. SAFFI mobilizes religious leaders and religious communities from African Traditional Religion, Bahai Faith, Hinduism, Islam and Judaism to address violence against women using resources within their religions.

While SAFFI's approach calls for the use religious resources in addressing violence, it has to be noted that the role of religion in public life has not been taken seriously because of persistent secularization theories that do not appreciate the role of religion in the public sphere. Thus, religion continues to suffer neglect from development theory and practice. Clarke highlights how religion has been downplayed as a force of change with no benefit (Clarke 2013). The potential of religion in addressing violence against women has been overlooked. I therefore argue for the need to appreciate the interventions of faith/religious-based organizations in addressing violence against women. I contend that faith-based organizations that are addressing violence against women can be important stakeholders in the development agenda given the negative effect of violence against women on development. I agree with Clarke that although religion is not the answer to development, an understanding of its place in the social lives of people may enhance development outcomes (Clarke 2013).

Granted that addressing violence against women has positive effects in social and economic development in general, in this chapter I particularly focus on the impact of addressing violence against women in relation to attaining the Sustainable Development Goals (SDGs). I highlight that addressing violence against women has a huge impact in meeting targets of SDGs goal 5 (empowerment of women) and 10 (overcoming inequality). Using ethnographic methods, I will give an account of the impact of the intervention of SAFFI in reducing inequalities, promoting gender equality, empowering women and girls and eliminating all forms of violence against women (Babu and Kusuma 2017; Chirongoma 2020). I

8 INTERFAITH APPROACHES TO VIOLENCE AGAINST WOMEN... 133

begin by providing the background of SAFFI, its vision, mission and key activities. I then connect the relationship between SAFFI's work and development.

HISTORICAL BACKGROUND OF THE SOUTH AFRICA FAITH AND FAMILY INSTITUTE

The South Africa Faith and Family Institute is a multi-faith organization concerned with issues of gender-based violence and the family. The organization intends to bring people from different faiths together for the common goal of addressing violence against women. It began its operations in 2008 and it was founded by Elizabeth Petersen. Elizabeth's[1] personal life, early career and her Master's research motivated her to establish this particular organization.

Elizabeth Petersen' Life Trajectory

In a TV series, *I am woman Leap of Faith*, Season 2 Episode 21 which was broadcast by the South African Broadcasting Cooperation (SABC 3) in 2013, Elizabeth shared her life history and how that history shaped and influenced her current work. Elizabeth Hoorn Petersen was born in a humble family and she has eight siblings. Her family was deeply religious, with strong ties to the Pentecostal church. Elizabeth shared how at the age of 8 she had an unusual experience for someone of her age.

> When I was playing in the sand, I had an ache in the heart. I had an extraordinary sense that I am supposed to help people. (Petersen, 1 September 2013)

In the same documentary, her sister, Susan, indicated that Elizabeth was so sure and convinced that she was going to be helping people (Susan, 1 September 2013).

Elizabeth went to the University of Western Cape and studied for a Bachelor of Social Work. In 1993, she started working as a social worker at St Anne's Homes, an Anglican shelter for abused women situated in Woodstock, Cape Town. Three years later she was appointed the Director of St Anne's Homes and served for fourteen years until the time of her resignation. Elizabeth shared how she was deeply affected by seeing

---

[1] A deliberate choice to use her first name has been made.

women who had been abused, raped, rejected and abandoned in their intimate relationships. Her career as a social worker and a Director at a shelter for abused women motivated her involvement in coming up with strategies to address violence against women (Petersen, 1 September 2013).

In 2006, Elizabeth pursued a Master's degree by research. Her research focused on the experiences of the clergy within the Anglican Church in Southern Africa in dealing with domestic violence. Elizabeth highlighted that her research motivated her need to train religious leaders in understanding and addressing the root causes and effects of domestic violence and gender-based violence (Petersen 2017). From what I gathered in the documentary, Elizabeth believes that;

> South Africa is diverse in its faith traditions, violence against women happens in every faith tradition. We have called everybody to account for violence against women. We have called the police, the magistrates, the justice system, everybody! But we have not yet called religious leaders to account for the violence against women that happens in women's intimate relationships... Religious leaders are very, very powerful people in the lives of people coming into their faith communities. I believe that religious leaders have a crucial role in the faith formation and people's beliefs. (Petersen, 01 September 2013).

Elizabeth expressed how the above hypothesis and the realization that there were no organizations working with religious leaders in responding to violence against women in South Africa influenced the establishment of the South Africa Faith and Family Institute (Petersen, 01 September 2013).

Given the above, Elizabeth's personal life, religious experiences, education and career were all influential in motivating the establishment of SAFFI. SAFFI, though established in 2008, was officially launched on the 2nd of December 2010 at the University of Western Cape. The event was co-hosted by the Department of Religion and Theology of the University of Western Cape (Official Launch Report 2010).

The SAFFI Vision

SAFFI indicates that its vision is;

> To see individuals live their full potential in intimate relationships and families in a society that is free from gender-based violence. (http://saffi.org.za/ Date accessed 09 October 2019).

SAFFI's Mission

The organization states that its mission is to advance a coordinated, multi sectoral, culturally competent restorative justice response to violence against women and children by:

- Being a resource to religious leaders, institutions and faith communities as they hold offenders accountable and ensure the safety and empowerment of victims/survivors by offering opportunity for truth telling and healing of individuals and families.
- To challenge, from a theological perspective, patriarchal traditions and other root causes of intimate partner abuse and violence that destroys the dignity of women, children and men and
- To encourage the promotion of scriptural and theological teachings that encourage intimate relationships that set people free to live their full potential in supportive unions (extracted from SAFFI website http://saffi.org.za/ date accessed 09 October 2019).

In the section to follow, I turn to present the key activities of SAFFI.

South African Faith and Family Key Activities

SAFFI's primary goal is to mobilize faith leaders to address violence against women (West 2019). SAFFI achieves this by providing training to faith leaders. For SAFFI, if religious leaders are transformed in their thinking and knowledge about gender power relations as hierarchical, their teaching, preaching and pastoral care interventions will transform the way women and men relate to each other in society (SAFFI 2017). Based on this hypothesis, SAFFI developed a training model for religious leaders. The aims of these sessions are mainly to create awareness on violence against women among religious leaders and unpack the responsibilities of religious leaders in helping individuals affected by violence against women. The trainings also provide room for religious leaders to share their experiences in dealing with violence in their respective religious congregations and get support and guidance from fellow religious leaders.

Assessing these trainings, it is clear that scriptures and traditions are integral to their discussions of violence against women. While on the one hand some scholars regard religion as a source of gender inequality and oppression of women (Rakoczy 2004; Greiff 2010; Rwafa 2016), on the other hand, some scholars regard religion and religious leaders as useful resources in addressing violence against women (Phiri 2001; Nadar 2005; Pyles 2007; le Roux et al. 2016; Njagi 2017).

Apart from religious leaders' trainings, SAFFI conducts sensitizer workshops on violence against women in various religious communities. These workshops aim to raise different religious groups' awareness of violence against women. In addition, pilgrimages constitute another method that SAFFI uses to provide education on violence against women. Davis (2007) indicates that pilgrimages are intentional learning journeys that are recognized as a transformative experience of learning. SAFFI conducted pilgrimages to Robben Island. Robben Island is a site of historical importance to South Africa and beyond. During the apartheid era, black political leaders who opposed the apartheid regime were imprisoned on this island (Buntman 2003). This includes political leaders such as Nelson Mandela who was imprisoned in the Robben Island for eighteen years. For SAFFI, Robben Island is symbolic of the tension of oppression and freedom which also exists in intimate relationships (SAFFI Annual Report 2015–2016). SAFFI therefore, symbolically uses the site to engage in dialogues on how to address abuse. The journeys also create a platform that allows women to reflect on their experiences of violence.

In addition, campaigns are recognised as crucial in raising awareness and educating the public about the unacceptability of violence against women (Reid 2003). To provide education and raise awareness on violence against women, SAFFI also uses advocacy and campaigns. To achieve this, SAFFI mainly uses mass media such as radio, television, and the internet to reach its audience. The organization is actively involved in international campaigns such as the 16 Days of Activism Against Gender Based Violence and in South Africa, the Women's Month campaigns (Annual Report 2015–2016).

Further, as part of its interventions to address violence against women, SAFFI developed strategies to engage men in addressing violence against women. Research indicates that most of the interventions to address violence against women tend to focus on women (Chitando and Chirongoma 2012; Graaff and Heinecken 2017). However, for Flood, while some men are part of the problem of violence against women, all men are part of the solution in addressing violence against women (Flood 2011). Flood (2011) adds that preventing violence against women can only be effective if some attitudes and beliefs of some men which promote violence are changed. To involve men in addressing violence, I observed that SAFFI

8 INTERFAITH APPROACHES TO VIOLENCE AGAINST WOMEN... 137

mainly targets changing the attitudes and perceptions of male religious leaders: from all the SAFFI religious leaders' forums' that I attended, male religious leaders dominated the spaces (Participant Observation June 2017–November 2018). In addition, SAFFI conducts men only pilgrimages with the intention of bringing together men from different walks of lives to share on and discuss about living in healthy relationships and respecting women in society to end violence against women (SAFFI 2012/2013 Annual Report).

What I have presented above is a summary of the key activities of SAFFI in addressing violence against women. In this chapter, I focus on only two of SAFFI's strategies to address violence against women in detail. In the section to follow I present the religious leaders' campaign that SAFFI commissioned and the establishment of the Theological Advisory Council on Gender based violence.

'As people of faith we take a stand—will you?' Campaign

As a multifaith organization that brings different religions into dialogue to address violence against women, SAFFI filmed nine 30 seconds messages from religious leaders from the Baha'i Faith, Christianity, Hinduism, Islam, Judaism. In these short videos, religious leaders took a stand against violence using resources within their respective religious traditions. These are resources that are affirming and discourage violence against women. The campaign also aimed at creating awareness among fellow religious leaders and the society at large to take a stand against violence. As stated in SAFFI's annual report, these campaigns were aired on Cape Town TV around October 2014 (SAFFI 2013–2014 Annual Report). These videos are also available on YouTube. Below are some of the messages that I transcribed from the YouTube videos;

> **African Traditional Religious Leader**: I am Bongile Mawawa, an *injoli*, a leader of African Traditional Religion. In our tradition we say, '*Induku hai-vake umuzi*' which means you cannot build your house with violence. As religious leaders we say you cannot unite a nation with violence. We call upon all South Africans to treat each other with respect. As people of faith we take a stand: will you?! (https://www.youtube.com/watch?v=r-dJ760BSL8 Date accessed 13/01/2020)

Hinduism: I am Guru Krishna, a spiritual head of the Hindu community in the Western Cape. Hinduism teaches non-violence to women through thought, word and action. Violence against women and children is a sinful act and it has its own karmic consequences. I call upon all faith leaders to step into true leadership on this issue. Let's send a message of love, peace and blessings. Love ever, hate never! As people of faith we take a stand: will you?! (https://www.youtube.com/watch?v=prRhV-GKoaU Date accessed 13/01/2020)

Islam: I am Imam Dr Rasheid Omar, chairperson of the Western Cape Religious Leaders Forum. As people of faith, it is our moral responsibility to reflect seriously on how we can support the struggle of women and children for full dignity in our homes, in our communities and in our religious institutions. We call for gender-based violence to be placed high on the agenda of all religious institutions and communities. As people of faith we take a stand: will you?! (https://www.youtube.com/watch?v=yXrOtSV0KGU Date 13/01/2020)

Judaism: Hi my name is Warren Goldstein, the chief rabbi of South Africa. The Talmud says to destroy one life is to destroy a world and to save a one life is to save a world. And if there is one woman or one child out there anywhere in South Africa that is harmed in any way that means the whole world have been destroyed. If we as people of faith across the country come together to protect our women and children even if it's only one person, we would have saved an entire world. As people of faith we take stand: do you?! (https://www.youtube.com/watch?v=omrZtmm6_i8 Date accessed 13 January 2020)

Christianity: I am Stephen Brislin, president of the Catholic Bishops Conference. Family is fundamentally important in our Christian tradition yet so much violence and abuse take place within the family and beyond. We believe that each and every person is made in the image of God. We as people of faith need to break the silence on violence against women and children. We need to take it into our own hearts to act with integrity and courage. As people of faith we take a stand: will you?! (https://www.youtube.com/watch?v=omrZtmm6_i8 13 January 2020)

Bahai Faith: I am Tahirih Matthee, representative of the Baha'i Community in South Africa. The Baha'i community is founded on the principles of unity and peace. Our sacred teachings implore us to take care of women and firmly uphold the principles of gender equality. Violence against women and children is society's yardstick that measures violation of all human rights. We

8 INTERFAITH APPROACHES TO VIOLENCE AGAINST WOMEN... 139

call upon all South Africans to embrace peaceful living. As people of faith we take a stand: will you?! (https://www.youtube.com/watch?v=4_WrA5FSmkM Date accessed 13 January 2020)

Islam: I am Maulana Abdul Khaliq Allie, secretary general of the Muslim Judicial Council SA (South Africa). The honour of women and children is the foundation of a healthy society. Almighty Allah in the glorious Quran says *wa 'ashiruhunna bi al-ma'ruf* 'and live with women in kindness'. We cannot turn a blind eye to domestic violence, and we cannot deny that it exists. I call for a decisive stand for the protection and dignity of women and children. As faith leaders we take a stand:-will you?! (https://www.youtube.com/watch?v=nN4eA9kQnYA Date accessed 13 January 2020)

Assessing the above, one can identify that religious leaders aimed at creating awareness of violence against women through campaigns. I found it significant that most of the religious leaders were wearing their respective religious regalia and that they drew attention to their respective religious titles. The regalia and their religious titles command authority in their respective religious communities, thus these messages were likely to be respected by their followers. It is believed that religious leaders command authority and they are respected and trusted in their communities, therefore they have the power to influence beliefs and behaviours of their communities (le Roux et al. 2016).

Theological Advisory Council on Gender Based Violence

As a strategy to address violence from a faith perspective, SAFFI established the Theological Advisory Council on Gender Based Violence (TACGBV). The TACGBV brings together religious leaders, scholars and theologians from different religions to address easily interpreted religious texts, teachings and practices related to violence against women (SAFFI 2017). The Council comprises leaders from Islam, Hinduism, Judaism, the Baha'i Faith, African Traditional Religion and Christianity. This Board assists in producing material that is used in SAFFI's trainings and workshops. Some of the material that this Council produces is used to provide a guide to religious leaders in addressing violence against women within their communities.

In 2016 TACGBV produced a reading material entitled '*Theological reflection on the root causes of abuse of women in intimate relationships: a resource for faith leaders.*' In the publication, religious leaders and representative from Islam, Christianity, the Baha'i faith, Judaism, African Traditional Religion and Hinduism discussed the causes of women abuse and offered positive scriptures and traditions from their respective religions that can be used in addressing such violence (TACGBV 2016). In addition, in 2017 the Council produced another resource entitled, '*Faith based interventions with male perpetrators of intimate partner abuse: what guidance can we get from holy scriptures and ancient teachings?*' The publication provided different religious perspectives that guide male perpetrators of violence to regard women as equals. The reading materials expressed how scriptures and traditions condemn any form of violence. According to the authors of the material, religious scriptures and ancient teachings provide a guide to transform the hearts and minds of perpetrators and they have life giving essence that guides perpetrators to respect women (TACGBV 2017). Having discussed SAFFI's strategies in addressing violence against women, in the section to follow, I discuss the impact of SAFFI's work on development, particularly in attaining the Sustainable Development Goal 5 target 2, which calls for the elimination of all forms of violence against women and girls.

THE SOUTH AFRICAN FAITH AND FAMILY INSTITUTE AND SUSTAINABLE DEVELOPMENT

SAFFI's efforts to eradicate violence against women through its violence against women trainings for religious leaders, sensitizer campaigns and the production of reading resources that I have discussed above largely contribute to development. SAFFI's work contributes to economic development, given the economic costs that violence against women has on development. Violence against women strains development by increasing demand on health and legal issues. This is a waste economic resources that could be used for other development projects.

As I mentioned earlier, violence against women is a development issue. In 2014, KPMG, a global network of firms that provides audit and advisory services, produced a report on the economic cost of gender-based violence in South Africa. According to this report, based on the assumption that one in every five women experiences violence (some statistics present that one in every three women experiences violence in South Africa), the minimum economic cost of gender based violence is R28,

4 billion (Khumalo et al. 2014). Khumalo et al add that such an amount could be used to pay student tuition fees for 900,000 Engineering students. These scholars added that this amount can also cover one quarter of the South Africa's population national health insurance cost. In addition, the same amount of money could pay over 200,000 primary school teachers' salary for a period of one year or it could be used to build over half a million Reconstruction and Development Program (RDP) houses (Khumalo et al. 2014). Although I acknowledge that statistics are sometimes exaggerated to achieve certain agendas, the above figures provide a reflection of the intensity of violence and its cost and impact on the economic development of South Africa. Based on this report, Khumalo et al concluded that the cost of gender-based violence in South Africa is too costly to ignore (Khumalo et al. 2014).

In the same vein, Sen also presents violence against women as a strain to development. For Sen, violence against women increases health and legal demands and it wastes resources that could be used for other development projects (Sen 1998). Kusuma and Babu agree with Sen that violence against women is a barrier to women's equal participation in society and it affects overall development (Kusuma and Babu 2017). Similarly in a 2015 study, Moreno and others reiterated that violence against women is a development problem. They therefore concluded that elimination of violence against women should be a top priority of the Sustainable Development Goals given its impact on other Sustainable Development Goals, mainly those related to maternal, infant mortality and HIV (García-Moreno et al. 2015). Thus, SAFFI's efforts to address the root causes of violence against women and gender inequalities makes it a key partner in attaining two closely related SDGs 5 and 10. These goals present ways of thinking about equality and promoting human rights. Broadly, the vision and mission of SAFFI that I mentioned earlier, is in line with the target of SDG 10 target 2 which aims to reduce inequalities and promote equal treatment of all irrespective of gender, age, race, ethnicity, religion and economic status. While SDG 10 targets reducing inequalities for all, as one of the most disadvantaged groups, women largely benefit from this SDG.

More precisely, the work of SAFFI in addressing violence against women makes it a key partner in attaining SDG 5 which targets to achieve gender equality and empower all women and girls. SAFFI's work directly relates to target 2 of the Sustainable Development Goal 5 which aims to end all forms of discrimination against all women and girls and the elimination of all forms of violence against women and girls (Babu and Kusuma 2017; Chirongoma 2020). This target tallies with SAFFI's vision of ending all forms of violence against women that I referred to in foregoing sections. SAFFI, therefore, becomes a partner in attaining Sustainable Development Goal 5 through providing strategies to address violence against women in a society were laws have not been very effective in addressing the problem (Mogale et al. 2012). As detailed in the earlier sections, SAFFI has made a major milestone by bringing different religions into the fore in addressing violence. SAFFI is one of the first organizations in South Africa to speak about the importance of religion in addressing violence against women. SAFFI believes that religious leaders have the power to influence behaviour change which may result in changing the way men and women relate in society (SAFFI Research Report 2017). This hypothesis reflects SAFFI's emphasis in promoting equality between men and women.

At the time of writing, SAFFI had reached more than 1500 religious' leaders in the Western Cape Province (SAFFI Newsletter, 2015). A major contribution of SAFFI is how it has managed to change patriarchal perceptions of some religious through its trainings. Based on the feedback of religious leaders, I gathered that SAFFI's trainings changed the perceptions of some religious leaders. Below are some of the feedback that the religious leaders who received SAFFI's trainings provided:

> I used to believe that women have no say and everything must come from the man. SAFFI's trainings have changed my perception. I now preach about domestic violence and there are many people who come to ask for help. (Pastor, http://saffi.org.za/ 13 January 2020)

> We did not talk much about domestic violence in my congregation. But after the training I began to have conversations during church hours about domestic violence. SAFFI has opened my mind. (Khayelitsha Pastor, 2015)

> SAFFI's training changed my perception of what domestic violence is. I was not understanding violence if it was not physical violence. Now I understand the emotional, financial, psychological types of abuse...I now see the root causes of violence. (Khayelitsha Pastor, 2015)

Based on the above, one can appreciate the efforts that SAFFI has made in changing the attitudes of some religious leaders from non-involvement to positive engagement in addressing violence against women. However, one challenge that I observed relates to how most of SAFFI's work was centred on Christian communities. As shown by the above examples, the monthly forums on gender-based violence were mostly offered to Christian leaders. According to SAFFI, this was mainly as a result of the lack of programme facilitators who had the capacity to facilitate in other religious communities. There is, therefore, need for SAFFI to recruit more staff with the capacity to facilitate in other religious traditions given that the organization is a multifaith organization.

In addition, another challenge that SAFFI faces relates to funding. In a 2015/2016 Annual report, the treasurer of SAFFI reported that;

> In the light of global recession, increased corporatisation and competition, reduced government funding, intangible government funding criteria and a general lack of government support, the non-profit sector in South Africa currently faces many challenges. For the period under review, SAFFI was also significantly affected by the drastic drop in donor and/government funding. (Annual Report 2015/2016)

The treasurer further indicated that in 2015 SAFFI had revenues of R1 352,100, whereas the operating expenses where R1 528,036 and this resulted in a deficit of R1 75,936 (Annual Report 2015/2016). She added that the financial challenge resulted in reducing staff to cut expenses (Annual Report 2015/2016). While SAFFI has negotiated this challenge by seeking donations and using voluntary workers, the issue of funding creates a major limitation to the work of SAFFI. During my fieldwork, SAFFI was short-staffed. The organization had only two permanent staff and in terms of secretarial and administrative work, the organization relied on volunteers and internship students (Participant Observation June May 2017–November 2018). Moreover, due to lack of funds, the organization could not employ a Xhosa speaking facilitator. I observed how this posed as a serious challenge in providing training and support to religious leaders in Xhosa speaking communities. Be that as it may, the work of SAFFI in addressing violence against women should not be overlooked. Despite the challenges that organization faces, it remains a key partner in attaining the SDGs 5 and 10 through its efforts to reduce inequalities and eliminate all forms of violence against women.

Conclusion

While the modernization theory has neglected the role of religion in development theory and practice, religion has the potential to influence development goals. SAFFI, a multifaith organization, through its strategy of bringing different religions into dialogue to address violence against women, becomes a key partner in the development agenda. SAFFI's initiative of addressing violence contributes significantly to development given the economic, legal and health costs of violence against women to development. If violence against women is addressed, it reduces a strain on the economy and creates room for resources that are wasted through violence against women to be used for other development projects. More precisely, SAFFI's attempt to address inequalities and to end all forms of discrimination and violence against women and girls presents it as a key stakeholder in attaining SDG5 and SDG 10, as I mentioned earlier. Despite the challenges that SAFFI faces in its operation, its initiative of proposing other strategies to address violence against women in a society where the law has proved not be very effective should be acknowledged and strengthened. While this is not to dismiss laws and policies as strategies to address violence against women, I agree with Petersen that religion has a potential to address violence against women in a society where 90% of the population adhere to religion and in a society were religion determines gender power relations (Petersen 2016). I, therefore, interpret the work of SAFFI as a key contribution to development given its effort to end violence against women which is a key issue in development.

Although a lot more still needs to be done in South Africa in terms of addressing violence against women, the work of SAFFI with religious leaders is a major milestone in the quest for holistic development. Of particular significance is how SAFFI has equipped many religious leaders to change their perceptions regarding GBV and become involved in demystifying easily misinterpreted religious texts and traditions that have been used to promote violence against women. Most importantly, being a multifaith organization, SAFFI embraces diversity in its quest to address violence against women. Its multifaith approach fosters cooperation and dialogue among religious leaders from African Tradition Religion, the Baha'i Faith, Christianity, Hinduism, Islam and Judaism in addressing the same challenge of violence against women.

References

Babu, B. V. and Y. S. Kusuma. 2017. Violence against women and girls in the Sustainable Development Goals. *Health Promotion Perspectives* 7(1): 1–3.e

Buntman, F. L. 2003. *Robben Island and prisoner resistance to apartheid.* London: Cambridge University Press.

Chirongoma, F. 2020. Pentecostal churches' involvement in addressing gender inequalities: A move towards attaining Sustainable Development Goal 5 in ZAOGA FIF Church. In J.N. Amanze et al (eds.), *Religion and development in Southern Africa.* Volume 2. Mzuzu: Mzuni Press.

Chitando, E. and S. Chirongoma. Eds. 2012. *Redemptive masculinities: Men, HIV, and religion.* Geneva: World Council of Churches.

Clarke, M. 2013. Understanding the nexus between religion and development. In M. Clarke (ed.), *Handbook of research on religion and development.* Cheltenham, UK: Edward Elgar Publishing: 1–13.

Davis, D. C. 2007. The pedagogy of experience: A case study of pilgrimage as experiential learning. Adult Education Research Conference. https://newprairiepress.org/aerc/2007/papers/27.

Flood, M. 2011. Involving men in efforts to end violence against women. *Men and Masculinities* 14(3): 358–377.

García-Moreno, C. et al. 2015. Addressing violence against women: A call to action. *The Lancet* 385 (9978): 1685–1695.

Graaff, K. and L. Heinecken. 2017. Masculinities and gender-based violence in South Africa: A study of a masculinities-focused intervention programme. *Development Southern Africa* 34(5): 622–634.

Greiff, S. 2010. No justice in justifications: Violence against women in the name of culture, religion, and tradition. *Resource Paper, Global Campaign to Stop Killing and Stoning Women,* 1–44.

Khumalo, B., et al. 2014. Too costly to ignore—The economic impact of gender-based violence in South Africa. Johannesburg: KPMG Services.

Kusuma, Y. S. and B. V. Babu. 2017. Elimination of violence against women and girls as a global action agenda. *Journal of Injury and Violence Research* 9(2): 117–121.

Le Roux, E. et al. 2016. Getting dirty: Working with faith leaders to prevent and respond to gender-based violence. *The Review of Faith & International Affairs* 14(3): 22–35.

Mogale, R. S. 2012. Violence against women in South Africa: Policy position and recommendations. *Violence Against Women* 18(5): 580–594.

Nadar, S. 2005. Searching the dungeons beneath our religious discourses: The case of violence against women and the 'unholy trinity'. *Agenda* 19(66): 16–22.

146 F. CHIRONGOMA

Njagi, C.W. (2017). The role of Faith Based Organizations in curbing gender-based violence in Nairobi County, Kenya. PhD thesis, Masinde Muliro University of Science and Technology, Kenya.

Petersen, E. 2016. Working with religious leaders and faith communities to advance culturally informed strategies to address violence against women. *Agenda* 30(3): 50–59.

Phiri, I. A. 2001. Domestic violence in Christian homes: A Durban case study. *Journal for the Study of Religion* 14(2): 85–101.

Pyles, L. 2007. The complexities of the religious response to domestic violence: Implications for faith-based initiatives. *Affilia* 22(3): 281–291.

Rakoczy, S. 2004. Religion and violence: The suffering of women. *Agenda* 18(61): 29–35.

Reid, S. 2003. *Preventing violence against women: A European perspective.* Strasbourg: Council of Europe Publishing.

Rwafa, U. 2016. Culture and religion as sources of gender inequality: Rethinking challenges women face in contemporary Africa. *Journal of Literary Studies* 32(1), 43–52.

Sen, P. 1998. Development practice and violence against women. *Gender and Development* 6(3): 7–16.

South Africa Faith and Family Institute (SAFFI). 2017. SAFFI responding to gender-based violence in South Africa: Documenting the history, theory and methods and training model 2008–2017, SAFFI, Issue 1, July.

Sweetman, C. 1998. *Violence against women.* Oxford: Oxfam.

Wael, R. 2019. *Negotiating the power of NGOs: Women's legal rights in South Africa.* New York: Cambridge University Press.

West, T.C. 2019. *Solidarity and defiant spirituality: Africana lessons on religion, racism, and ending gender violence.* New York: New York University Press.

PRIMARY SOURCES

Abdul Khaliq Allie, Muslim leader (https://www.youtube.com/watch?v=nN Date accessed 13 January 2020).

Anonymous Pastor, http://saffi.org.za/ 13 January 2020.

Bongile Mawawa, African Traditional Religion leader, (https://www.youtube.com/watch?v=r-dJ760BSL8 Date accessed 13/01/2020).

Brislin, Stephen, Christian leader, (https://www.youtube.com/watch?v=om 13 January 2020).

Elizabeth Petersen Documentary, I am Woman, Leap of Faith aired on SABC 3 1 September 2013, YouTube link https://www.youtube.com/watch?v=2lXbv1V5CFo Date accessed 02 October 2019.

Guru Krishna, Hindu leader, (https://www.youtube.com/watch?v=prRhV-GKoaU Date accessed 13/01/2020).

Interview with Elizabeth Petersen, 13 April 2017, SAFFI Offices, Cape Town.
Khayelitsha Pastor 1, SAFFI, Newsletter, Issue 1, July 2015.
Khayelitsha Pastor 2, SAFFI, Newsletter, Issue 1, July 2015.
Khayelitsha Pastor 3, SAFFI, Newsletter, Issue 1, July 2015.
Omar, Rasheid, Muslim leader, (https://www.youtube.com/watch?v=yXrOtSV0KGU Date 13/01/2020).
Participant Observation, SAFFI, June 2017–November 2018.
SAFFI 2012/2013 Annual Report.
SAFFI 2013/2014 Annual Report.
SAFFI 2014/2015 Annual Report.
SAFFI 2015/2016 Annual Report.
SAFFI Official Launch, December 2010 Report.
SAFFI, Newsletter, Issue 1, July 2015.
SAFFI Website: http://saffi.org.za/ Date accessed 9 October 2019.
TACGBV. 2016. Theological reflection on the root causes of abuse of women in intimate relationships: A resource for faith leaders. Cape Town: Desmond Tutu Centre or Spirituality and Society.
TACGBV. 2017. Faith based interventions with male perpetrators of intimate partner abuse: What guidance can we get from holy scriptures and ancient teachings? Cape Town: Desmond Tutu Centre or Spirituality and Society.
Tahirih Matthee, Bahai Faith representative, https://www.youtube.com/watch?v=4_ Date accessed 13 January 2020).
Warren Goldstein, religious leader from Judaism, https://www.youtube.com/watch?v= Date accessed 13 January 2020).

CHAPTER 9

Interfaith Collaboration, Sexual Diversity and Development in Botswana

Tshenolo Jennifer Madigele

INTRODUCTION

Religion is one the most powerful resources for societal transformation. It dictates all dimensions of human existence, be they social, political, psychological, economic and spiritual. It is arguably an institution of conflict management and a resource to development (Casson et al. 2009). According to a Pew Study in 2012, the world population was 6.9 billion and 84% of the world population professed to a faith/religious affiliation. Particularly in Africa, the entire life cycle or every single stage of life revolves around religion (Idowu 1973: 1). Idowu sees religion as an entity that holds a community together, so that life was one invisible whole, with no divisions between the sacred and the secular (1973: 3) hence pivotal to government structures.

Religious leaders are, however, normally expected to back the government's initiatives on development instead of being engaged as

T. J. Madigele (✉)
University of Botswana, Gaborone, Botswana
e-mail: Madigeletj@ub.ac.bw

© The Author(s), under exclusive license to Springer Nature Switzerland AG 2022
E. Chitando, I. S. Gusha (eds.), *Interfaith Networks and Development*, Sustainable Development Goals Series,
https://doi.org/10.1007/978-3-030-89807-6_9

149

development actors (Jinkins 2012). They should instead speak back to government policies to ascertain the rights of the people, instead of being relegated to a religious corner that serves only the religious interests of the people (Nthontho 2020). They should also use a person and need-based approach. Their work should be shaped by the needs of the people, their organizational goals rather than traditions and doctrines. The latter may be used as an authoritative means of service (Nthontho 2017). In that way, interreligious networks play a pivotal role in promoting mutual understanding and in fostering consensus on common aspirations.

Human sexual diversity and inclusion is a critical dimension of the work of religious communities, yet an overlooked development issue directly implicating people who comprise an estimated 0.3–0.5% (25 million) of the global population. Despite their demographic significance, LGBTIQ persons have mostly been unrecognized in development programmes, policies, and discourse. Hence many countries are behind in developing capacities to address the health needs of LGBTIQ people. These needs are wide-ranging, with alarmingly high rates of abuse and higher HIV risk and vulnerability among younger LTGBTIQ persons.

This chapter begins by exploring an understanding of sexual diversity, challenges and health issues experienced by LGBTIQ people. The chapter deliberates on reasons for denying sexual and gender minorities HIV prevention and health services. It then highlights the urgent need for the Botswana Faith-Based Organizations Network on HIV and AIDS (BOFABONETHA) to co-create a more inclusive and equal world by 2030. The chapter calls for service inclusion to become the moral norm of service provision. It argues that BOFABONETHA could reduce health service exclusion that responds to sexual diversity by adopting an egalitarian approach that encourages collaboration with other service providers. The chapter also uses the paradigm of transformed masculinity to redress this gross scenario. Its further advocates for linking of the LGBTIQ sexual reproductive health and welfare to SDG 10 of Agenda 2030 that emphasizes reducing inequalities within and among countries.

SEXUAL DIVERSITY

In order to put the discussion into proper perspective, it is important to clarify some key concepts.

Definition and Practice in Botswana

Sexual diversity refers to the broad spectrum of sex characteristics, sexual orientations and gender identities and no more value is attached to the one or the other. Sexual health, on the other hand, is associated with a person's overall physical, emotional, and social well-being (WHO 2006). Despite its significance to holistic identity and well-being, sexuality remains a taboo topic in Botswana (Dube 2001). The purpose of this chapter is to increase our understanding of the nature of sexuality in adolescents of sixteen years and older whose experiences do not fit within the heterosexual model of sexual orientation. It is important to provide a brief description of sex characteristics, sexual orientations and gender identities.

Sexual characteristics refer to behavioural traits that suggest biological sex (Diamond 2008). Human beings are born as male and female depending on characteristics such as vagina, penis, ovaries and testes (Igartua et al. 2009). An intersex person is born with sex characteristics that may be found in both males and females including, among others, sex hormones, chromosomes or genitals. Thus, they do not fall in the conventional definitions for male or female (Morrow and Messinger 2006: 8). This biological spectrum shows that there are more than just two sexes. More research reveals that our brains have a role in how we experience our gender (Igartua et al. 2009). Therefore, a binary view of sex cannot adequately capture the biological aspect of gender. Gender identity does not always match the sex based on genitalia.

Sexual orientation, on the other hand, refers to sexual feelings, feelings of love and commitment towards the other (Diamond 2008). It provides a description of whom were are consensually and intimately attracted to. Some people are attracted to members of the same sex. These are referred to as homosexual and commonly called gays (lesbians if they are women). Heterosexuals are those that are attracted to people of the opposite sex while bisexuals have both homosexual and heterosexual feelings and are emotionally, physically and sexually attracted to people of both sexes (Vrangalova and Savin-Williams 2012). There are, however, other people who identify as queer and asexual. Queer people feel that they do not fall in any of the gender binaries or in any of the above-discussed categories of people. Asexual people feel that they are not sexually attracted to people (Vrangalova and Savin-Williams 2012). Above discussions show that sexual orientation occurs on a continuum.

Sexual orientation is interpersonal. Gender identity, on the other hand, is personal. Thus, "Gender identity refers to an individual's sense of identity as masculine or feminine, or some combination thereof" (Morrow and Messinger 2006: 8). It is informed by people's unique intersection of identities, experiences, and personal characteristics. It can either correlate with a person's assigned sex or differ from it (Diamond 2008). People can express behaviours, attitudes and appearances consistently with a gender role. However, that expression does not necessarily mirror their gender identity. Nonetheless, many communities and cultures dictate how individuals should express their sexuality. Communities and cultures are authoritative sources of human behaviour. Through their values, norms, rules and expectations, they shape sexual beings, and what is looked at as normal, natural, good, bad, right, or wrong (Maizes 2015; Madigele 2017). Thus, masculinity and femininity are characterized by certain physical attributes. In this context, people can be labelled as more or less 'man' or 'woman' based on the degree to which those attributes are present. Gendered norms and expressions are acquired through socialization rather than being natural or genetic. In most cases, these norms give men power, position and privilege over resources on a preferential basis to women (Maizes 2015).

The gendering of bodies is a controversial issue because it affects how people feel about themselves and how they are perceived and treated by others (Michael 2000; Madigele 2017). They would, therefore, be a conflict between social and personal gender. Communities and cultures enforce gender norms. Hence, they expect members to conform to gender roles and expectations. On the other hand, other people fail to feel comfortable and in harmony with their gender. They do not see themselves consistently with the way other people see them and cannot express themselves fully normally due to the fear of stigma and ill-treatment (Lombardi et al. 2008). These people normally experience gender distress because of the discordance of biological sex and experienced gender (Maizes 2015: 745). Some people do not identify with most of the aspects of gender assigned to their biological sex. These people are commonly considered to be transgender, gender fluid, and/or genderqueer (Altilio and Otis-Green 2011). Transgender is an umbrella term that is used for people whose gender identities, gender expressions, and/or behaviours are different from those culturally associated with the sex to which they were assigned at birth (Forsyth and Copes 2014). Transgender people, therefore, challenge traditional gender roles and gender identity (Chrisler and McCreary

9 INTERFAITH COLLABORATION, SEXUAL DIVERSITY AND DEVELOPMENT... 153

2010). On the other hand, people whose gender identity aligns with their assigned sex are commonly considered to be cisgender.

This chapter is particularly concerned with the health and wellbeing of the LGBTIQ people in Botswana in particular. It argues that for the most part sexual health is denied to LGBTIQ. Sexual health is understood as,

> A state of physical, emotional, mental and social well-being concerning sexuality; it is not merely the absence of disease, dysfunction or infirmity. Sexual health requires a positive and respectful approach to the possibility of having pleasurable and safe sexual experiences, free of coercion, discrimination and violence. For sexual health to be attained and maintained, the sexual rights of all persons, at all ages and in all contexts must be respected, protected and fulfilled.

The chapter will highlight health issues faced by the LGBTIQ people of Botswana and argues for the need for the interfaith network to integrate LGBTIQ health into health activists' demand.

Challenges the LGBTIQ People in Botswana Face

LGBTIQ persons in Botswana have for many years faced legal issues more than any group of citizens in the country. In 2016, the High Court of Botswana ordered the Registrar of Societies to register the Lesbians, Gays & Bisexuals of Botswana (LEGABIBO) as a society after many years of struggle. In 2017 the High Court of Botswana ruled that transgender people have a constitutional right to change their legal gender. The Registrar of National Registration was ordered to change a transgender man's marker and to issue new an identity document that reflected his gender identity. Another case of a trans woman in 2017 was heard. Similarly, her gender identity was recognised, and she was issued new identity documents (Legabibo fact sheet 2020).

In 2019, there was yet another milestone achievement by the LGBTIQ community in Botswana. Homosexuality was decriminalized and realized as sexual orientation, although the ruling was being appealed at the High Court. Legally, the LGBTIQ community in Botswana is given rights to dignity, privacy, freedom of expression, equal protection of the law, freedom from discrimination and freedom from inhumane and degrading treatment. However, they are many people in Botswana who still oppose LGBTIQ people for different reasons, including on moral, cultural, personal, political, and religious grounds. These are the same reasons that were used to oppose sexual diversity. In this context, human rights and LGBTIQ people are considered as foreign entities that are threatening the tradition of the people. This is a communalistic community that believes in consensus and belonging. Sexual expressions that are inconsistent with societal expectations are considered as alien (Kenyon 2019). Social intolerance towards the LGBTIQ people in Botswana contributes to the failure to provide adequate appropriate services to this community.

Health Issues Faced by the LGBTIQ People in Southern Africa

LGBTIQ people have specific health needs, including mental health challenges and sexually transmitted infections. It has been noted that globally, one-third of all new HIV infections are attributed to key vulnerable populations (Lane et al. 2011). In response to these high incidences of new infections, some countries have adopted punitive laws targeted at key vulnerable populations, hoping to minimize and/or possibly eliminate the risks of new infections. For instance, in 2012, it was reported that about 60% of national governments had laws, regulations and/or policies in place specifically aimed to serve as obstacles for vulnerable groups such as the LGBTIQ populations. Consequently, same-sex relations were reportedly criminalized in about 76 countries globally. The approach of some governments insofar as the LGBTIQ population is concerned has ignited homophobic behaviours among the populace. Notwithstanding such resistance, it is estimated that 10% of the population falls with the LGBTIQ group. A large array of social, structural and behavioural factors affects the health of such individuals. They are exposed to several health risks. However, their health risks are often not addressed, especially by public health care practitioners, primarily due to lack of requisite knowledge on human sexuality by health care providers, and partially due to homophobia and ignorance of specific health care issues.

In Botswana, only 44.9% of those classified as vulnerable and/or key affected populations have access to HIV prevention programmes. The remaining majority is not yet being reached. By implication, of the minority with access to HIV prevention programmes in Botswana, arguably, some are not served in a culturally sensitive and appropriate way, aligned to their needs. A study of women who have sex with women in South Africa, Botswana and Namibia, found that HIV prevalence of women who have sex with other women (WSW) is 9.6%. According to this study, these women contract HIV through vaginal fluid and menstrual blood. Almost half of them are reported to have consensual sexual relations with heterosexual men and that is how the virus spreads further (Sandford et al. 2013). According to Muranda et al. (2014), during healthcare interactions some lesbians shy away from talking about having sexual relations with heterosexual men because they do not want to be accused of "not being lesbian enough." Additionally, being women and queer puts lesbians as targets of sexual violence. Therefore, they experience increased risk of contracting HIV (Sandford et al. 2013).

Women, whether queer or not, have long been the most receivers of HIV-related burden. It is argued that gender inequities continue to drive the HIV epidemic. The consequences of gender inequities are evident in gender-based violence, inability to negotiate during sexual practices, and the dilemmas of "transactional sex" (Jewkes and Morrell 2010). Violent men are more likely to have HIV and their violent practices are from cultural ideals of gender identities. In many African contexts (as elsewhere), masculinity is characterised by toughness, control of women, strength and expression of prodigious sexual success. The dominant ideal of womanhood, on the other hand, is characterized by tolerance. These women are at risk because they lack control of the circumstances of sex, particularly during violent encounters. Hence these gender identities are models of behaviour in societies and may be hard for individuals to critique and exercise a choice (Jewkes and Morrell 2010). Men enjoy social and cultural privileges over women and inequities in sex and power translate into increased HIV risk and spread. Jewkes and Morrell (2010), therefore, argue that change in gender identities, rather than a focus on individual sexual behaviours, could successfully optimize care and HIV prevention.

A study in Botswana reveals high rates of men who have sex with men also engaging in heterosexual relationships. This underscores the necessity of creating programmes specific to LGBTIQs to effectively promote their health and wellbeing. The study suggests that sexual health interventions should continue to target men who have sex with men. Interventions should focus on the social, cultural, and structural factors that interact with individual behaviours to elevate HIV risk for this group of people (Selemogwe and White 2013). Another study that was done in Botswana, Namibia, South Africa and Zimbabwe examined the demographic and social factors contributing to female-to-female STI/HIV transmission knowledge among women who have sex with women using an integrated model of health literacy. The results of the study show that 64.4% (n =

362) of women had high knowledge; 35.6% (n = 200) had low knowledge. The study suggests opportunities for peer-led sexual health programming and expanded HIV prevention campaigns addressing women who have sex with women (Paschen-Wolff et al. 2019).

Accessing Health

Apart from healthcare needs, LGBTIQ people are likely to have difficulties in accessing health care services. One of the barriers of healthcare accessibility is the heteronormativity of healthcare providers and the broader society (Muranda et al. 2014). Other established barriers are patriarchy, moral judgments, homophobia and information need. Due to fear of stigmatization, many people within the LGBTIQ community remain 'in the closet' and do not seek medical help. It is estimated that almost two-thirds of health care practitioners never ask their patients about their sexual orientation because of either their homophobia and hostility or the presumptions they hold that all the people are heterosexual. It is suggested that ideals of masculinities that emphasize male dominance and relationship control are harmful to everyone's health, including men, youth, adolescents and women's health.

The negative influence of endorsing and enacting dominant norms of masculinity, therefore, includes lack of health care access, as well as HIV testing. In this chapter, the lack of information is seen as a catalyst for ill-treatment or lack of access or providing inadequate health care services. The information on health care risks available to both health care providers and the LGBTIQ community is limited (Moenga 2015). Most studies do not address issues related to sexual diversity. Lack of knowledge of human sexuality has an impact on services rendered by health care professionals. Due to misinformation, health professionals sometimes stigmatize people with anal problems rooting from anal sex. Due to stigmatization, some LGBTIQ persons are afraid of accessing health care services. In effect, HIV and AIDS infections are not addressed. Notwithstanding, some individuals in the LGBTIQ community are bisexual. By implication, such individuals are also having sexual relations with people who are heterosexual. Technically, there is a chain of sex that connects heterosexuals and the LGBTIQ. Some gay men, due to social pressure, have also engaged in marriage with women. Therefore, failure to render health care to the LGBTIQ works against the efforts to attain zero new infections of HIV in Botswana, as well as in sub-Saharan Africa (Moenga 2015). This challenges the achievement of the Sustainable Development Goals, particularly SDG 3, "Ensure healthy lives and promote wellbeing for all at all ages." Further, it is contrary to SDG 10 that seeks to address inequality, as LGTIQ will continue to be marginalised.

INTERFAITH COLLABORATION AND LGBTIQ HEALTH CHALLENGES

Given the urgency of including LGBTIQ in health, there is need for faith-based organisations to be actively involved in this quest. The following discussions are based on data collected during fieldwork in Botswana in May 2020. The chapter analyses the information from BOFABONETHA on its formation, polity, work, and achievements. Interviews were conducted with religious leaders from different religions who sit on the board of the organization. Members of faith-based organizations and an LGBTIQ organization that does work focusing on adolescent and youth reproductive health were also interviewed virtually to establish if there was partnership between them and BOFABONETHA and to fill gaps on literature review. Participants were, therefore, faith-based and secular. To protect the identities of the participants, names and organizations have been kept confidential. There is currently one interreligious network in Botswana by the name of Botswana Faith-Based Organizations Network on HIV and AIDS (BOFABONETHA) which was founded in 2011. This organization is composed of different religions and denominations in the country that are committed to working together in contributing to the national priorities for the national response to HIV and AIDS for the period 2019 to 2023 (and beyond). The following are founding member organs of the interfaith network:

1. Organizational African Independent Churches
2. Botswana Council of Churches
3. Evangelical Fellowship of Botswana
4. Botswana Islam Association
5. Baha'i
6. Botswana Hindu Association
7. Botswana Christian AIDS Intervention Program
8. Scripture Union
9. Open Baptist Church
10. Seventh Day Adventist.

Objectives of BOFABONETHA

1. The overall objective will be to provide strengthened coordination of targeted HIV prevention, care and support initiatives for outstanding service of BOFABONETHA towards the reduction of HIV infections and mitigate the impact.
2. To coordinate, harmonize and align the faith sector to the national HIV/AIDS response at all levels.
3. To capacitate her organs to effectively design, implement, coordinate, monitor and evaluate their HIV/AIDS programs.
4. To enhance and improve the advocacy role of the faith sector on matters relating to HIV and AIDS.
5. To facilitate and improve the recourse capacity of faith-based organizations, for effective delivery of HIV and AIDS interventions.
6. To be an information hub on faith sector activities on HIV and AIDS work.
7. To enhance networking and increase strategic partnerships in the field of HIV and AIDS.
8. To promote the development of family units nurtured and anchored on faith beliefs.
9. To report periodically all the HIV and AIDS work done by the faith sector to the Ministry of Health and Wellness (National AIDS Coordinating Agency), National AIDS Council, BOFABONETHA members and its stakeholders.

BOFABONETHA, Sustainable Development Goals and Sexual Diversity

The focus of the organization is mainly on SDG 10 that aims at reducing inequalities within and among countries. Its mandate is on enhancing partnerships at the connection of religion and development. BOFABONETHA is doing a great job in the area of Adolescent Sexual and Reproductive Health (ASRH) services and information. It is reported that adolescents and youths are at risk of contracting HIV/AIDS and other STIs more than other age groups, especially in Southern Africa. UNAIDS 2019 reports that in sub-Saharan Africa, three in five new HIV infections among 15–19-year-olds are among girls. BOFABONETHA is not only providing services and information, but it is also engaged in promoting access to health services and developing frameworks to shaping religions, traditions, social institutions, and promoting knowledge, awareness, and empowerment. The frameworks are necessarily made to avoid conflicts aggravated by opposing worldviews connected to how to inform and provide services on sexual reproductive health and what packages to offer to adolescent and youths (Shakile 04/05/2020). The frameworks may also help with overcoming resistance in the community by reaching out to religious and community leaders.

There is currently a lot of information circulated on the roles of adolescents and youth on HIV and AIDS prevention, as well as in other development-related areas because of the level of trust that the religious community has with the people at large. "It is however unfortunate that sometimes political leaders use that trust relationship to their gain" (Morakga 04/05/2020). Although BOFABONETHA through its services promotes healthy adolescence for a healthy future, it does not cover all sexual reproductive health rights of all adolescents. From this background, this chapter maintains that BOFABONETHA should increase its involvement in sexual diversity activism, focus on extending services on HIV and AIDS prevention and treatment, ending stigma, discrimination and violence that threaten the lives of the LGBTIQ people. BOFABONETHA is also challenged to develop and implement strategies to deal with discrimination against the LGBTIQ people, through turning to transformative masculinities as part of the development discourse and advocacy for intervention for legal changes. Thus, BOFABONETHA can work with organizations such as LEGABIBO, health care professionals, lawyers and other relevant professional networks for institutional change.

BOFABONETHA's role in HIV and AIDS is particularly made effective by their holistic approach. The organization participates in advocacy, education and awareness creation, capacity strengthening, provides health services, preventing and managing gender-based violence (GBV), counselling, and HIV/AIDS prevention and treatment (BOFABONETHA Summary Sheet 2020). According to Clinebell (1984: 31–50), a holistic approach includes all dimensions of life. Therefore, in order for a service to be holistic, there is need to analyse social structures to see if they contribute to the suffering of human beings (Louw 1999: 39–40) and meet people at their multiple points of need. Literature has shown that the

LGBTIQ people experience multidimensional oppression based on gender, culture and religion. The social system and culture predominately contribute to their suffering. Therefore, there is need to listen to their grievances in order to address their needs holistically. There is need to take it into account the underlying factors, including in-depth knowledge of the individual. Transformation in this context should be dual; it should have an individual therapeutic effect and socio-political transformation (Clinebell 1984: 29, 75). In other words, health service providers need to listen to those in distress and their account of their life situation and the reason for it, since counselees ultimately must decide what can be done. A health service provider's adherence to treatment preferences of the client, therefore, leads to increased client engagement in HIV treatment and intervention.

According to the BOFABONETHA information sheet, the organization is disseminating key "Messages of Hope." It aims at strengthening justice for children through engaging the faith, traditional structures and justice sectors. The approach considers the emotional, spiritual, physical and material aspects of the person. This approach is in conjunction with the WHO definition of health. As noted earlier, according to WHO (2006), health is understood as a state of physical, emotional, mental, and social wellbeing concerning all aspects of sexuality and reproduction. Therefore, the objective of BOFABONETHA should not simply be achieving an absence of disease among adolescents, but also acknowledging that adolescents and youth have the right to make decisions governing their bodies and to access services supportive of that right (WHO 2006).

BOFABONETHA is also engaged in advocacy and their advocacy work must influence both faith-based organizations and the wider community. According to the BOFABONETHA information sheet, the organization identifies gaps/barriers in systems, actors and processes that are involved in responding to cases of sexual violence against children and offer assistance to deal with these. The organization collaborates with secular organizations, media houses and the government of Botswana through its Ministry of Health and Wellness in its advocacy deliberations. Partnerships in advocacy have a lot of influence at the national legislative level, but the problem is with political leaders who would try to politicize sexual reproductive rights (Moraaka 08/05/2020). Apart from a holistic approach, BOFABONETHA uses a need-based approach that is driven by the needs of the people. This approach dictates that health care delivery must be aligned to the defined care beneficiaries and their needs (Clinebell (1984)

9 INTERFAITH COLLABORATION, SEXUAL DIVERSITY AND DEVELOPMENT... 161

2011). BOFABONETHA is thus informed by faith values such as love, respect, care so that they can authentically reach out to the needs of the people (Information Sheet, 2020). However, neglecting health needs of the LGBTIQ people shows that BOFABONETHA generally assumes that the challenges and needs of individuals are the same. It misses the fact that people's needs differ. With the usage of Maslow's psychotherapeutic tool (1968), this chapter suggests the thorough investigation of challenges and needs of the people so that their services would be more appropriate. There is also a need for understanding multiple systems of human existence and the underlying motivations of humanity. The organization is challenged to develop a method of allocating health care resources among the LGBTIQ people according to their levels of need for health care independent of their sexuality.

BOFABONETHA is also challenged to realign its development strategies to include ensuring that the LGBTIQ people are meaningfully engaged and represented at all levels of the national and regional response to HIV and AIDS. Botswana is one of the countries that has been most affected by HIV and AIDS. BOFABONETHA has managed to mobilise a strong response to the epidemic which has resulted in the scaling up of a more harmonised and holistic response. However, one significant gap has been the meaningful engagement of the LGBTI people in the planning, delivery, and monitoring of programmes, and in decision-making. HIV is a global health issue and also a development issue. It threatens social and economic stability and the achievement of SDGs 3 and 10. Botswana has accepted the call to halt and begin to reverse the spread of HIV and AIDS, and to achieve universal access to treatment for HIV for all those who need it.

CHALLENGES

The discussions above show that there are current societal barriers to HIV-related service provision to the LGBTIQ people. There is also a lack of resources and capacity to respond to the health needs of this minority group. Because of lack of information, sexual minorities have been more vulnerable to HIV. Hence a lot of stigma and discrimination in health facilities. In that regard, health services and systems are failing LGBTIQ people. It is worth noting, however, that denying them health services may increase the risk of anal cancer, especially among men who have sexual relations with other men and breast cancer among queer women.

Health care professionals are neither educated on these issues nor are they implementing programmes to address them.

Meanwhile, discrimination may generate mental health challenges which are particularly common among LGBTIQ people (Moenga 2015). HIV and AIDS are in a way challenging how we think about the relationship(s) between public health services, sexuality and religion, and how this is a threat to development and sustainable livelihoods. The 2030 Sustainable Development Agenda encourages working towards a world that reflects equity with universal respect for human dignity, pledging to leave no one behind. Although there are high rates of HIV infection among LGBTIQ people, they experience reduced access to medical services. The best possible way to achieve this is to adopt a transformative masculinity approach that holds that all people have equal rights and dignity. Women, children and other marginalised groups share equal human rights to healthcare, security, gender equality, freedom from discrimination, and to self-determination. In principle, BOFABONETHA has shown its willingness to engage with women and children but the decriminalisation of LGBTIQ people and HIV is still outstanding.

One of the respondents mentioned that BOFABONETHA prevents and responds to violence against women and girls. It aims at dealing with harmful practices such as domestic violence and sexual violence (Sera 14/05/2020). There is no evidence of the same services being extended to the LGBTIQ people. Neither is there evidence of the organization advocating for the sexual and reproductive health rights to this group. This chapter argues for gender-transformative approaches towards increasing protective sexual behaviours, preventing violence, advocating for inequitable attitudes, and reducing the spread of HIV. One of the reasons for the denial of health services to the LGBTIQ people by religion might be conformity to societal norms and values. It might be to this effect that some faith communities in Botswana would not to fully participate in sexual reproductive health prevention and intervention. According to a respondent, it is only some of the Christians, Muslims and Baha'i people who are active. The Zezuru, International Pentecostal Churches, are not participating in the coalition. Many issues connected to adolescent sexual and reproductive health are a no-go area. They are taboo and have misleading conspiracy news around them. They are also highly politicized. Besides, the organization lacks funds to fully execute its mandate (Banele, 30/04/2020).

Most religions in Botswana offer guidance and counselling about HIV and AIDS, to the youth, children and women in abusive marriages. Followers are encouraged to practice abstinence and faithfulness in marriage to avoid contracting HIV. The teaching of abstinence and marriage is done through organizations such as the Botswana Christian AIDS Intervention Programme (BOCAIP). The Islamic religion also encourages abstinence until marriage. Abstinence, which is seen as a powerful deterrent against the spread of HIV and AIDS, is viewed as an act of faith and compliance with the expectations of the religion. Baha'i followers also emphasise abstinence, marriage and the importance of living morally upright live towards reducing the spread of HIV and AIDS (Religious Education Form 3 Learners Book 2010). Buddhism, likewise, encourages people not to engage in promiscuity and pre-marital sex. People are advised to be aware of their actions to avoid harmful actions. It also encourages people to adopt positive behaviour (Ibid, 2010).

In this chapter, hegemonic masculinity is seen as the main perpetrator of inequalities, violence and the spread of HIV and AIDS. However, practices such as polygamy that are found in the African Traditional Religion, can expose everyone to HIV and AIDS including men and women. Cultural practices such that assume that marriage should happen within heterosexual relationships are not considerate of other sexual and gender identities. Therefore, sexual and reproductive health care services may be denied to the LGBTIQ by service providers who are in favour of cultural values of heterosexual marriages or traditional families. Moreover, attaching HIV and AIDS to morality and one's action is problematic as it may perpetuate fear of stigma, discrimination, denial of health services and self-blame. On the other hand, adolescent and youth may fear to seek health services where sexual contact is encouraged only within marriage unions. LGBTIQ people are therefore excluded not only because of their sexual and gender identities, but also because of engaging in sexual activities before marriage. Some lesbians who also engage in heterosexual sexual contact might resort to silence than be accused of immorality and receiving multiple blames. Failure to recognise sexual diversity is one of the contributing factors to the spread of HIV and AIDS. This is because the societal values and norms favour marriage, heterosexuality and privilege men.

From the above assertions, it could be argued that the outcome of gender-based violence is shaped by religious socialization of gender roles. Religious leaders, therefore, are the main targets for interventions as they are seen to have holder authority and power to influence gender norms and values. Moreover, such interventions imply that social transformation such as masculinity transformative approaches that may be used to interfere in norms and values that perpetuate gender inequalities, violence and the spread of HIV. It has also been maintained that religion provides a definition and understanding of social values. There is an intersection between religion and values because religion was founded in a society that has cultures, norms and values. This means that religion was not formed in a vacuum. Cultural norms, values, traditions and sacred text remain sources of religion. Conforming to these sources of religion shows a true sense of belonging (Ives and Kidwell 2019). Religion may also express a sense of belonging through conforming to societal norms.

Transformed Masculinities

The discussions above show that cultural norms may pose as a de facto barrier to the full exercise of human rights of the LGBTI people, including access to health. Social attitudes about sexuality, including the values of healthcare providers, govern adolescent and youths' access to sexual and reproductive health services. Information on BOFABONETHA shows that the organization assumes that adolescents and youths identify as heterosexual, and exclusively engage in sexual activity with partners of the opposite sex or gender. There is absolutely nothing on how the needs of sexual and gender minority adolescents are met. A study (Müller et al. 2018) that was done in Malawi, Mozambique, Namibia, Zambia and Zimbabwe analysed data from fifty in-depth qualitative interviews with representatives of organisations working with adolescents, sexual and gender minorities, and/or sexual and reproductive health and rights. According to this study, LGBTIQ adolescents and youths experience double-marginalisation while in pursuit of sexual and reproductive health services. They experience barriers to accessing sexual reproductive health services from LGBTIQ organisations. The organizations fear being associated with adolescents and extending reproductive health services to this group because they have been painted as "homosexuality recruiters." They are also excluded from heteronormative adolescent and youth sexual and reproductive health services (Müller et al. 2018). In the mentioned countries in Southern Africa, barriers to health services are attributable to the criminalisation of consensual sexual behaviours between partners of the same sex.

However, in Botswana consensual sexual behaviours between partners of the same sex have since been decriminalized. Societal heteronormativity, which is a social construct that assumes heterosexual identities as the norm, is the main barrier in healthcare provision. Because of heteronormativity, sexual and gender minority identities become invisible in all facets of life. This normative influences BOFABONETHA and the healthcare sector, to assume that everyone is heterosexual and cisgender. Consequently, the LGBTIQ people's diverse health needs are not known and recognized. The following discussions are on how the local interfaith network could work on a 'transformation of masculinities'.

Proposed Interventions

Throughout our discussions, men and societal structures that favour men have been condemned as subordinating women, children and men that do not act according to the norms set by these structures. Men are the culprits of marginalization of gender or sexual identities and by extension, the major perpetrators of the further spread of HIV and AIDS and gender-based violence that pose high HIV risk. According to Chitando, to provide effective responses to the HIV epidemic, men should not be left out of prevention, care and support programmes. Against this background, BOFABONETHA in collaboration with other reproductive health service providers, sexual minority organizations, legal fraternity and policymakers are challenged to engage men and boys' organizations in transformation of masculinities. HIV and AIDS affect all gender and sexual identities all and should be included in the eradication of this pandemic. Men and boys' organizations should be engaged in activities to prevent violence against women, children and other sexual/gender minorities. Experienced mediators such as these are mechanisms that could foster the transformation process. This approach should not continue with the blame game but focus on transforming masculinity relations of all people, norms and social structures that sustain inequality and violence (WHO 2011).

This chapter maintains that interfaith networks must move beyond cultural and religious boundaries in extending their services as well as organising and implementing programmes for the welfare of the LGBTIQ people. Health services and supporting treatment or interventions should be extended to everyone regardless of sex or gender (Balogun and Durojaye 2011). Interfaith networks, therefore, should embody positive religious values. Values such as tolerance, compromise, shared responsibility that cut across all religions should be used to allow different professionals to contribute to the general good of the people. Religious values could be powerful tools that could counter the harmful hegemonic masculinity approach. Besides, maintaining health is more important than conforming to hegemonic masculinity ideals.

Collective values, however, do not have a lasting impact if masculinity transformative approach is not tagged along. Listening is a very important aspect of the intervention. As one listens, he or she is expected to cross over to understanding one's thought pattern, behaviour, principles, values and religion. In that way, a health service provider will get to know the problems and needs of their clients. People's specific needs should be considered. They would also be able to explore the causes and effects of gender-based health inequities. Values of respect, appreciation, understanding, care, altruism may be essential at this stage. This entails careful listening, observing the care seeker, as well as his or her context. Intentional listening is a process of attending and exploring, explanation, expanding, and enquiring into the person's life. It is the ability to interpret the cause of suffering and to identify what is essential. Human experiences are to be taken seriously and should thus be allowed to challenge and inform understanding.

At this stage, a sexual and reproductive health provider would put his or her values, principles or religion aside in favour of the need of the other. Listening and getting to know underlying problems, challenges and needs of the LGBTIQ persons itself might bring understanding and a paradigm shift from hegemonic masculinity. Hegemonic masculinity is understood as a social construct of power, privilege and hierarchy that favours men over women, children and other gender or sexual minorities. This approach has been made popular by its influence in the spread of HIV, gender violence and subordination of other gender and sexual minorities (Fleming et al. 2016). Added effects of hegemonic masculinity are multiple sexual relationship and refusal to use condoms (Fleming et al. 2016). This harmful concept of masculinity is, therefore, to be challenged towards more gender-equitable and sensitive aspects. According to WHO, a gender-transformative approach is the one that "address the causes of gender-based health inequities through approaches that challenge and redress harmful and unequal gender norms, roles, and power relations that privilege men over women" (2011).

It could be adopted by individual adolescent and youth sexual reproductive health service providers in their deliveries. For maximum impact, however, men and boys' organizations should be engaged to work with other sexual reproductive health service providers in the transformation of masculinities, HIV prevention strategies and interventions. There are different ways of transforming a hegemonic masculinity approach. One way is to engage in critical reflection and exposure to gender norms, roles, and men's position of privilege in society and assess if there are justice and equality between people. Harmful gender norms, roles and relations would be deconstructed or reconstructed (Ruane-McAteer et al. 2019). Hegemonic masculinity has harmful effects on everyone, including men. As indicated, it hurts sexual reproductive health and rights. It puts everyone at risk in the context of HIV. Therefore, introducing transformative masculinity approaches could be beneficial to everyone as it improves sexual reproductive health relations (Fleming et al. 2016). The approach should specifically critique how gender norms, roles, male privilege, power, position and relations affect access to and control over resources (Ruane-McAteer 2019).

Another transformative masculinity approach investigates the use of religious and cultural concepts considered patriarchal to promote an alternative type of masculinity for men (Ruxton 2004). Other men had adopted counter-hegemonic practices (Connell 2005). These men would get to do the work that is culturally considered to be of women and girls, such as participating in childcare and caretaking. They would even engage in addressing violence against women and children. In other instances, socio-economic changes may challenge the traditional system that perceives men as family sole providers. Here men could either be loving and caring hence participating in caregiving or may consequently seek affirmation of their masculinity in other ways such as reckless sexual behaviour or domestic violence (Ruxton 2004). It is only through listening, dialogue and critical thinking that men would be able to explore the causes and effects of gender-based health inequities and subsequently decide on the more gender-equitable masculinity approaches (Gibbs et al. 2015). Men should be conscious of gender as something that also affects their lives. They should be aware that positive effects of gender equality are also of benefit to men and boys. It can also contribute to the eradication of HIV and AIDS, eliminating violence of women and human rights. Ideologies of hegemonic masculinity, though rooted on societal values and norms bring more harm in the society and hence limit men's capacity to express care and love, thereby narrowing their experience of what it is to be fully human (Gibbs et al. 2015).

Knowing problems, challenges and needs of the LGBTIQ people either through individuals from this group or through LGBTIQ groups is essential because it facilitates authentic adolescent and youth sexual reproductive health care. This knowledge may also allow victims to negotiate their painful experiences as sexual and gender minorities; an emotional appeal in the quest for gender and sexual transformation. The knowledge may also facilitate awareness on the matter of sexual and gender-based violence and promote collective responses to perpetrators and sexual gender-based violence. Knowledge gathered may ultimately reinforce BOFABONETA's strategy to mobilize religious communities fostering the engagement of worshippers in the public sphere to include all people in their health deliveries. Engaging men and boys groups in facilitating societal changes and furthering the inclusion of sexual and gender identities in care is essential as it may address the root cause of the problem hence exposing societal structures that perpetuate violence towards others and the spread of HIV and AIDS. Adolescent sexual reproductive health care service providers should also be enlightened on how to deal with specific health needs of the LGBTIQ people. Policymakers also need awareness on LGBTIQ people, sexual health rights, exclusion and further spread of HIV and AIDS. BOFABONETHA's starting point towards authentic intervention should, therefore, start with the realization of the need to facilitate partnership with other service providers and the concerned people in promoting gender equality for sexual and reproductive health needs of the LGBTIQ community.

The Sustainable Development Goal number 10 (SDG 10) dictate that no one should be left behind. This means that LGBTIQ people should be treated equally and not be excluded in health services. BOFABONETA is therefore challenged to bring more attention to LGBTIQ health issues within the framework of SDG 10 implementation at all institutional, policy, data and dialogue levels. The organization should facilitate change of thought and practice for improved health and social relations. Partnering with relevant service providers and concerned people is essential as the organization does not currently have the technical knowledge and resources.

CONCLUSION

This chapter sets off by deliberately using the term 'sexual diversity' to emphasize that there are different forms of sexual expressions against the ideal that maintain that there is single sexual normality. It specifically questions heterosexual norms that are used to legitimize disregard of non-heterosexual sexualities. Likewise, the concern of hegemonic masculinity is deliberate. It is made unpopular by its influence in excluding other sexual and gender identities, heightening the risk of HIV, homophobic and transphobic stigma and discrimination, human rights violations, the absence of legal frameworks offering protection, denial of sexual reproductive health services to the LGBTIQ people and gender-based violence. Against this background, the SDG 10 advocates for the regard of humanity and social inclusion hence the use of transformative masculinity approaches. These approaches entail considering how norms, relations and male privilege affect access and authority of health resources to transform them and promote gender equality. They also encourage the knowledge of the underlying causes, effects and specific needs of the LGBTIQ people. Interventions include strategies to foster feasible changes in power relationships between people for better sexual and reproductive health for all. BOFABONETHA is a local interfaith network that has been engaged in offering sexual reproductive health services to the people. The organization has a specific focus on women and children. This means that its approach targets "victims." This chapter argues for the inclusion of LGBTIQ people, men and boys' organizations and further collaboration with other health service providers for maximum impact of the intervention. Thus, inclusion is an egalitarian system that provides LGBTIQ people with fair access to sexual reproductive health service and fair treatment during service.

The inclusivist approach in health service and deliberations should be a moral imperative for BOFABONETHA. If such a moral imperative becomes a norm, services would become as inclusive as possible by 2030. If the organization advocates that service norms, policies and practices should be transformed to include all people by 2030, a new era of health service and delivery would be envisioned. Linking LGBTIQ advocacy to the sustainable development enterprise should be considered as an opportunity. Furthermore, the chapter argues that there is a need for an exclusive adolescent and youth sexual and reproductive health and HIV-preventative and coping strategies towards improved health outcomes of the LGBTIQ people. Also, literature has shown that there a demand for LGBTIQ health needs training for healthcare professionals, with a specific focus on the LGBTI identities in Botswana and Southern Africa. Interventions at policy, service and community levels are also recommended. There is need for a policy framework that is related to gender equity. The education system should also adopt transformative masculinity approaches to build more gender-equitable caring masculinities in our communities. By acknowledging sexual diversity and meeting the needs of LGBTIQ people, an interfaith organisation such as BOFABONETHA can make more effective contributions to SDG 10 and ensure that everyone is treated equally.

References

Altilio, T. and S. Otis-Green, 2011. *Oxford Textbook of Palliative Social Work.* Oxford: Oxford University Press.

Balogun, V. and E. Durojaye, 2011. The African Commission on Human and Peoples' Rights and the Protection of Sexual and Reproductive Rights. *African Human Rights Law Journal* 11(2): 268–395.

Casson, M.C. et al. 2009. Formal and Informal Institutions and Development. *World Development* 38(2): 137–141.

Chrisler, J.C. and D.R. McCreary. 2010. *Handbook of Gender Research in Psychology*, vol. 1. New York: Springer.

Clinebell, H. (1984) 2011. *Basic Types of Pastoral Care & Counselling: Resources for the Ministry of Healing and Growth.* Nashville: Abingdon Press.

Connell, R. 2005. *Masculinities.* Cambridge: Polity Press.

Diamond, L.M. 2008. *Sexual Fluidity Understanding Women's Love and Desire.* Cambridge: Harvard University Press.

Dube, M.W. (ed.) 2001. *Other Ways of Reading: African Women and the Bible.* Atlanta: SBL.

Fleming, P.J. (et al.) 2016. Masculinity and HIV: Dimensions of Masculine Norms that Contribute to Men's HIV-Related Sexual Behaviors. *AIDS and Behaviour* 20(4): 788–798. https://doi.org/10.1007/s10461-015-1264-y. Retrieved on May 10, 2020.

Forsyth, C.J. and Copes, H. 2014. *Encyclopaedia of Social Deviance.* Sage Publications. Retrieved on April 29, 2020.

Gibbs, A. (et al.) 2015. Beyond 'Working with Men and Boys': (Re) Defining, Challenging and Transforming Masculinities in Sexuality and Health Programmes and Policy. *Culture, Health & Sexuality* 17 (Suppl 2): 85–95.

Idowu, B.I. 1973. *African Traditional Religion.* London: SCM.

Igartua, K. (et al.) 2009. Concordance and Discrepancy in Sexual Identity, Attraction, and Behaviour among Adolescents. *Journal of Adolescent Health*, 45(6): 602–608.

Ives, C.D and Kidwell, J. 2019. Religion and Social Values for Sustainability. *Sustainability Science* 14: 1355–1362. https://doi.org/10.1007/s11625-019-00657-0.

Jewkes, R. and Morrell, R. 2010. Gender and Sexuality: Emerging Perspectives from the Heterosexual Epidemic in South Africa and Implications for HIV Risk and Prevention. *Journal of the International AIDS Society.* https://doi.org/10.1186/1758-2652-13-6

Jinkins, M. 2012. Religious Leadership. In B. J. Miller-McLemore (Eds), *Wiley-Blackwell Companion to Practical Theology.* Chichester: Blackwell Publishing Limited: 308–317.

Kenyon, K.H. 2019. Health Advocacy on the Margins: Human Rights as a Tool for HIV Prevention among LGBTI Communities in Botswana. *Journal of Contemporary African Studies* 37(2–3): 257–273.

Lane, T. et al. 2011. High HIV Prevalence among Men Who Have Sex with Men in Soweto, South Africa: Results from the Soweto Men's Study. *AIDS Behaviour* 15: 626–634.

Legabibo fact sheet, 2020.

Lombardi, E.L. (et al.) 2008. Gender Violence: Transgender Experiences with Violence and Discrimination. *Journal of Homosexuality* 42 (1): 89–101.

Louw, D.J. 1999. *A Mature Faith: Spiritual Direction and Anthropology in a Theology of Pastoral Care and Counselling.* Louvain: Peeters.

Madigele, T.J. 2017. Informed by Heterosexual Moral Norms? Raising Some Moral Questions for Traditional Leaders, Lawyers and the General Public of Botswana. *BOLESWA* 4(3).

Maizes, V. 2015. *Integrative Women's Health,* p. 745: Retrieved on May 14, 2020.

Michael, K. 2000. *The Gendered Society.* Oxford: Oxford University Press.

Moenga, T.J. 2015. Pastoral Care to the Gay Community in Botswana. Thesis. University of Botswana, Department of Theology and Religious Studies.

Morrow, D.F. and Messinger, L. Eds. 2006. *Sexual Orientation and Gender Expression in Social Work Practice: Working with Gay, Lesbian, Bisexual and Transgender People.* New York: Columbia University Press.

Müller, A, (et al.) 2018. The No-Go Zone: A Qualitative Study of Access to Sexual and Reproductive Health Services for Sexual and Gender Minority Adolescents in Southern Africa. *Reproductive Health* 215: 12. https://doi.org/10.1186/s12978-018-0462-2. Retrieved on May 12, 2020.

Muranda, T.M. (et al.) 2014. HIV is Not for Me: A Study of African Women Who Have Sex with Women's Perceptions of HIV/AIDS and Sexual Health. *African Human Rights Law Journal AHRLJ* 36.

Nthontho, M.A. 2017. Is It Possible to Be Accommodative of Other Religions as a School Principal? *Journal of Religious Education* 65: 35–50. https://doi.org/10.1007/s40839-017-0049-1. Retrieved on May 7, 2020.

Nthontho, M.A. 2020. School Principals Managing Policy Change: The Case of Religion Policy. *Religion & Education* 47(1): 77–97. https://doi.org/10.1080/15507394.2019.1668254. Retrieved on May 14, 2020.

Paschen-Wolff, M.M. (et al.) 2019. HIV and Sexually Transmitted Infection Knowledge among Women Who Have Sex with Women in Four Southern African Countries. *Culture, Health & Sexuality.* https://doi.org/10.1080/13691058.2019.1629627. Retrieved on May 27, 2020.

Religious Education Form 3 Learners Book. 2010. http://www.collegium.co.bw/share/0222%20. Retrieved on May 15, 2020.

Ruane-McAteer, E. (et al.) 2019. Interventions Addressing Men, Masculinities and Gender Equality in Sexual and Reproductive Health and Rights: An Evidence and Gap Map and Systematic Review of Reviews. *BMJ Global Health* 4(5).

Ruxton, S. (Ed.). 2004. *Gender Equality and Masculinity: Learning from Practice.* London: Oxfam.

Sandford, T.G.M. (et al.) 2013. Forced Sexual Experiences as Risk Factor for Self-Reported HIV Infection among Southern African Lesbian and Bisexual Women. *PlOs ONE* 8(1).

Selemogwe, M., and White, D. (2013). An Overview of Gay, Lesbian and Bisexual Issues in Botswana. *Journal of Gay & Lesbian Mental Health* 17(4): 406–414. https://doi.org/10.1080/19359705.2013.793223

Vrangalova, Z. and Savin-Williams, R. 2012. Mostly Heterosexual and Mostly Gay/Lesbian: Evidence for New Sexual Orientation Identities. *Archives of Sexual Behaviour* 41(1): 85–101.

WHO. 2006. *Defining Sexual Health: Report of a Technical Consultation on Sexual Health.* Geneva: WHO, pp. 28–31.

WHO. 2011. *Gender Mainstreaming for Health Managers: A Practical Approach—Participant's Notes.* Geneva.

PART III

Case Studies of Interfaith Networks and Development in Selected African Countries

CHAPTER 10

The Inter-Religious Council of Uganda and Development

Andrew David Omona

INTRODUCTION

The Inter-Religious Council of Uganda (IRCU), founded in 2001, is a network of religious organizations in Uganda "that works through its leadership and structures to mobilize and organize Ugandans to work for harmony, unity, peace, prosperity, good health and freedom for the common good" (IRCU 2017f, g: 2). Its membership comprises the Roman Catholic Church (RCC), the Church of the Province of Uganda (COU), the Uganda Orthodox Church (UOC), and the Uganda Muslim Supreme Council (UMSC). It also includes the Seventh-day Adventist Uganda Union (SDAUU), the Born Again Faith in Uganda (BAF), and the National Alliance of Pentecostal and Evangelical Churches in Uganda (NAPECU). Besides, IRCU works in partnership with the Spiritual Assembly of the Baha'i, the Methodist Church and Lutheran Church (IRCU 2017: 2). Among many programmatic areas, the IRCU deploys its efforts to peacebuilding so to realize harmonious coexistence in a

A. D. Omona (✉)
Uganda Christian University, Mukono, Uganda

© The Author(s), under exclusive license to Springer Nature
Switzerland AG 2022
E. Chitando, I. S. Gusha (eds.), *Interfaith Networks and Development*, Sustainable Development Goals Series,
https://doi.org/10.1007/978-3-030-89807-6_10

175

multi-ethnic and multi-religious context. The IRCU is an affiliate of the Religions for Peace International (RfP), the African Council for Religious Leaders, (ACLR), the East African Community—Inter-Religious Council (EAC-IRC), and the Global Women and Youth of Faith Networks.

The Council delivers services through religious leaders, structures and infrastructure that cascade from national to the grassroots levels. It also works with institutions, including health facilities, universities, schools, vocational/post-secondary institutions and regional and district governance structures (dioceses, deaneries, fields and Muslim districts, counties and villages). The IRCU plays the coordination function to ensure coordinated approaches, coherence of effort, maximization of synergy and sharing of resources to enable these structures and infrastructure to provide quality services to God's people. It mainly focuses on promoting peace and conflict transformation, sustainable human development and network development among the religious leaders, communities, women and youths (IRCU 2017: 2). Although, as an independent country, Uganda is slightly half a century old at the time of writing this chapter, the myriad of upheavals that the country has gone through far exceed what the state could manage. Whereas some of the upheavals predate Uganda as an independent country, the vestiges of such conflictual relations continued right into the postcolonial time. Since religion is an aspect of human culture, even in times of peace and conflict in Uganda, religious leaders stood as a vanguard of development. In the case of Uganda, even before and after the introduction of missionary religions, religion helped people to understand their environment and relate to it in ways that brought about social development. As we shall see later in the chapter, religion in general and the Inter-religious Council in particular, has played a great role in socio-economic, political, democratic, and educational development in Uganda.

Historical Background to the Emergence of the Interreligious Council of Uganda

The creation of the IRCU was in the context of the need to respond to human suffering. As the HIV and AIDS pandemic was sweeping across the world, at the international level, religious leaders saw the need to respond to the plight of children affected or infected by HIV and AIDS. Probably, because Uganda is lauded as a success story in addressing

10 THE INTER-RELIGIOUS COUNCIL OF UGANDA AND DEVELOPMENT 177

the challenge of HIV and AIDS, the then Secretary-General of Religions for Peace (RfP) International, Doctor William Fray Vendley, visited and held private meetings with senior Islamic and Christian religious leaders, about the need to establish a body to coordinate religious actions in the same area. The private meetings held on 31st March and 3rd April 2001 were attended by; His Eminence Sheik Shaban Ramathan Mubaje (Islamic Faith), His Eminence Metropolitan Jonas Lwanga (the Uganda Orthodox Church), His Grace Doctor Cyprian Kizito Lwanga (Roman Catholic Church), and His Grace, the Most Reverend Henry Luke Orombi (the Anglican Church {Church of Uganda}) (IRCU n.d. –e). During the meetings, Dr. Vendley introduced the mission and vision of the then "World's Council of Religions for Peace (WCRP)," now RfP. After elaborating on the "emerging initiative and unique opportunity for religious communities to address the plight of orphans affected by HIV/AIDS," he also "offered to facilitate the formation of a national inter-religious structure" (IRCU n.d. –e).

The members in attendance welcomed the idea. Actually, to the religious leaders present, this meeting came as an answer to the felt needs of the religious leaders of collectively participating in addressing issues that affect common humanity in Uganda. They unanimously agreed that the time was ripe for a national inter-religious council be co-built by both Christians and Muslims. Possibly, at the back of their minds, they thought working together could afford the opportunity to bridge existing historical gaps between members of the two religious groups, let alone the strife within their denominations. Among other things, during the meeting the WCRP team and major religious groups in Uganda brainstormed on how forming a national inter-religious council could strengthen their activities. Accordingly;

> The first preparatory meeting for the formation of the Inter-Religious Council of Uganda (IRCU) was held on 4th April [2001], at Nile Hotel in Kampala. The committee consisted of representatives appointed by the heads of four religious communities in Uganda. The participants agreed to officially constitute the preparatory committee mandated to work for the establishment of IRCU. The committee designated six members to form an ad-hoc committee to conduct preliminary work for the committee, including the drafting of the Council's constitution. (IRCU n.d. –e)

Indeed, the meeting set the stage for speeding up the process of forming the IRCU. Although at the beginning only leaders from four religious groups welcomed the idea, as time went by the membership kept increasing because other religious leaders also saw the need for joint participation in addressing issues that affect humanity regardless of religious or denominational affiliation. The expansion of the membership also propelled the expansion of the programmatic areas of operation, given that the members realized many life-threatening issues that affected people in Uganda apart from HIV and AIDS. Since development is a multi-sectorial issue, the IRCU identified many areas that they felt they could augment the efforts of the government. The fact that even before the creation of IRCU Christians and Muslims had been attending to developmental concerns through the Uganda Joint Christian Council (UJCC) and the Uganda Muslims Supreme Council, pulling together to address issues of concern meant expanding the coverage of areas in the country. With already existing structures at the grassroots, the IRCU uses the religious leaders, structures and infrastructure to deliver services from national to the grassroots levels. Consequently, because the health facilities, universities, schools, vocational/post-secondary institutions, regional and district governance structures have people from faith groups, this facilitates the cascading of services to the lower levels. The IRCU office at the national level plays a coordination function so to ensure the realization of "coordinated approaches, coherence of effort, and maximization of synergy and sharing of resources to enable these structures and infrastructure to provide quality services to God's people" (IRCU 2017: 2).

THE ACTIVITIES AND ACHIEVEMENTS OF THE IRCU

The IRCU works through seven programmatic areas to ensure the realization of human development in the country. Whereas there is still a lot that requires streamlining, what the IRCU does still sustains the livelihood of many. To ease operational oversight, the IRCU has regional arms that work with local communities, including;

- West Nile Inter-Faith Network,
- Acholi Religious Leaders Peace Initiative Forum,
- Lango Religious' Leaders Peace Forum,
- Teso Religious Leaders' Efforts for Peace and Reconciliation,
- The Interim Inter-Faith Steering Committee for Eastern Region,

10 THE INTER-RELIGIOUS COUNCIL OF UGANDA AND DEVELOPMENT   179

- Busoga Religious Leaders' Forum,
- Bunyoro Inter-Religious Council,
- Western Uganda Inter-Religious Forum,
- Moroto-Nakapiripirit Religious Leaders' Initiative for Peace (MONARLIP), and
- Kigezi Inter-Faith Forum (IRCU n.d. –f1).

The national and the regional coordination offices have worked through religious and denominational leaders at the grassroots to achieve the IRCU mandate of; building the capacity of FBOs and religious leaders so that they rise to today's challenges; mobilizing resources for addressing the challenges, influencing public policy advocacy; and taking action as an agent of social change and transformation. The subsection that follows is devoted to analyzing some of the programmatic areas through which the IRCU participates in holistic human development.

The Public Health Programme

At the time of writing, in Uganda, communicable diseases accounted for over 50% of morbidity and mortality. According to the 2018 World Health Organization's "Country cooperation strategy at a glance", the leading causes of illness and death in Uganda were malaria, HIV and AIDS, Tuberculosis (TB), and respiratory, diarrheal, epidemic-prone and vaccine-preventable diseases. Besides, the report indicates that Uganda was registering a growing burden of non-communicable diseases (NCD) including mental health disorders, maternal and child prenatal conditions having a direct impact on mortality. Neglected Tropical Diseases (NTDs) had also become a big problem in the country's rural communities (WHO 2018). In an attempt to augment the efforts of the government to address the health challenge, the IRCU came up with a programme that focuses on addressing public health concerns. In collaboration with the Uganda Aids Commission (UAC), the Ministry of Health, and as a member of the Uganda National Aids Service Organization, the IRCU participates in responding to the HIV and AIDS epidemic in Uganda. Besides being a member of the National Prevention Committee, the Country Coordinating Mechanism (CCM) of the Global Fund to Fight AIDS, TB and Malaria, the Health Policy Advisory Committee (HIPAC), the IRCU actively participates in addressing health concerns of the citizens of Uganda. In doing this, it is contributing towards the attainment of the Sustainable

180   A. D. OMONA

Development Goal (SDG) 3, "Ensure healthy lives and promote well-being for all at all ages."

In following up on this dimension, the IRCU supports the comprehensive faith and community-based HIV/AIDS programme through sub-grants for capacity building to religious structures and organizations. Through this programme, the IRCU has participated in HIV prevention, care, treatment and mitigation services for orphans and vulnerable children (OVC) in Uganda. In line with the Ministry of Health's campaign to scale up Biomedical HIV and AIDS Prevention, the IRCU has conducted Safe Medical Circumcision to thousands of uncircumcised males who turn up for the exercise. In one of the free Safe Medical Circumcision (SMC) camp organized by IRCU with support from USAID and Mengo hospital, 1886 males aged between 10 and 50 years got circumcised. While adults made their own decision for the services, they sought the consent of parents or guardian in case of children. Given the fact that "the 2011 National HIV/AIDS survey indicated that the prevalence rate among the sexually active population (15–49 years) has risen from 6.4% to 7.3% over the past five years" (IRCU n.d. -f2), the IRCU strategically drew up a five-year proposal to continue the fight. In a way of addressing a reproduction health concern, the IRCU unveiled actions to end Female Genital Mutilation in Karamoja and Sebei sub-regions (Vision Reporter 2017). While earlier attempts had been made to address this, the persistence of the practice has drawn the concern of the religious body to act along the same lines. With the local religious leaders scattered around the sub-region, the IRCU's understanding is that constant appeal to the community about the dangers of the practice will help in curbing the practice among the local communities.

The IRCU has trained religious leaders to monitor issues of health in the community who act as community sensitizers and educators. For example, when there was an outbreak of cholera in Kasese, the IRCU's field representatives facilitated the IRCU to make a swift report about the outbreak to the Minister of Health so that the situation was put under control (IRCU 13 June 2019b). In keeping with the health concerns of women, the IRCU in collaboration with UNICEF rolled out the Key Family Care Practices (KFCP) in Northern Uganda and Karamoja Sub-region. KFCP are simple practices which, when practised, could significantly reduce morbidity and mortality. These practices include promoting immunization, hand washing, taking family members to the hospital when

10 THE INTER-RELIGIOUS COUNCIL OF UGANDA AND DEVELOPMENT 181

sick, keeping children in school, using of pit latrines for defecation, attending antenatal care, educating children and so forth. Accordingly;

> The program was conceived out of the need to reduce maternal and child mortality that is endemic in both regions of Uganda. It was precipitated by the resolutions of a conference on Maternal, Reproductive and Child Health (MRNAH) that took place in Kampala in July 2015 where religious leaders across the country resolved to take a more active role in the promotion of child and maternal health in the country. (IRCU 15 June 2017)

Through this initiative, many religious leaders were trained and were now advocating for the practices in their different localities. Through this programme, the communities that were opposed to using pit latrines had been sensitised about the effects of open disposal of faecal matter to the health of the people (IRCU 25 May 2017). Although the IRCU does not have a health unit in its name, these programmes are run in the health units of the different faith groups. Alongside this, in the different health units, attention is given to addressing health challenges in the community. Many of these health facilities provide testing, treatment, and counselling services for the people who go to them for assistance.

Peace, Justice, and Governance

Given that Uganda's postcolonial political landscape has been replete with all kinds of conflict, religious groups have been key stakeholders in addressing emerging issues in peace, justice and governance. Some of the conflicts are a continuation of the suppressed conflicts during the British Colonial Administration. Serve for only the first two years after independence, the country has witnessed conflict of different forms and magnitude (Omona 2015), just like in other formerly colonized countries (Senyomo 1996: 76). Although the IRCU came into existence way after some of these conflicts, knowing that what manifests at present are vestiges of the previous conflicts, the IRCU has actively participated in creating peaceful coexistence within and between communities. This reflects the spirit of Pope Paul VI's statement;

> May the shining sun of peace and brotherly love rise of the land, bathed with their blood by generous sons of the Catholic, Christian, and Muslim converts of Uganda, to illuminate all of Africa! And may this, our meeting with

you respected representatives, be the symbol of, and the first step towards that unity for which God calls us all to strive for His great glory, for the happiness of this blessed continent!!! (Rwehikiza 1986: 75)

The IRCU has, over the years, mobilized assets of the religious communities throughout the country so to analyse problems such as violence and conflict. Working with the grassroots and knowing that religious places of worship have moral assets that build upon and unfold the great strength of their spiritualties, both Christian and Muslim leaders deploy their unique position and moral status, to influence and encourage moral understanding within their communities. Since religious visions are a guide to the meaning of human life because spiritualties can provide to believers enormous courage and strength amid tragedy and human wickedness, members of the IRCU have been available during times of hardships in local communities. For example, the Foundations for Islamic Development, Christian Mother's Union, Catholic Action, and others, as members of the IRCU at local levels, have been actively ensuring peace at family levels. Through giving strength to the believers to bear the unbearable, have hope even when all seems hopeless, and encouraging forgiveness even to the unforgivable, their advocacy for peaceful coexistence (Senyomo 1996: 25) yields fruits at the community level.

In fulfilling such a mandate, the Acholi Religious Leaders Peace Initiative (ARLPI), an arm of the IRCU, has walked with the people of northern Uganda during and after the protracted conflict in northern Uganda between the government of Uganda and the Lord's Resistance Army (LRA). They have initiated peace talks between the warring parties, participated in the Juba Peace Process (Latigo and Ochola 2015: 12–20), and was now dealing with the post-conflict land issues in the sub-region at the time of writing. In a related development, during the consultation on the International Criminal Court's trail, the religious and cultural leaders plus women and youth groups from Acholi, Lango, Madi, and Teso agreed on the need to use the traditional mechanism as part of the process to restore peace and reconciliation (JRP 2007). Besides, in the other sub-regions, the Teso Religious Leaders' Efforts for Peace and Reconciliation, the Interim Inter-Faith Steering Committee for Eastern Region, the Busoga Religious Leaders' Forum, and Bunyoro Inter-Religious Council were also doing a great deal of work in addressing issues of conflict. Furthermore, the Western Uganda Inter-Religious Forum, the Moroto-Nakapiripirit Religious Leaders' Initiative for Peace (MONARLIP), and

10 THE INTER-RELIGIOUS COUNCIL OF UGANDA AND DEVELOPMENT   183

Kigezi Inter-Faith Forum were also actively attending to conflict mitigation processes so to realize peaceful coexistence between parties in conflict.

By launching the Inter-Religious Institute for Peace (IRIP) in August 2012, the IRCU became strategic in addressing itself to issues that divide, instead of uniting, Ugandans. With the backing of the Peace, Justice and Governance (PJG) Committee that had created a special sub-committee to support the operationalization of this proposal and see the growth of the institute, the IRCU found fertile ground of operation. Through this institute, the IRCU has been pushing the agenda for peaceful coexistence to another level, notwithstanding the challenges encountered on the way. The IRCU has also deployed itself to nurturing integrity, peace, justice and good governance by popularizing shared vision and values so as to make Uganda a truly peaceful and justice loving country. In particular, it has identified and strongly advocated for the need to address the main challenges that undermine integrity, peace, justice and good governance. To create and strengthen impartiality and provide independent space for dialogue and conciliation, the IRCU and the Elders Forum of Uganda (TEFU) have seen the need for national dialogue so as to address the historical injustices that the country has experienced over the years. The Uganda National Dialogue (UND) was set to address 8 agenda items, including:

- A national political consensus
- A national consensus on constitutionalism and the rule of law
- A national values consensus
- A national diversity consensus
- Land, land justice, access to natural resources and the environment
- A national consensus on an economy that works for everybody
- A national consensus on minimum standards for quality public service delivery.
- A national consensus on implementation mechanism for the outcomes of the national dialogue
- Establishing of Working Committees (IRCU 10 May 2019a).

Deliberating on the aforementioned agenda items of the UND is necessary because it will help to clear historical misinformation and injustices perpetrated over the years. It is, therefore, hoped that the UND will help to clear;

184 A. D. OMONA

- Competing alternative narratives about the present and the future of [our country] Uganda.
- More than half a century of political instability and violence.
- More than 3 decades of contested elections, election violence and increasing monetization of the electoral process.
- Emerging fault lines that continue to divide us rather than building a united strong nation.
- Incomplete economic, democratic and political transitions (IRCU 10 May 2019a).

Whereas the dialogue process has remained murky and marred by a lot of animosities, if the process kick-started, it would achieve the most yearned for the state in the lives of Ugandans, namely, that of sustainable peace. TEFU and the IRCU hoped the UND would provide a safe space for dialogue, and conciliation. Seeking every opportunity to address political candidates on the challenges along the way; before, during and after the elections, helps in maintaining peace. To this end, during the period leading up to the 2016 presidential elections, the IRCU and TEFU organized presidential debates so as:

- To enable presidential candidates to unpack their manifestoes and visions to the citizens of Uganda
- To promote the spirit of tolerance and consensus-building among candidates.
- To strengthen the individual/party cooperation and statesmanship despite political differences
- To promote issue-based discussions among candidates and the citizens
- To amplify citizens voices and nurture their participation in the democratic processes.
- To put on the record promises made by the Presidential candidates to which they will be held accountable once elected into office. (IRCU 7 Jan 2016).

Indeed, for the first time in many years, some of the candidates were able to shake hands and interact with one another. Besides, the debate also allowed the population who could not go to attend any of the presidential campaigns to listen to the candidates during the debate. Further still, in continuing to build on the achievements of its interventions during the

2011 and 2016 presidential elections that helped to minimize the potential for violent political conflict, the IRCU released a series of press statements covering different areas of concern in the country to maintain peace. Among the issues the press statement addressed included corruption, the violence of different kinds, strikes of teachers in public schools, the prevailing state of insecurity (IRCU 17 May 2017) and others. It further intensified prayer for peace in the country for the common good. The IRCU continued to be the voice of the nation on political and election reforms, critical for the consolidation of good and democratic governance, and continuance of peaceful and harmonious co-existence. Given that consensus building, transparency, rule of law, participation, and inclusiveness are aspects of good governance, the IRCU, during the contentious debate on lifting the presidential age cap and extending the presidential tenure of office from five years to seven years, appealed to the government to allow the decisions to be made through a referendum. This suggestion was to allow the people of Uganda to determine their destiny. Since their role as religious leaders is to guide the nation and to preach against bad laws and actions that do not honour God, keeping quiet at such a critical time would have been tantamount to betraying their nation. Besides, the religious leaders felt since they were supposed to lead by example and sow seeds of justice and peace, if they did not awaken the society whenever it deviated from the right path (Ninsiima 18 March 2018), history would judge them harshly. Consequently,

> ...the religious leaders have advised that the debate on the extension of the president's term of office from five to seven years should not be monopolised by politicians. That matter calls for the participation of all citizens through national dialogue. It is worth ... noting that people have divergent views on national matters hence fairly balanced and transparent platforms should be provided for people to listen to contending views. (Ninsiima 18 March 2018)

Although the above advice was issued to quell the tension of the previous year, to inculcate the spirit of consensus building on matters that affect the citizenry, the government did whatever was in its interest. After the gruesome attack on the palace of the King of Bakonzo and in expressing concern and advocating for peaceful coexistence, the IRCU and TEFU extended a pastoral visit to Kasese and Bundibugyo. They consoled the people who lost their dear ones and the families of those arrested and jailed, also held a reconciliation meeting (IRCU 16 April 2017). Also in collaboration with the Adventist Development and Relief Agency (ADRA), it provided food relief to the victims of the conflict in Kasese and Bundibugyo (IRCU 16 April 2017). These activities are consistent with SDG 16, "Promote peaceful and inclusive societies for sustainable development…" and are contributing towards national integration in Uganda.

Advocacy, Policy, and Partnership

In following up with influencing policy, advocating, and working in partnership with others for the good of the people it serves, the IRCU has come up with the advocacy, policy and partnership programme. Through this, IRCU has worked "to influence policies, improve partnerships as well as advocate for the voices of the voiceless" (IRCU n.d. -a-b). Under this function, IRCU deliberately works to improve its partnership with government, stakeholders, and most importantly, Faith-Based Organizations (FBOs). As its main objective is to promote peace, reconciliation, good governance and holistic human development through advocacy, influencing policies and creating effective partnerships; in following with its specific objectives, IRCU is;

- Influencing policies at different levels so that they serve the common good
- Providing an effective corporate focus for all IRCU staff involved in coordination and partnership interventions
- Actively seeking out the best partners that can support IRCU's mission and vision to bring greater access to services to its beneficiaries
- Speaking for and on behalf of sections of Ugandans that do not have a voice (IRCU n.d. -a-b).

There are many examples that one could cite to show that the IRCU has lived to its commitment as shown above. With regards to influencing policies, whenever the government wants to come up with a new bill or policy, it consults with the IRCU so they also give their input. In case they see the policy is not going to work for the good of the people, they will either make amends or inform the government to shelve it. A case in point was the Domestic Relations Bill, 2003 meant

10 THE INTER-RELIGIOUS COUNCIL OF UGANDA AND DEVELOPMENT 187

...to reform and consolidate the law relating to marriage, separation and divorce; to provide *for* the types of recognised marriages in Uganda, marital rights and duties, grounds for a breakdown of the marriage, rights of parties on the dissolution of marriage and for other connected Purposes...

The IRCU stood opposed to the bill, arguing it was not necessary. Even after renaming the bill to "Marriage and Divorce Bill 2009", the IRCU felt it was not wise to have such a bill passed into law because the subject matter contained in the Bill was provided for in other existing Acts. Referring to cohabitation that the bill provided for, in particular, Archbishop Stanley Ntagali reasoned that if ascended into law it "may destroy the fabric of society" (Akullo 2018: 10). Instead of hurrying such a bill, the faith body urged it to be subjected to "a wider consultation and sensitization of the masses since this is a bill that concerns the family which is the basic unit of society" (Akullo 2018: 10). Indeed, given the advocacy, the bill was subjected for scrutiny by the masses.

The participation of the IRCU in such events is not by accident. Since the majority of Ugandans are religious, it is within the mandate of the IRCU to participate in the formulation, and or vetting of policies meant to be applied on the very people for which they advocate. For example, among others, the IRCU has given input on the Petroleum Extraction, Development and Production Bill; participated in drafting the Regulation of Faith-Based Organization (RFBOs); vetted the Sex Education policy, Health Policies, and others. Through such participation in the policy-making process, the IRCU contributes by raising salient issues which, when not taken care of, can cause more harm than good. In as far as a partnership is concerned, the IRCU has collaborated with both international and local organizations to mitigate health, economic, educational, political and social challenges affecting the country. In health, for example, the IRCU collaborated with UNICEF and the Coalition of Uganda Private School Teachers Association (COUPSTA) to roll out KFCP (see above). Then it partnered with the Ministry of Education and Sports (MoES) to implement the elimination of Violence against Children in Schools (VACiS) by providing clear guidelines on reporting, tracking, referral and responses to children, teachers, parents, members of the community, and schools (Ainengonzi 13 June 2017). On gender-based violence (GBV), it collaborated with the Government of Uganda and other development partners to address the vice in the community (elaborated on

188   A. D. OMONA

later in this chapter). It is also collaborated with the Rhino Fund Uganda and WildAid in campaigning to save rhinos (IRCU 26 April 2017). Through such strategic partnerships, the IRCU has been touching lives in Uganda at all levels. To ensure peace prevails in Uganda, the IRCU in collaboration with TEFU, Government of Uganda and Religion for Peace (RfP) plus other stakeholders have been working towards ensuring a peaceful Uganda, as described earlier. Between March 27th and 31st 2017, a research team from the IRCU visited the Rwenzori sub-region to appraise the situation relating to peace in the sub-region. After visiting different districts and noting the fragility in the sub-region, the body voiced the need to support the efforts of the religious leaders there in bringing calm in the face of the animosity (Reporter 24th April 2017).

Research, Documentation, and Strategic Information

The Research, Documentation and Strategic Information (RDSI) helps in gathering, keeping and sharing information. It is on such information it gathers, analyses, and keeps that credible information is passed to the population. To ensure accurate data collection in all the IRCU interventions to promote evidence-based programming and service delivery, the unit helps the IRCU to act when a gap is identified to address the challenge. Whenever research is done, the findings are shared (disseminated) with other stakeholders for accountability purposes and the promotion of networking and building partnerships (IRCU n.d. -g). In collaboration with universities, the RSDI implements action-based research and develop options to influence public policy and direct programming at the IRCU. The outcomes of the research are published in the form of annual reports, books, pamphlets, and newsletters that are shared with concerned parties and others are kept in the IRCU Resource Centre. Each of the programme activities that the organization specializes in has some sort of research documentation so to inform what is done or give a report of what was done so far (IRCU n.d. -g).

A case in point of the IRCU team researching to inform their situational response was the Ruwenzori region tension conducted between 27 and 31 March 2017. After collecting data from the districts of Kabalore, Kamwenge, Ntoroko, Bundibugyo, and Kasese, faith groups found out that the situation was volatile. The research aimed to identify emerging issues and gaps in the peace process that would form the basis for remobilizing religious leaders into a strong lobby group for their continued pursuit of joint action for peace and reconciliation within the sub-region (IRCU 24 April 2017). After identifying the underlying causes of the tension, the IRCU and TEFU were able to spearhead a peace process that resulted in the signing of a memorandum of understanding between the principal leaders, the Obusinga Bwa Rwenzururu and Obudingya Bwa Bamba. The joint communique issued on 14th April 2017 and signed by both Kings spells out the conditions required to create peace in the Rwenzori districts of Kasese and Bundibugyo (IRCU 16 April 2017).

Faith-Based Gender-Based Violence (GBV) Prevention

Despite the Government of Uganda's endeavour to establish a supportive GBV legal framework, for instance, the Domestic Violence Act and the National Policy and the National Plan for the Elimination of GBV in Uganda, both the 2011 and 2016 Uganda Demographic Health Surveys (UDHS) confirm that GBV is still prevalent in the country. While most people see this state as men battering women, there are instances where women do batter men. As such, GBV is still a problem in the communities at all levels. Therefore, in augmenting the work of the Government of Uganda and other stakeholders, the IRCU works to enhance the quality of alternative dispute resolution services provided by faith leaders in target communities that focus on safety for women and processes centred on the person who has experienced violence (IRCU n.d.). Through this, the IRCU has assisted many GBV survivors to overcome trauma (IRCU; 27 July 2017). In keeping with its mandate, the IRCU continues to lobby, and support other stakeholders to advocate, for appropriate resourcing and implementation of gender-based violence laws and systems at national and local levels. The organization is using the Domestic Violence Act (2010) and the Gender-Based Violence Policy and Action Plan (2016) as a basis for their advocacy work. With generous support from Trocaire/ Irish Aid, the IRCU runs a programme to mitigate GBV that commenced in March 2017 and would end in 2022. The objectives of the programme are,

- To advocate for the implementation of the GBV policy to promote communities where women are free from violence...
- Support female religious leaders to be at the forefront of advocating for issues that concern them...

- Advocating for effective implementation of the GBV laws and policies for the elimination of Violence Against Women in Uganda through senior religious leaders... (IRCU n.d. -d).

The IRCU set these objectives purposely so to empower and promote women's participation in all aspects of society, and to bring women religious leaders into the team of the champion religious leaders and the GBV reference group. This was also to give women of faith network space in different fora to advocate on issues affecting women. Besides, given the fact that violence against women is a violation of human rights, thus using the rights-based approach, the IRCU will strategically place itself to lobby government as key duty bearers to addressing the vice (IRCU n.d.). To attain intermediate outcomes, the IRCU organized a series of training for women and male religious leaders so to know about GBV prevention and associated HIV risks. A series of activities so to implement have been in place, including;

- The orientation of religious leaders on GBV laws and policies
- Surveying religious leaders' attitudes on the GBV Act
- Conducting a safeguarding plan for staff and develop an act
- Disseminating the research findings of the baseline survey of religious leader's Gender-Based Violence Knowledge, attitudes and practices in Acholi, Teso and Kampala to senior religious leaders at the national level.
- Disseminating the research findings of partners of Trocaire on the violence of women/girls and HIV/AIDS in Gulu and Soroti districts.
- Having interface with the partners in Justice, Law and Order sector by sharing their experiences in preventing and mitigating GBV/SGBV in Uganda.
- Strategize and develop an advocacy agenda for policy engagement on the salient issues affecting women/Girls and HIV/AIDS.
- Interfaith intercession prayers during the National Women's week.
- Leadership conference for women of faith to envision their effective participation in the decision making processes within the church and mosque structures.
- GBV Camp on prevention and mitigation during the 16 days of activism.

- Follow up meetings after the women's conference to consolidate strategies with the women structures of Islamic women, catholic women and Born again faith. (IRCU n.d. –d).

Ambitious as they are, some of the set activities have been achieved in the different parts of Uganda where incidences of GBV are high. Knowing that IRCU advocate against GBV, during the time running towards the celebration of the Day of the African Child on June 16th 2016, children asked religious leaders to lobby government to put in place a system that fast track cases of sexual violence through the Justice and Child Protection Unit (IRCU 15 June 2016). These activities by the IRCU contribute towards the attainment of SDG 3, "Achieve gender equality and empower all women and girls."

The Business, Livelihood and Environmental Governance (BLEG) Programme

The IRCU has also deployed its energy in the area of the Business, Livelihood and Environmental Governance (BLEG). This programme focuses on ensuring household income security, food security and environmental stewardship. Given that there is a lot of vulnerability among women and youth, the IRCU works with women under the Uganda Women of Faith Network (UWOFNET) and youth under the Uganda Youth Inter-faith Network (UYIN) to roll out this programme in the deserving communities.

Women and youth were selected for this project for a purpose. As 'mothers of the nation' and bearing more of the responsibility of ensuring the well-being of their families, empowering women means empowering the whole household. Regarding the youth; as leaders of today and tomorrow, inculcating in them the necessary skills, knowledge, and information on business, livelihood, and environmental governance would help them to be responsible citizens by undertaking profitable and meaningful livelihood engagement.

The programme has its thematic focus on promoting:

- Enterprise development and Financial Literacy
- Group formation and cooperatives growth
- Environmental Stewardship through climate change effects mitigation and adaptation

192   A. D. OMONA

- Disaster Risk Reduction and community resilience
- Climate-smart Agriculture, crop and animal value chain development (IRCU n.d. –c)

The IRCU, through the B LEG, has achieved the necessary skilling of the local population who attended their programme. In some instances, after equipping people with entrepreneurial skill and financial literacy, the IRCU extended assistance so the people can fend for themselves and their families. An article entitled "From a pauper to Millionaire: An IRCU beneficiary's testimony," (IRCU 16 January 2014a) is a testimony to such empowerment. In the testimony, the beneficiary applauded the IRCU and USAID's support to the Buddu Social Development Association, BUSODA—a local faith-based organization that trained and encouraged them to form a group. With the support given to them in the group, the members were able to support their families (IRCU 16 January 2014a). Another success story was the training of women groups in Mukono in making soap, candles, jellies and paper beads (IRCU 11 March 2014b). In doing this and other activities, the IRCU has been achieving its aims of enterprise development and financial literacy, and group formation and cooperatives' growth. This is very strategic towards achieving SDG 1, "End poverty in all its forms everywhere."

The IRCU has been in collaboration with the National Association of Professional Environmentalists (NAPE) has taken an environmental campaign by creating awareness on environmental stewardship to mitigate the effects of and adapt to climate change. The joint body conducted an awareness campaign on climate change targeting different churches and mosques. NAPE chose to team up with the IRCU because they knew religious organizations command a lot of respect and trust from their followers and by becoming active and aggressive in climate change advocacy, a lot would be achieved. To this end, many awareness workshops for different groups of religious leaders were conducted across the country to educate religious leaders about the effects of climate change and how they could be involved in climate change discussions at local and national levels (NAPE n.d.: 12). Although previously some faith organizations under the umbrella of the IRCU had been actively preaching against destroying the environment and encouraging their followers to plant more trees, teaming up with NAPE acted as energizer to push the same agenda. On many occasions, the IRCU has responded to disaster risk reduction, community resilience and climate-smart agriculture, crop and animal value chain development. Through its affiliate organizations, the IRCU has responded to the plight of the mudslide victims in the Mount Elgon area of Uganda, the crisis in Kasese when there was a standoff between the government of Uganda and the Rwenzururu Kingdom, and many other similar situations. Such responses helped in disaster risk reduction, and building community resilience in the face of disasters. They also contribute towards the attainment of SDG 13, "Take urgent action to combat climate change and its impacts."

The Challenges Encountered by the IRCU in its Work and Measures Towards Addressing the Challenges

Despite the notable achievements of the IRCU, there are many challenges. This section highlights a few of the main challenges. The major challenge is funding given the mega programme. Since the IRCU does not have income-generating projects, but rather depends on the goodwill of donor support, achieving certain programmes in the way they ought to have been implemented has not been easy. Many times programmes have stalled or even the implementation of certain projects ends abruptly because of insufficient funds. In trying to overcome the challenge of finances, the team constantly keeps writing more proposals and contacting more organisations for support.

The silent voices coming from upcountry places is that the IRCU is an urban programme because many upcountry centres do not feel its presence. In other words, whereas in the different regions of Uganda the IRCU has a representative structure that it works with, the local person in some of the upcountry places where the IRCU does not have running programmes does not know that it exists. In some instances, the IRCU has programmes but faces delays in the delivery of such programmes, leaving many people in suspense. The existing structures upcountry do not have their funding to operate and in some parts of the country, there are no full-time employees to run the programmes. Despite this, whenever there is a project, it runs in a particular area the faith-based body tries to show presence and get some people responsible for such projects. What now remains is to get permanent staff to run the upcountry structures and or creating committees that are visible at the grassroots.

194 A. D. OMONA

There have also been some reports of financial diversion and misappropriation at the IRCU. As noted above, the faith body depends on donor funding. These funds come for specific programmes or projects within the programme. However, in times of emergencies, there could be vote transfers but in case no funds come for the programme or project for which funds were transferred from another vote, then replacing what was transferred so to achieve what it was intended for becomes a challenge. As such, improper implementation of some programmes is evident. As noted earlier, the team at the IRCU is continually trying to write project proposals and seeks links with new funding agencies to have funds available for the good of Ugandan citizens. In most cases, the IRCU acts like the fire-brigade institution. It only acts where there is an emergency because of the sustainability of some of the projects it rolls out. For example, the Peace, Justice, and Good Governance programme is active when elections are coming or when there is unrest in some part of the country. The lack of sustained rolling of Peace, Justice, and Good Governance programmes during times of normalcy makes inculcating the spirit of peace, justice and good governance difficult in the lives of people. In a bid to address this, individual members of the clergy in the different faith-based organizations take it upon themselves to play the role of raising moral consciousness in their communities.

Further, in some cases, the IRCU does not have any notable impact. Whereas the IRCU issues press statements on pertinent issues, if the government or the community does not back what they are calling for, such statements just remain in the realm of the press. In most cases, whenever such statements touch the political lives of some people directly, they rebut the statement by saying religious leaders should not be involved in making political statements. Yet, wherever the religious leaders are silent, the same people complain that religious leaders under the umbrella of the IRCU, or even as individuals, are not playing their role of being the conscience of society. However, on some occasions, the leadership has been meeting the head of state to clear the air on certain things, as well as to ensure the implementation of what they think should be done. It was through such an arrangement that they got the discourse on National Dialogue started. Translating some of the activities that the IRCU runs in the real lives of the people at local levels is still a challenge. For example, even when people trained in skills of mitigating GBV, some of the very trainees remained the ones perpetrating acts of GBV in the community. A high-ranking religious leader in one part of the country at one time beat up his wife badly to the extent that the wife had to run away and spent the night in the bush. Although not often, some errant clergy are reprimanded by their faith leadership. To some extent, despite the team spirit in achieving progress for Uganda, there still exist mistrust among the members. At times there is a feeling that members have just been forced to accommodate each other for the sake of being seen working together. Urgent attention ought to be paid to this so as not to affect the valuable work that the IRCU is doing for the good of the people in Uganda and beyond.

Conclusion: Reiterating the Role of the Interfaith Network to Development

Over the years, the IRCU has been an active participant in development in Uganda. From the foregoing discussion, through the various programmes, the interfaith body in augmenting the efforts of the government in realizing the SDGs. It is contributing to different SDGs, highlighting the importance of interfaith groups to development. Notwithstanding some challenges, if the IRCU maintains its push towards the goals for which it was established, it will remain a major player in the quest to improve the lives of the majority of Ugandan citizens. Further, through bringing diverse faith groups together, the IRCU confirms the value of interfaith groups in promoting sustainable development.

References

Primary Sources (IRCU Material)

IRCU. (16 January 2014a. From Pauper to Millionaire: An IRCU beneficiary's testimony. Available from https://ircu.or.ug/from-pauper-to-millionaire-an-ircu-beneficiarys-testimony/, Accessed 1/4/2020.

IRCU. 11 March 2014b. IRCU trains Mukono Women in Soap Making. Available from https://ircu.or.ug/ircu-trains-mukono-women-in-soap-making/, Accessed 01 April 2020.

IRCU. 7 Jan 2016. Press Release. Available from https://ircu.or.ug/press-releases-press-release-07th-january-2016/, Accessed 21 April 2020.

IRCU. 16 April 2017a. IRCU, ADRA provide relief to Kasese-Bundibugyo conflict victims. Available from https://ircu.or.ug/ircu-adra-provide-relief-to-kasese-bundibugyo-conflict-victims/, Accessed 31 March 2020.

196 A. D. OMONA

IRCU. 15 June 2017b IRCU and UNICEF Partner to roll out Key Family Care Practices in Karamoja and Northern Uganda. Available *from* https://ircu.or.ug/kfcps/, Accessed 31 March 2020.

IRCU. 25 May 2017c. "KFCPs: Success stories from Karamoja and the Northern region. Available from https://ircu.or.ug/kfcps-success-stories-from-karamoja-and-the-northern-region/, Accessed 31 March 2020.

IRCU. 16 April 2017d. IRCU-TEFU take custody of memorandum of protocol between the Obusinga Bwa Rwenzururu and Obundigya Bwa Bamba. Available from https://ircu.or.ug/ircu-tefu-take-custody-of-memorandum-of-protocol-between-the-obusinga-bwa-rwenzururu-and-obundigya-bwa-bamba/, Accessed 31/3/2020.

IRCU. 16 April 2017e. IRCU-TEFU, pay solidarity visit to Kasese and Bundibugyo. Available from https://ircu.or.ug/ircu-tefu-pay-solidarity-visit-to-kasese-and-bundibugyo/, Accessed 31 March 2020.

IRCU. 26 April 2017f. Partners with WildAid in campaign to save rhinos. Available from https://ircu.or.ug/ircu-partners-with-wildaid-in-campaign-to-save-rhinos/, Accessed 31 March 2020.

IRCU. 17 May 2017g. Press release: Religious leaders' concern on the prevailing state of insecurity and acts of torture in the country. Available from; https://ircu.or.ug/religious-leaders-concern-on-the-prevailing-state-of-insecurity-and-acts-of-torture-in-the-country/, Accessed 31/2020.

IRCU. 10 May 2019a. Press Statement Second Meeting of the UNaDiCoT. Available from https://ircu.or.ug/press-statement-second-meeting-of-the-uganda-national-dialogue-coordinating-team/, Accessed 31 March 2020.

IRCU. (n.d.-a-b), Advocacy, Policy, and Partnership Program. Available from https://ircu.or.ug/program/advocacy-policy-and-partnership/, Accessed 02 April 2020.

IRCU (n.d.-c), Business, Livelihood, and Environmental Governance. Available from https://ircu.or.ug/program/business-livelihood-and-environmental-governance-bleg-program/, Accessed 01 April 2020.

IRCU (n.d.-d), Faith-Based Gender-Based Violence (GBV) Prevention. Available from https://ircu.or.ug/program/trocaire-ircu-program/, Acceessed 01 April 2020.

IRCU, 13 June 2019. Health Alert! Ebola Outbreak. Available from https://ircu.or.ug/health-alert-ebola-outbreak/, Accessed 31 March 2020.

IRCU, (n.d.-e), History. Available from https://ircu.or.ug/ircu-history/, Accessed 30 March 2020.

IRCU. (n.d.-f1) Our Achievements. Available from https://ircu.or.ug/our-achievements/, Accessed 02 April 2020.

IRCU (n.d.-f2), IRCU scale-up Biomedical HIV/AIDS Prevention: Thousands turn up for Safe Medical Circumcision. Available from https://ircu.or.ug/ircu-scale-up-biomedical-hivaids-prevention-thousands-turn-up-for-safe-medical-circumcision/, Accessed 31 March 2020.

10 THE INTER-RELIGIOUS COUNCIL OF UGANDA AND DEVELOPMENT

IRCU, (n.d.-g), Research, Documentation and Strategic Information. Available from https://ircu.or.ug/program/research-documentation-and-strategic-information-rdsi/, Accessed 02 April 2020.

SECONDARY SOURCES

Ainengonzi, A. 13 June 2017. RTRR guidelines to promote safe learning environments. Available from https://ircu.or.ug/rtrr-guidelines-to-promote-safe-learning-environments/, Accessed 31 March 2020.

Akullo, G. M. 2018. How long shall we wait? An analysis of the Marriage and Divorce Bill, 2009. Available from *Error! Hyperlink reference not valid.* http://cepa.or.ug/analysis/how-long-shall-we-wait-an-analysis-of-the-marriage-and-divorce-bill-2009/, Accessed 8 April 2020.

JRP. 11th August 2007. *Lira Declaration on agenda item 3 of the Juba Peace Talks (Accountability and Reconciliation) by cultural and religious leaders, women and youth from Madi, Teso, Lango and Acholi sub-regions.* Lira: St. Augustine Hall.

Latigo, O. A. & M. B. Ochola, 2015. Northern Uganda – The Acholi Religious Leaders' Peace Initiative: Local mediation with the Lord's Resistance Army", In Haspeslagh, S. & Z. Yuusuf, (eds.), *Local engagement with armed groups in the midst of violence, Accord insight 2*, London: Conciliation Resources. pp. 15–20.

NAPE (n.d.), *20 years of NAPE's environmental advocacy in Uganda.* Kampala: NAPE.

Ninsiima, P. 19 March 2018. Hold dialogue before referendum, Monitor News Paper. Available from https://www.monitor.co.ug/OpEd/Commentary/-dialogue-referendum-Inter-Religious-Counci/689364-4347162-14buav5/index.html, Accessed 31 March 2020.

Omona, A. D. 2015. Management of Postcolonial Intrastate Conflicts in Uganda: A case of Northern Uganda. Kenyatta University: *PhD Thesis.*

Reporter. 24th April 2017.Peace in Rwenzori sub-region still fragile- IRCU findings. Available from https://ircu.or.ug/peace-in-rwenzori-sub-region-still-fragile-ircu-findings/, Accessed 31 March 2020.

Rwehikiza, F. 1986. Let us understand each other: An attempt at Fostering Mutual Understanding between Christians and Muslims. Gaba Publications, AMECEA PASTORAL INSTITUTE, Eldoret Kenya.

Senyomo, A. 1996.Interreligious relations in Uganda: A case study of Kawempe South Sub-division of Kampala, Stavanger School of Mission and Theology"-Norway: *MA Dissertation.*

The Domestic Relations Bill, 2003. Available from https://ulii.org/node/25008, Accessed 8 April 2020.

Vision Reporter, 2017. Inter-religious council moves to fight FGM. Available, https://www.newvision.co.ug/new_vision/news/1461767/inter-religious-council-moves-fight-fgm, Accessed 26 February 2020.

World Health Organization. 2018. Country cooperation strategy at a glance. Available from https://s.docworkspace.com/d/AlvWKC_t1JEBoNbXz52dFA, Accessed 7 April 2020.

CHAPTER 11

Religion and Sustainable Development: The Role of the Zambia Interfaith Networking Group (ZINGO) in Contemporary Times

Nelly Mwale

INTRODUCTION

This chapter qualitatively engages with religion and development through interfaith networks and the global goal to reducing inequalities within and among countries using the example of the Zambia Interfaith Networking Group (ZINGO) in Zambia. Contrary to perceptions of religion as irrelevant to modern societies and a constraint on progress (Tomalin 2013), faith communities, actors and assets continued to occupy a critical space in discourses on development. The chapter is premised on the growing acknowledgment of religion's potential to contribute towards Sustainable Development Goals (SDGs). For example, Tomalin et al. (2019) acknowledge that global development discourse and practice has seen a new wave

N. Mwale (✉)
University of Zambia, Lusaka, Zambia

© The Author(s), under exclusive license to Springer Nature Switzerland AG 2022
E. Chitando, I. S. Gusha (eds.), *Interfaith Networks and Development*, Sustainable Development Goals Series,
https://doi.org/10.1007/978-3-030-89807-6_11

199

indicating a turn to recognising the significant role of religion as it is increasingly recognised as a human resource rather than an obstacle to development. Despite these conclusions, Zambian scholarship on religion and development has been preoccupied with individual religious initiatives (Hinfelaar 2009; Mwale 2013; Mwale and Chita 2019) to the neglect of interfaith initiatives. Therefore, this chapter seeks to contribute to existing knowledge on religion and development by extending religion's interconnectedness with development to the role of interfaith networks in promoting sustainable development, particularly reducing inequalities within and among countries (SDG 10) from the Zambian context.

The chapter purposively focuses on ZINGO based on its relevance (Mason 2002) to discourses on interfaith networks and development in Zambia. ZINGO is a multi-religious networking group which consists of four major Christian umbrella faith bodies in Zambia, namely, the Council of Churches in Zambia (CCZ), the Evangelical Fellowship of Zambia (EFZ), the Independent Churches of Zambia (ICOZ) and the Zambia Conference of Catholic Bishops (ZCCB), as well as the Islamic Supreme Council of Zambia, the Baha'i and Hindu Association of Zambia.

ZINGO's mandate is to coordinate, network, mobilise resources and build competencies among ZINGO members for a holistic and compassionate approach to responding to the impact of HIV and AIDS and other related development issues. By mandate, ZINGO activities are closely related to the SDGs in general and to SDG 10 in particular, hence the need to understand its role in fostering sustainable development in the country. The chapter shows that although reducing inequalities within and among countries was recently conceptualised as one of the indicators for sustainable development, ZINGO was long engaged in activities that are directly linked to SDG 10 and thus religion remained significant to the attainment of SDGs.

Approaches to Religion and Development

The chapter focuses on the functionalist definition that stresses what religion does for society as opposed to the substantive definition of religion which focuses on how religion is carried out (Rakodi 2012: 638). Religion is, thus, understood in terms of its dimensions as articulated by scholars like Durkheim (1995) and Smart (1969) which have been narrowed down to the four ways of linking religion and development, namely; religious ideas, practices, organisation, and religious actors (Basedau et al. 2017). By this, religious ideas are the foundation of any consideration of religion which provide meaning to believers. The chapter therefore takes the view that religious ideas, both formal and informal, shaped ZINGO's approach to development and stance on addressing inequalities, just as religious practices which were centred on religious behaviour such as worship. ZINGO is also related to the actor's dimension which refers to individuals and the formal organisational expressions of religious communities such as religious networks or associations of several religious groups (Basedau et al. 2017). Similarly, the organisational and actors dimensions were considered significant for facilitating the expression of religious ideas on sustainable development. Religion is also related to sustainable development, defined as development that meets the needs of the present without compromising the ability of future generations to meet their own needs (World Commission on Environment and Development (WCED) 1987). Sustainable development is thus understood in relation to the global goals that have seemingly become acceptable indicators for development for 2030.

The chapter situates the role of ZINGO in the global goal of reducing inequalities context partly because of the limited scholarly attention given to religion's role in attaining the SDGs. For example, discourses on religion and development in Zambia have often been at a single religion and denominational level Hinfelaar (2009) and Mwale (2013) have explored political and socio-economic development from a Catholic Church perspective, while Mwale and Chita (2019) have trailed the work of the Jesuit Centre for Theological Reflections (Catholic) in development). The nature of SDGs and the quest to reduce inequalities also closely resonates with religion. By this, SDGs seek to ensure a more grassroots and locally owned type of development based on the recognition that local people (who constitute faith communities) are better placed to both understand and respond to development challenges (UN 2015). Additionally, the commitment of leaving no one behind not only points to an inclusive approach but also resonates with the golden rule of showing concern to others, that is shared among many religious traditions. Given the interconnectedness of the SDGs and the emphasis that development ought to balance social, economic and environmental sustainability (UN 2017), the chapter relates the work of ZINGO to SDG 10 for purposes of depth. This SDG focuses on reducing inequalities in income including those based on age, sex, disability, race, ethnicity, origin, religion or economic or other status within a country. It also addresses inequalities based on representation, migration and development assistance among countries (as shown in the figure below):

> 10.1 By 2030, progressively achieve and sustain income growth of the bottom 40 per cent of the population at a rate higher than the national average.
> 10.2 By 2030, empower and promote the social, economic and political inclusion of all, irrespective of age, sex, disability, race, ethnicity, origin, religion or economic or other status.
> 10.3 Ensure equal opportunity and reduce inequalities of outcome, including by eliminating discriminatory laws, policies and practices and promoting appropriate legislation, policies and action in this regard.
> 10.4 Adopt policies, especially fiscal, wage and social protection policies and progressively achiever greater equality.
> 10.5 Improve the regulation and monitoring of global financial markets and institutions and strengthen the implementation of such regulations.
> 10.6 Ensure enhanced representation and voice for developing countries in decision making in global international economic and financial institutions in order to deliver more effective, credible, accountable and legitimate institutions.
> 10.7 Facilitate orderly, safe, regular and responsible migration and mobility of people including through the implementation of planned and well managed migration policies.
> 10.a Implement the principle of special and differential treatment for developing countries, in particular least developed countries in accordance with World Trade Organisation agreements.
> 10.b Encourage official development assistance and financial flows, including foreign direct investment, to States where the need is greatest, in particular developed countries, African countries, small island developing States and landlocked developing countries, in accordance with their national plans and programmes.
> 10.c By 2030, reduce to less than 3 per cent the transaction costs of migrant remittances and eliminate remittance corridors with costs higher than 5 per cent.
>
> Source: UN (2017).

CONTEXT

The role of ZINGO in the country's sustainable development is situated in the religious and developmental context. In terms of the religious landscape, Zambia is a multi-religious society with Christianity as the dominant religion. Other religions, including Islam, Hinduism, Zambian Indigenous Religions, the Baha'i Faith, Buddhism and Sikhism, despite accounting for smaller percentages in terms of following, are part of the religious landscape and are contributing to development. The composition of ZINGO was thus a reflection of the religious landscape in the country. The country's developmental agenda is driven by, among other guidelines, the Vision 2030 (2006–2030) which is Zambia's first ever long-term plan expressing the country's aspirations of being a prosperous middle-income country by the year 2030 (GRZ 2006). The policy document embodies values of socio-economic justice underpinned by the principles of gender responsive, sustainable development, democracy, respect for human rights, good traditional and family values, positive attitude towards work, peaceful co-existence and private –public partnerships (GRZ 2006: 7). The country's developmental agenda was also shaped by the international developmental agenda. Of particular interest, are the global goals, or the SDGs which were adopted in 2015 by all United Nations (UN) member states as a universal call to action to end poverty, protect the planet and ensure that all people enjoy peace and prosperity by 2030. President Edgar Lungu has emphasised the importance of the fight against poverty and the need to enhance all partnerships in ensuring that the SDG targets were fully realised (Minister of Foreign Affairs 2014, Ministerial statement 7th October 2015).

THE EMERGENCE OF ZINGO

The emergence of ZINGO is traced back to 1997 when the Interfaith Networking Group on HIV and AIDS was established to help religious communities become more involved in the prevention and mitigation of HIV under the name, the Lusaka Interfaith Networking Group on HIV and AIDS (LINGO). It changed its name to ZINGO after the religious leaders reaffirmed the efficacy of a well-co-ordinated HIV response and called for the expansion of the interfaith model to all areas of the country in 2002 (Ndhlovu 2008). Consequently, it was formalised in 2003 with gaining a Non-Governmental Organisation (NGO) status and being registered with the Registrar of Societies. ZINGO was established to provide information, technical and financial support to religious organisations and communities responding to the needs of vulnerable groups such as people living with HIV and AIDS, women, widows, youth and vulnerable children, including those orphaned by HIV and AIDS (ZINGO report for 2002 activities, unpublished). This was underpinned by the concern for a lack of consolidated interfaith platform for addressing HIV and AIDS in the country. It can also be stated that ZINGO was established to encourage greater participation of the minority religious groups into the HIV and AIDS response through strengthening existing weak HIV and AIDS responses of faith mother bodies into fully fledged HIV and AIDS programmes with full time HIV and AIDS programme coordinators.

Additionally, ZINGO was initiated to respond to the challenges of HIV and AIDS and in turn promote and preserve life. Before the inception of ZINGO, HIV and AIDS were seen to reflect badly on any religious institution that acknowledged its presence among its faithful. It was realised that HIV and AIDS was a universal problem that affected everybody and which all people of all faiths needed to collectively address and that HIV and AIDS arose from the inability to address the socio-economic challenges facing humans holistically as opposed to immoral behaviour (Zambia Country Report 2008). The emergence of ZINGO was, therefore, a mirror of how HIV and AIDS had impacted on faith communities and the resulting response to HIV and AIDS. The emergence of ZINGO could also be understood within changing context of faith and HIV and AIDS interface from the religious ideas, practices, organisation and actors perspective.

Activities and Achievements of ZINGO

ZINGO was involved in numerous activities that cut across HIV and AIDS, children and gender in ways that reveal religion's connectedness with the global goal to reducing inequalities in the country as informed by interfaith ideas, practices, organisation and actors.

ZINGO's Activities and Strides to Reduce Inequalities

ZINGO has undertaken diverse activities that are consistent with the global goal to reducing inequalities within the country and among countries. In this section, the chapter reviews some of these key activities.

ZINGO's activities which were aligned to reducing inequalities were centred on HIV prevention, education and gender, and promotion of economic growth among vulnerable households and individuals, orphans and children. To begin with, ZINGO was involved in HIV prevention programmes. For example, through partnership with Corridors of Hope III, children and young people between the ages of 7 and 24 were targeted for Abstinence and Being Faithful interventions through peer education, sport, and youth-Adult communication (ZINGO 2016). With Support to the HIV/AIDS Response in Zambia II (2015) (SHARe II project), ZINGO trained religious leaders who reached others with prevention messages with results of referrals for accessing care and bio medical services to other stakeholders (ZINGO 2013). Additionally, ZINGO partnered with Save the Children International and the European Union to implement a sexual reproductive rights project that encompassed a series of outreaches to schools and places of worship aimed at increasing the number of people with age appropriate and comprehensive knowledge about HIV and AIDS. Other prevention activities included HIV Counselling and Testing, prevention of sexually transmitted infections (STIs), prevention of mother to child transmission, male circumcision and prevention with positives (to help discordant couples maintain their HIV status).

The examples of HIV prevention activities revealed ZINGO's role in networking and mobilising resources for the faith member groups on HIV prevention. ZINGO has, through its affiliated faith-based organisations at both national and sub-national levels (including community level), implemented a series of interventions using the combination prevention approach and focusing on prioritised epidemic drivers in line with national priorities to reduce new HIV infection (Centre for Health Marketing Innovations 2020). These roles were also closely linked to ZINGO's ideas on the value of human life and the consequent attempt to prevent HIV infections and contribute to zero HIV and sustainable development. For example, ZINGO's promotion of abstinence and faithfulness to the neglect of condom use could not be detached from faith inclined teachings on premarital sex and faithfulness in marriage, as concluded by Genrich and Brathwaite (2005). ZINGO's focus on prevention of HIV centred on behavioural change and consequent contribution to the promotion of health affirms Ellison and Levin (1998)'s argument that behaviour responses to religious ideas provide an important link between religion and health. The activities in HIV prevention also underpin the religious actors' efforts to promote the well-being for all ages and address health related inequalities.

ZINGO was also involved in the treatment, care and support through the home-based care and support programmes. Centre for Health Marketing Innovations (2020) affirmed that ZINGO through its partners intensified provision of home-based care services and strengthened its referral system to ensure that People Living with HIV (PLHIV) receive a continuum of care and support services. As such, ZINGO was a coordinator for the 2016 national consultation in Zambia on faith-based partnerships in the national HIV strategic priorities sponsored by the UNAIDS/PEPFAR Faith Initiative. This also pointed to ZINGO's contribution to reducing inequalities among the population irrespective of any status through networking and mobilizing resources.

Other activities closely linked to reducing inequalities in the country were in education and gender. ZINGO, through the support of cooperating partners like the Church Health Association of Zambia (CHAZ) and the Global Fund engaged in educational support for women, orphans and vulnerable children (OVCs) from across different faith communities. For instance, through this partnership, ZINGO was able to empower low income women with livelihood activities while OVCs were provided with education, including tertiary education, thereby giving them an opportunity to become self-sufficient. While these efforts closely resonate with the SDG goal of achieving inclusive and equitable quality education, they also point to ZINGO's strides to address social inequalities by being a channel for development assistance from international partners as envisioned in SDG 10. ZINGO also fostered child rights with organisations such as Save the Children International through child protection by building the capacity of the District Child Protection Committees to support community structures in the protection of children (ZINGO 2016). Other partnerships included the Protect and Educate the Girl Child project with First Quantum Minerals (FQM) with a focus on building capacity of communities to respond to challenges of teenage pregnancies and early marriages in the North—Western part of Zambia. The youth were trained in peer education skills while other activities were material support for in and out of school outreach activities, training of change agents, support to school outreach activities, village banks, parenting sessions and providing technical support to community change agents and peer educators (ZINGO 2016: Daily Nation 6th January 2016). These efforts in education were significant given the different forms inequalities (relating to access, quality, gender, equity and participation among others) in the current provision of education in the country (Mwanza 2015; Mwale and Simuchimba 2018).

Additionally, ZINGO had gender related activities by partnering with stakeholders such as the Joint Country Programme to train women for leadership so as to provide grounds for meaningful engagement of women in decision making. Women who had been exposed to some level of leadership and deemed as emerging leaders were therefore trained to usher them into recognised leadership positions (ZINGO 2013), thereby fostering some form of equality in leadership. Radio series were also conducted in which faith umbrella bodies discussed women leadership alongside other organisations working in the area of enhancing women's leadership. ZINGO was also engaged in addressing gender-based violence (GBV) through participation in International Women's Day commemorations, including the observation of 16 days of activism against gender-based violence. ZINGO also had community outreach activities through the GBV project. For example, the Centre for Health Marketing Innovations (2020) observed that:

> ZINGO mobilised men, women and traditional/ religious leaders ... to address stigma and discrimination and vulnerabilities among women that expose them to GBV. The project aims at empowering women with knowledge, skills and economic strengthening so that they are better placed to face domestic violence; works with men as equal partners to women in eliminating GBV; and uses the authority of religious and traditional leaders to advocate against GBV within their places of worship and traditional authorities.

While religion is often associated with promoting gender inequality (Tomalin 2013), the work of ZINGO demonstrated that it was striving to make a difference in reducing inequalities and that the organisational and actors' dimensions of religion were significant in addressing different forms of inequalities.

ZINGO's activities also encompassed coordinating, networking and mobilising resources for the promotion of sustainable income growth. This was through impact mitigation activities which targeted vulnerable households and individuals, orphans and children so as to have more people receive economic and psychological support and care at home and community level. This was largely done through economic strengthening projects with different partners such as Corridors of Hope (III) through mobilising financial safety nets through savings, maximising household production and increasing market readiness. For example, at the level of mobilising financial safety nets through savings, beneficiaries and their families were empowered to build group savings based safety nets in partnership with trusted friends and relatives (ZINGO 2013). The Centre for Health Marketing Innovations (2020) also observed that ZINGO was providing the target populations with follow-on economic empowering skills beyond the group savings and loans, namely; Generate Your Business Idea (GYBI) (aimed at giving beneficiaries basic skills and orientation to enable them make meaningful decisions about business selection) and Household Production Guidelines (HPG) (to help targeted beneficiaries value assets that surround them and transform them into productive ventures).

Beneficiaries were empowered to adopt productive behaviours for stabilising and expanding food security and household resilience (ZINGO 2013). Through peer to peer discussions, households learnt how to identify and better utilise household surplus, savings and assets to improve land, livestock and small business output. In practice, trainings were held in small plot horticulture and small livestock husbandry with success stories that enabled households to be resilient to economic shocks and the threat of HIV and AIDS. The beneficiaries were keeping small livestock like poultry and growing vegetables using sustainable methods while others developed small businesses such as selling of vegetables and groceries (ZINGO n.d.-a). This reveals that the economic strides were closely tied to achieving and sustaining income growth so as to reduce inequalities.

Religious actors may affect environmental attitudes and behaviour through their own initiatives as well as their influence on members, public debates and political decision makers (Djupe and Patrick 2009). Most importantly, those who were not trained were getting ideas from other trained group members, an indication that no one was being left behind in these communities directly and indirectly by adopting the spirit of entrepreneurship. By transforming beneficiaries from subsistence levels (consumption orientation) through training in plant production and organic farming to commercial entrepreneurship through increasing market readiness, ZINGO was contributing not only to sustainable income growth, but also empowering and promoting social and economic inclusion of all and fostering equal opportunities.

ZINGO was promoting economic support for vulnerable households and individuals by introducing them to sustainable agriculture to enable the beneficiaries to improve their yields, thereby promoting sustainable income growth. The close ties between the activities of ZINGO and the economic (income) growth signify the conclusions on the influence of religion on economic outcomes through shaping individual traits and creating a form of social capital (McCleary and Barro 2006). It has also been concluded that religious ideas positively correlated with certain personal characteristics relevant for development such as a positive work ethic (Feess et al. 2014), while religion fosters economic prosperity through its positive association with attitudes that favour free markers and improved institutions (Guiso et al. 2006).

The Achievements of ZINGO

ZINGO's achievements could not be detached from the fact that it was one of the few religious networks that managed to bring together a diversity of faith groupings for the purpose of responding to the HIV and AIDS pandemic both at the national and local levels in the country (Zambia Country Report 2008). This was to be understood in a context of different positions of the umbrella bodies on matters of sexuality. Despite having divergent views on sexuality within the context of HIV and AIDS, ZINGO (with support from the Family Health International (FHI) and Youth Net project) developed guidelines for all faith leaders and groups addressing adolescent sexual and reproductive health (Ndhlovu 2008). With a unified agenda, barriers to the promotion and preservation of life were erased. The approach to HIV and AIDS by ZINGO signified the pledge of leaving no one behind and resonated with the global goal to reducing inequalities of different forms.

ZINGO's achievements were further in relation to the growth of its programmes which expanded in scope, geography, and level of engagement (ZINGO 2016). For example, the scope of ZINGO programmes expanded to include not only HIV and AIDS, but also gender, human rights and economic strengthening targeting vulnerable women and other vulnerable groups which directly related to reducing inequalities in the country. Geographically, ZINGO programmes were implemented in almost all provinces of Zambia while the level of engagement equally deepened. The widened scope of ZINGO's programmes also reflected the strides made in resource mobilisation which facilitated the implementation of its programmes and in inclusion of all regardless of geographical location. By this, the network mobilised resources that resulted in a greater engagement of the various faith umbrella bodies in implementing its programmes and numerous collaborating partners. Some cooperating partners included FHI/ Corridors of Hope, Norwegian Church AID, Save the Children, SHARe II, Churches Health Association of Zambia (CHAZ), FQM, Global Fund, Plan International, United States Agency for International Development (USAID) and the President's Emergency Plan for AIDS Relief II (PEPFAR II) among others. As such, ZINGO was contributing to addressing inequalities by tapping in the local and international partnerships.

Similarly, ZINGO's collaboration with government intensified, making the interfaith network a partner in complementing government on efforts to deliver on some aspects of both the mid-term and long-term development goals of the government. This relates to the encouragement of development assistance and financial flows within and outside the country through strengthening the means of implementation and revitalising the global partnership for sustainable development. ZINGO's attractiveness to partners was also not detached from the religious factor. For example, it was highlighted that ZINGO was uniquely positioned to engage affiliates and increase HIV and AIDS leadership among religious leaders (SHARe II 2015).

Another achievement was the documentation of best practice. In view of a lack of documentation on what religious organisations were doing to respond to HIV, ZINGO embarked on a best practice documentation exercise aimed to document practices in existence that might have been unknown by the outside world, and subsequently propose them to UNAIDS for documentation. The objectives of the exercise were to generate information on the type of activities carried out by FBOs (Ndhlovu 2008).

ZINGO also produced a manual entitled *Treasuring the gift: how to handle God's gift of sexual learning activities for religious groups* (ZINGO n.d.-b). This manual helps youth groups to gain knowledge, attitudes and skills they would need to treasure the gift of sexuality beyond their religious barriers and also helps young people from various faith groups to put aside their doctrinal and denominational differences and work together in the fight against HIV (Ndhlovu 2008). This achievement signified the unity of purpose among the membership of ZINGO to address inequalities and promote the overall wellbeing of humanity.

In view of these achievements, it can be stated that ZINGO was contributing to the attainment of the SDG 10 in the country, especially in relation to achieving and sustaining income growth, empowering and promoting social, economic and political inclusion of all, equal opportunities and reducing inequalities of outcome, adopting policies for greater equality and encouraging official development assistance and financial flows to States where the need is greatest.

CHALLENGES OF THE INTERFAITH NETWORKING GROUP IN FOSTERING DEVELOPMENT

The challenges encountered by ZINGO were largely centred on marketing, decentralisation and capacity building. In this regard, while ZINGO had fared well in attracting the recognition of many stakeholders in HIV and AIDS response and contributing to addressing inequalities, it was held that more still had to be done to market ZINGO (ZINGO 2013). This challenge was as a result of not having a deliberate policy to manage the branding and marketing of ZINGO. In this regard, a conscious decision was made to engage a communication and resource mobilisation officer through the office of the Executive Director to help in marketing ZINGO and in turn reap the benefits of increased mobilisation of both technical and material resources to support the work on HIV and AIDS, gender and human rights. ZINGO also encountered the challenge of limited resources which affected the robustness of field offices which pointed to the need to address financial sustainability. As observed by UNAIDS (2015: 9):

> While efforts were being made to strengthen the sector [civil society] many of its members are fighting for survival, highlighting the urgency of addressing sustainability. Competition for specific opportunities to become sub recipients of the Global Fund for instance may limit the efficacy of coordination.

To address this, it was realised that there was need to develop strategies that would result in the mother bodies and field offices having the necessary capacities (skills, tools, and funding) to implement the interfaith response at community level and continue seeking partnerships in line the interfaith network's areas of focus. Additionally, capacity among some members of the network remained a challenge, especially with regard to technology. As such, ZINGO continues having a challenge with some of its members who still need to be helped to grow their technological level to a point where they are able to sufficiently process inputs from the external environment into quality output to benefit their constituencies (ZINGO 2013). In this regard, numerous trainings and skills development efforts were initiated. Notwithstanding these challenges, ZINGO's response and engagement with vulnerable groups of society confirmed religion's potential to be mobilised for reducing inequalities. By this, the religious ideas shared by the umbrella faith bodies were expressed in the concern for humanity through the approach to sustainable development carried out though the organisational and actors dimensions of religion.

CONCLUSION

The chapter explored the interconnectedness of religion and sustainable development through the work of ZINGO and its contributions to reducing inequalities in Zambia. Based on ZINGO's provision of information, technical and financial support to religious organisations and communities responding to the needs of vulnerable groups such as PLHIV, women, widows, youth and vulnerable children including those orphaned by HIV and AIDS, the chapter concludes that the work of ZINGO was closely aligned to the global goal to reducing inequalities. As an interfaith network that emerged long before the SDGs were spelt out, the chapter shows that what the global goal on reducing inequalities envisions has been at the centre of ZINGO as informed by religious ideas, practices, organisation and actors. While making a modest contribution towards addressing inequalities in the country and beyond, ZINGO signified that religion remained a significant aspect of the development discourses in Zambia. This was because the religious ideas and practices reflected in ZINGO were closely aligned to the aspirations of reducing inequalities within and among countries.

REFERENCES

Basedau, Matthias (et al.). 2017. *The Ambivalent Role of Religion for Sustainable Development: A Review of the Empirical Evidence*. GIGA Working Papers, No. 297. Hamburg: Institute of Global and Area Studies.

Centre for Health Marketing Innovations. 2020. *Zambia Interfaith Networking Group*. Accessed 2 January 2020. Retrieved from https://healthmarketinnovations.org/program/zambia-interfaith-networking-group

Daily Nation Reporter. 2016. ZINGO, FQM Scale Up Girl Child Education. *Daily Nation*, 6 January.

Djupe, Paul A. & Kieran H. Patrick. 2009. Beyond the Lynn White Thesis: Congregational Effects on Environmental Concern. *Journal for the Scientific Study of Religion* 48 (4): 670–686.

Durkheim, Emile. 1995. *The Elementary Forms of Religious Life*. Translated by Karen E. Fields. New York: Free Press.

Ellison, Christopher G. & Jeffrey S. Levin. 1998. The Religion-Health Connection: Evidence, Theory, and Future Directions. *Health Education & Behavior* 25 (6): 700–720.

Feess, Eberhard., Helge Mueller and Sabrina G. Ruhnau. 2014. The impact of religion and the degree of religiosity on work ethic: A multilevel analysis. *Kyklos* 67(4): 506–534.

Genrich, Gillian L. & Brader A. Brathwaite. 2005. Response of religious groups to HIV/AIDS as a sexually transmitted infection in Trinidad. *BMC Public Health* 5(12): 1–12.

Government of the Republic of Zambia (GRZ). 2006. *Vision 2030: A prosperous Middle-income Nation by 2030.* Lusaka: GRZ.

Guiso, Luigi (et al.). 2006. Does Culture Affect Economic Outcome? *The Journal of Economic Perspectives* 20(2): 23–48.

Hinfelaar, Marja. 2009. 'Legitimizing Powers: The Political Role of the Roman Catholic Church, 1972–1991'. In *One Zambia, Many Histories—Towards a History of Post-colonial Zambia*, ed. J. Gewald, M. Hinfelaar & G. Macola. Lusaka: Lembani Trust.

Mason, Jennifer. 2002. *Qualitative Researching.* London: Sage.

McCleary, Rachel M., & Robert J. Barro. 2006. Religion and economy. *Journal of Economic perspectives* 20(2): 49–72.

Minister of Foreign Affairs. 2014. *Ministerial Statement on the Presidential Participation at the High level segment of the United Nations General Assembly and the Summit for the Adoption of the Post 2015 Development Agenda. 7th October,* Lusaka.

Mwale, Nelly. 2013. Religion and Development in Zambia. *Alternation: Interdisciplinary Journal for the Study of the Arts and Humanities in Southern Africa* 11: 110–133.

Mwale, Nelly. & Chita, Joseph. 2019. Religion and Development in Zambia: A Case of the Jesuit Centre for Theological Reflection. In, *Religion and Development in Southern and Central Africa.* Ed. J. N. Amanze, M. Masango, E. Chitando and L. Siwila. Mzuzu: Mzuni Press.

Mwale, Nelly. & Simuchimba, Melvin. 2018. 125 years of Catholicism in Zambia: The History and Mission of the Church in the Provision of University Education. *Oral History Journal of South Africa* 6(1):1–16.

Mwanza, Peggy. 2015. The state of girl-child's education in Zambia: The case of Chongwe District. *Journal of International Cooperation in Education,* 17(2): 95–110.

Ndhlovu, Japhet. 2008. 'Combating HIV: A Ministerial Strategy for Zambian Churches'. *PhD Diss.* Pretoria: University of Pretoria.

Rakodi, Carole. 2012. A Framework for Analyzing the Links between Religion and Development. *Development in Practice* 22: 634–50.

Smart, Ninian. 1969. *The Religious Experience of Mankind*. New York: Charles Scribner's Sons.

Support to the HIV/AIDS Response in Zambia II. 2015. *The Five Years 2010–2015 of the United States President's t Emergency Plan for AIDS Relief and United States Agency for International Development Final Report*. John Snow Int and SHARe II.

Tomalin, Emma (et al.). 2019. Religion and the Sustainable Development Goals. *The Review of Faith and International Affairs* 17(2): 102–118.

Tomalin, Emma. 2013. Gender, Religion and Development. In *Handbook of Research on Development and Religion*, edited by Matthew Clarke. Massachusetts: Edward Elgar Publishing. pp. 183–200.

UNAIDS. 2015. *UNAIDS Engagement with Civil Society: Case Study 2-Zambia*. Geneva: UNAIDS.

United Nations. 2015. *Sustainable Development Goals-United Nations Environment Programme Annual Report*. Accessed 18 February 2020. Retrieved from https://www.unep.org/resources/annual-report

United Nations. 2017. *The Sustainable Development Goals Report*. New York: UN.

World Commission on Environment and Development (WCED). 1987. Discussion paper on Legal Principles for Environmental Protection and Sustainable Development. Vol 12 (WCED/SS/24A) Accessed 19 February 2020. Retrieved from https://idl-bncidrc.dspacedirect.org/bitstream/handle/10625/8942/WCED_79365.pdf

Zambia Country Report. 2008. *Multi-sectoral AIDS Response Monitoring and Evaluation Biennial Report 2006–2007*. Government of the Republic of Zambia: Lusaka.

ZINGO. 2013. Technical Report January to December Unpublished. 9140 Lufubu Road, Lusaka.

ZINGO. 2016. Three Year Technical Report 2014–2016 Unpublished. 28 Mwambula Road, Lusaka.

ZINGO report for 2002 activities—unpublished. 5055 Msanzara Road, Kalundu, Lusaka. n.d.-a

ZINGO Strategic Plan 2012–2016. Unpublished Document, Lusaka. n.d.-b

CHAPTER 12

The Role of the Council of Religions and Peace in Mozambique (COREM) in Peace and Reconciliation, 2012–2019

Júlio Machele and Mário Jorge Carlos

Introduction

In 1982, a meeting was held in Maputo between Samora Machel, the first president of the People's Republic of Mozambique and religious organizations in the country. This meeting, which had eagerly awaited, aimed at seeking commitment on the role of religious organizations in the development of the country. In the previous years, religious organizations had been relegated to the background (Silva 2017). The centralization of the economy in a context of one-party system, the ghosts of the commitment

J. Machele (✉)
University Eduardo Mondlane (UEM), Maputo, Mozambique

M. J. Carlos
ADPP-Mozambique, Matola, Mozambique

© The Author(s), under exclusive license to Springer Nature Switzerland AG 2022
E. Chitando, I. S. Gusha (eds.), *Interfaith Networks and Development*, Sustainable Development Goals Series,
https://doi.org/10.1007/978-3-030-89807-6_12

215

of some religious organizations to colonialism,[1] the reconstruction of the new nation with the Liberation Front of Mozambique (FRELIMO) still haunted the country. It was precisely from 1991 with the Freedom of Association Law that the participation of religious organizations in the development of the country was recognized. The war that had begun one year after national independence (1976) between the Movement of National Resistance (MNR), later renamed the National Resistance of Mozambique (RENAMO), continued to rage in the country[2] in conjunction with natural disasters (Coelho 2004), thus contributing to exacerbate inequalities within the country and among neighboring countries. The war ended 16 years later in 1992 and two years later the first multiparty elections were held in the country, which were won by FRELIMO.

From emergency aid, the country went to development aid (Ratilal 1990). It was, indeed, necessary to rebuild the country devastated by war which had collapsed all the components considered in the definition of development, namely;

> (1) universal access to healthy food, unpolluted air and water, hygienic clothing and shelter, (2) enhancement of the resource base while improving yields, (3) self-reliance and optimal use of the potential of each locality, region and nation in the perspective of better use of ecological (and human) resources, (4) harmony between the individual, the family and society. (Hettne, Karlsson & Magnusson (1990) in Adam 2006: 109)

It was also necessary to reduce the disparities between rural and urban areas that did not suffer directly from the conflict. Besides, it became common to ear that "the war ended long ago, but we are still poor" (Hanlon 2010).

In the reconstruction of the country and following the Freedom of Association Act of 1991, the country was continuously "assaulted" by various forms of organizations, including religious ones that, in a more favorable climate, engaged in the development of the country including their involvement in the achievement of the Millennium Development Goals (MDGs). These were succeeded by the Sustainable Development Goals (SDGs). In an attempt to achieve the set targets, the nation was

---

[1] For example, the leadership of FRELIMO admitted overtly that the Roman Catholics would not be part of the new order, because it supported colonialism.

[2] On the RENAMO see: Alex Vines 1996.

presented the 2025 Agenda (Agenda 2025), whose Commitment Note highlights that:

> As we celebrate 26 years of National Independence, our Homeland celebrates the unity of all Mozambicans regardless of their ethnicity, race, gender, social, cultural, religious origin and political choice. By promoting principles of unity and national reconciliation, Mozambique projects a future of peace, stability and progress for all its people and implements cooperation with countries and peoples around the world. In accordance with these principles, on 25 June 1998, the Head of State launched the initiative for all Mozambicans to reflect together on the future of the country over the next 25 years and formulate a national vision and strategies. (República de Moçambique 2003: 6)

In this Agenda, religious organizations were also called to participate in the eradication of extreme hunger and poverty, universal primary education, the promotion of gender equality and empowerment of women, the reduction of child immortality, the improvement of maternal health, the fight against HIV-AIDS, malaria and other diseases and ensuring environmental sustainability (Republic of Mozambique & European Union 2014). However, the achievement of these development goals depended fundamentally on the existence of a climate of peace so that there can be "self-reliance and optimal use of the potential of each locality, region and nation in the perspective of better use of ecological (and human) resources," but also on "harmony between the individual, family and society" (ibid.). In fact, religious organizations are in tandem with the SDGs because they are "determined to foster peaceful, just and inclusive societies which are free from fear and violence. There can be no sustainable development without peace and no peace without sustainable development" (United Nations 2015).

However, from 2013 to 2014, military hostilities were resuming between the government and the RENAMO military forces that made country lag behind in the achievement of the development objectives. This situation hinders the empowerment and promotion of social, economic and political inclusion of all irrespective of age, sex, disability, race, ethnicity, origin, religion or economic or other status, the 10.2 SDG (United Nations 2015).

The focus of this chapter is the Council of Religions and Peace of Mozambique (COREM). The aim this chapter is to contribute to the understanding of the role of COREM in promoting peace and reconciliation in Mozambique as a *sine qua non* condition for the achievement of the SDGs, specially the reduction of inequalities. Our point of departure is 2013, the year in which misunderstandings between RENAMO and the Government led to the military-political conflict until the signing of the definitive Peace and National Reconciliation Agreement in 2019.[3]

We argue that as the signs of threat to peace came to light, COREM, as an entity that brings together "all the faiths of Mozambique", strove to promote a culture of national dialogue and reconciliation by rescuing the *modus operandi* used during and after the 16-year armed conflict that consisted of appealing through the various media, contacting and bringing together leaders in conflict. We maintain that unlike the previous period characterized by conflicts among religions and among faith-based organizations, with COREM a common front coordinated for national peace and reconciliation was created. This common front has provided greater promise of meeting the National Peace and Reconciliation agenda. This study is justified by the fact that although studies on the role of religion in peace and national reconciliation abound, few or no studies focus on the role of interfaith organizations. When scrutinizing literature on religion and peace, we are usually faced with studies that analyze the role of churches in the peace process, focusing on Protestant churches through the Christian Council of Mozambique (CCM) and the Catholic Church of Mozambique, mainly through the Community of St. Egidio or simply studies focused on a single church or organization.[4] In general, these studies highlight the positive role of the religion in the search for peace and national reconciliation. Thus, by studying the COREM, we intend to fill this gap in the literature on interfaith organizations and development in Mozambique.

---

[3] In the north of the country, in the province of Cabo Delgado, a group called "insurgents" by the government, linked to religious radicalism, has emerged since 2017 and is carrying out attacks against military and civilian targets. This study does not cover the role of COREM in this new conflict.

[4] Alex Vines (1996), Gentili (2013), Sengulane and Gonçalves (1998), etc. are among those who have studied the role of Catholics and Protestants. Fernando da Silva, for example, studied the role of the CCM since the colonial period including the "2012–2014 civil war," leaving aside the other faiths (Silva 2015).

The Context

In 1992, Mozambique celebrated the signing of the General Peace Agreement (GPA) in Rome with joy. Religious organizations, namely the CCM and the Community of Sant'Egidio, linked to the Roman Catholic Church, were instrumental in bringing the Government closer to the leadership of the RENAMO, which led to the signing of the agreement. With the signing of the GPA, Mozambique embarked on a process of national reconciliation and reconstruction. It was indeed necessary to bring together fellow citizens who had been divided by the armed conflict. It was necessary to forgive. In fact, Mozambicans had to "endure one another and forgive one another" (Colossians 3:13). These Mozambicans who were doing badly had to, "Depart from evil and do good; seek peace and follow it" (Psalms 34:14). The forgiveness and reconciliation defended by religious community had already been echoed by them in the 1980s but in the version of amnesty. The "armed bandits," as they were stubbornly labelled by the government, were understood by the religious community as "brothers". The poster "FRELIMO's weapons kill bandits", "stop being a bandit", "give yourself up and you will be forgiven", "be free again and live in peace" is, in part, the religious understanding of how to deal with "bandits" who are "brothers" (Geffray 1990: 241).

Issues related to the GPA caused RENAMO to remain with a military guard and in control of some bases not yet dismantled, thus becoming a militarized political party in times of peace. Thus, during successive terms of government, Mozambique "learned" to live with militarized RENAMO. The armed wing has become a form of pressure in the face of the GPA's "non-compliance", especially in the integration of RENAMO's fighters into the army, the police, the secret service, at the National Electoral Commission (CNE) and the sharing of gas and coal revenues.[5] During President Armando Emílio Guebuza's term, disagreements with RENAMO led to what the government labelled as political instability in central Mozambique. In practice this was an armed conflict in which both RENAMO and the government used military force to achieve their objectives.

Thus the central region of Mozambique became politically and militarily unstable and whose spark was the rejection of the election results. It

---

[5] The "cocktail" of factors that have washed away instability and also relevant to the sustainability of future agreements are summarized in Alex Vines (2019).

was following this that Afonso Dhlakama installed a military base in the Gorongosa region in 2014, and began training former veterans, thus demanding a new political order. In one of his statements, he said, "Yes, I authorized an attack… But two days later I ordered a ceasefire, because we felt sorry when a civilian was injured, the objective was not to attack a civilian, it was to attack the army" (DW África/Correspondentes/LUSA 2014). So, from 2014 until 2019 Mozambique lived in a situation of instability. With the death of Afonso Dlhakama and the election of the contested Ossufo Momade surged another military wing of RENAMO that does not recognize the new leadership and which is leading the same model of attacks in the centre of the country thus extending the political-military instability to the present. However, "the renewed conflict of 2015–2016 was more serious than the insurgency of 2013–2014. The attacks conducted by RENAMO remained low cost but high in impact, "with the intention of frightening the people and demonstrating that the government was unable to guarantee security, especially that of its employees" (Vines 2019: 2018).

The RENAMO strategy also impacted on non-governmental institutions and rural communities in central Mozambique. Non-Governmental Organizations redirected their projects and in some areas agricultural activities stopped. Inequalities within regions were exacerbated. It in this context that the COREM has sought to champion development in Mozambique.

The Council of Religions and Peace of Mozambique, Peace and National Reconciliation

The Council of Religions of Mozambique

One of the characteristics of Mozambique with regard to religion is the existence of several religions, giving the country the status of a religious mosaic. Other religions have joined the African Traditional Religion. First, Islam along the coast is linked to the Arab world through traders; second, Christians are linked to the European expansion through missionaries, and third are the Ethiopian separatist churches. The list includes Jews, Buddhists and other minority groups. Mozambique is marked by religious diversity and there is no one dominant church. "We find a varied religious society there, with roughly equal numbers of Catholics, Protestants, and

Muslims" (Morier-Genoud 2013: 185). In the search for a relationship with the state through a valid interlocutor, these religious denominations have created faith-based organizations.

The genesis of some faith-based organizations is remote, having their orings from the colonial period. For example, the Mahometana community, an organization of Muslims based in India, is closely linked to the group of Indians who were not expelled from Mozambique in 1961 (Morier-Genoud 2002). Religious organizations such as the CCM of Protestants, the Episcopal Conference of Mozambique of the Catholics, the Christian Charitable Association (ABC) of the Universal Church of the Kingdom of God, the Islamic Council of Mozambique (CISLAMO),[6] the Islamic Congress of Mozambique,[7] the Islamic Community of Mozambique (CIMO), Johrei Community, the Buddhist Community, Brahma Kumaris, the Greek Orthodox Church and so many other faith-based organizations, each in their own way, have become part of the Mozambican religious landscape and have engaged various fronts for the well-being of Mozambicans. Given the enormous religious diversity in the country and in an effort to ensure the greater coordination of peace, reconciliation and development, the COREM was created. The Council of Religions and Peace of Mozambique, brings together religious communities, faith-based associations, people of good will, to share, develop the culture of peace, promote the ideals of the Kingdom of God, justice, equality, joy among people, in a universal and humanitarian perspective.

The COREM dates back to the signing of the General Peace Accords in 1992, when an Inter-Religious Forum was created to facilitate and mediate the signing of the agreement. The Forum was transformed into the Mozambique Inter-Religious Council (CIRM) in 1998 until its current name, COREM, was established in February 2004. Throughout its evolution, this interreligious group has worked to bring together various

[6] The first nation-wide Islamic organization created in Mozambique was the Conselho Islâmico de Moçambique (Islamic Council of Mozambique, CISLAMO). It was founded at a meeting between the government and Maputo imams in January 1981, and it elected Abubacar Ismael 'Mangira' as coordinator and later the first national secretary. Later and up to the time of writing, Shaykh Aminuddin Mohamad has been the president.

[7] The Islamic Congress of Mozambique was created by many sheiks, Imams and influential Muslims in Maputo. The organization was founded in January 1983 after the "historic" meeting between the government and all religious confessions in the country—a meeting that officially and, above all, publicly marked the change in the attitude of power towards religion (Morier-Genoud 2002).

religious groups in order to promote peaceful coexistence. Members include the CCM, the Jewish Community, the Baha'i Community, the League of Scouts of Mozambique, the Hindu Community, the Islamic Council of Mozambique, the Aga Khan Community, the African Traditional Religion, the Brahma Kumaris and the Greek Orthodox Church (Reisman and Lalá 2012: 43). Like other associations in the country, COREM was the fruit of the new multi-party constitution of 1990 and more specifically the Freedom of Association Act of 1991. It is a Council that has taken a rather winding road at a time when several faith-based organizations were individualistic and contesting for dominance.

Its creation and designation as the Council of Religions for Peace in Mozambique reflects the concerns of the moment. The war that had begun in 1976 had ended in 1992 with the signing of the GPA in Rome. In this long road to peace there was a great involvement of the religious leadership with emphasis on the CCM and the Roman Catholic Church through the Sant'Egidio Community. It was necessary to contain and demobilize the forces of the belligerents. It was also necessary to lead the country to the first general elections and above all to reconcile the Mozambicans who were divided during the 16 years of war. For instance, "in 1993, at the request of the government of the Republic of Mozambique, UNESCO established a programme called Culture of Peace, a concept broadened and appropriated by many people..." (London/News in Portuguese 2016). As time passed, new concerns arose. To start with, the centralization of spirituality and peace was aggregated in the Social Action or Ministry of Access and Human Development. In fact, Pastor Albino Luis Mussuei, Secretary General of COREM in an interview with UN News in 2014 referred to these major areas of action (UN News 10 June 2014).

The extension in the areas of action is reflected in the 14 themes in the "Religious Leaders' Guide for Promoting Health, Education and Child Protection": (1) Care during pregnancy and childbirth (2) Birth registration (3) Newborn health (4) Vaccination (5) Infant and young child feeding (6) Prevention and treatment of malaria (7) Prevention of diarrhea and cholera 8. Prevention and treatment of HIV and AIDS (9) The importance of the family in the child's development (10) Protection of the most vulnerable (orphaned children) (11) Rights of children with disabilities (12) Physical violence against children (13) Sexual abuse and exploitation (14) Premature marriage (COREM 2014: 5). Therefore, in addition to peacekeeping and national reconciliation, COREM promotes equity and gender equality, rights of women and girls and promotes a culture of continuous inter-religious dialogue where tolerance and peace prevail. All these activities are quite consistent with the SDGs. In particular, these activities address SDG 10 in a direct way by seeking to reduce inequalities relating to health, age, disability and gender.

The Council also undertakes socio-cultural and community mobilization on behaviour change, advocates against violence and early marriage, promotion of child protection, inclusion of people with disability, disaster risk reduction for the management and mitigation of environmental disasters, promotes inter-religious dialogue from the community level to the central area and vice versa, advocate for health with an emphasis on HIV-AIDS. According to the statutes approved after its General Assembly, held on July 29, 2010 it had the following composition: Marcos Efreime Macamo—President of the General Assembly; Aminudine Mohamed—Chairman of the Council of Leaders; José Guerra—Vice Chairman of the Council of Leaders; Bantual Prabul—Chairman of the Supervisory Board; Albino Luis Mussuei—General Secretary (Boletim da República 2017: 6974).

The COREM and the Quest for Peace and Reconciliation

There can be no development without peace. In 2013 Sheik Aminudine Mohamed,[8] president of the Council of Religions and Peace of Mozambique and also president of the CISLAMO predicting the future of Mozambican children for 2025 said:

> ... I see Mozambique very focused on the issue of peace for the next 10 years, a peace that cannot be reduced simply by silencing weapons. I see peace as the happiness of citizens, the possibility of moving anywhere in search of better living conditions, without fear. In 10 years' time, children

---

[8] Shaykh Aminuddin Mohamad, is a prominent Islamic scholar. Besides of propagating modern Islamic education he established several madrassas of a new kind, incorporating formal secular curricula along with the Islamic one. "Some of these madrassas enjoy support from the Al-Azhar University in Egypt that regularly sends teachers of Arabic language. This is the case with an Islamic centre called Hamza founded in 1996 in Matola city near Maputo under the direct control of Shaykh Aminuddin. It includes a mosque, a madrassa, and a boarding school for boys" (Bonate 2005: 41–42).

should have safe transport to school. We must become a country that never allows a child to go to war. (UNICEF 2014: 9)

The message was a clear reaction to the growing disagreements between the government and RENAMO whose solution through dialogue appeared to be a mirage. The Sheik, aware of the damage caused by the previous conflict, showed greater concern for the consolidation of the hard-won peace. But to his disappointment Afonso Dhlakama, the president of RENAMO, set up a military base in the Gorongosa region of central Mozambique a year later and began training former veterans, demanding a new political order. From here several armed attacks were reported in central Mozambique. Thus since 2014 many civilians, means of transport, social infrastructure were caught up in the middle of the conflict. Due to the use of arms, it has become easy to understand the criticism of religious leaders regarding the "lack of coherence" in political discourses on peace. In fact, in the view of the Mozambican Catholic bishops, "what is said does not correspond to practice and the relationship between the government and RENAMO is still marked by confrontation" (Beck 2016). Since the arms race showed no signs of slowing down, in 2015 the Archbishop of Beira, Mons. Claudio Dalla Zuanna, spoke about the need to "put an end to proliferation of guns in the country". In his understanding, which was also the COREM understanding, he argued that it was "certainly necessary to do a job, to convince that guns cannot be spread in the country in the hands of any citizen" (Beck 2016). In its turn, the president of the COREM, Artimiza Franco, reproved Dhlakama's departure to the Gorongosa forests in Sofala, central Mozambique saying that he needed to come out of the woods to achieve genuine reconciliation (Silva 2018).

In January 2014 the Mozambican Council of Religions facilitated a National Summit on Peace and Reconciliation to find solutions to the conflict that followed the 2014 general elections. The summit was widely attended by religious and political leaders from throughout the country, as well as the international community (United States Department of State 2018: 5).COREM and its members constantly appealed to the involvement all the living forces of Mozambican society for peace and national reconciliation. It made constant calls for the resumption of dialogue and the abandonment of arms. In its constant quest for peace, COREM together with the Islands of Peace Association organized, for example, a dinner at which Noel Chicuecue, representative of the UNESCO in

12 THE ROLE OF THE COUNCIL OF RELIGIONS AND PEACE...

Mozambique, was invited in October 2016. In his speech, which began with the role of UNESCO after the 16-year conflict, Chicuecue, addressing the need for a constant quest for peace, stressed that:

> Peace is like a plant that must be cultivated and watered. When we forget, it withers. We must all remember that it must be cared for by Mozambicans, without exception, and only if we are all united can we promote peace... (London/Notícias em Português 2016)

COREM also organized conferences for the search for peace. In January 2018 it organized a two-day national meeting in search of solutions to the post-election conflicts in the country. It was the National Summit on Peace and National Reconciliation that took place in the city of Beira, central Mozambique (Lusa 2018). It is important to remember that the 2013–2014 conflict has been linked, among other things, to non-acceptance of the election results by RENAMO. Besides, "the Head of State, Filipe Jacinto Nyusi, held on 8 September 2015 the opening ceremony of the III National Religious Conference, in the city of Quelimane, Zambezia province. The event, which was attended by over 500 participants, had as its motto "Contribution of Religious Confessions in Peacekeeping in Mozambique" (Presidency of the Republic 2017: 6). For his part, José Guerra, Vice-President of COREM and President of the Universal Church of the Kingdom of God, said that "peace is a supreme good that places itself above individual or ideological interests", so religious denominations should be increasingly involved, since they have an important role in the peace process (Presidency of the Republic 2017: 6). The recommendations arising from this meeting guided in part, the subsequent commitment of COREM to peace and reconciliation. Also in the context of meetings, COREM organized a Seminar for Discussion and Approval of the Action Plan of the Platform on Women, Peace and Security, an initiative supported by the Programme, Women, Peace and Security of UN Women Mozambique funded by the governments of Iceland and the Kingdom of Norway.

At the IV National Religious Conference in 2017, the Prime Minister, recognizing the efforts and the role of religious denominations emphasized that they, together with Civil Society Organizations, are challenged to assume an increasingly active role in the pursuit of the national agenda, especially with regard to achieving definitive peace and creating conditions for the well-being of the population". Still according to the Prime Minister

"Only with effective Peace can we consolidate national unity, guarantee sovereignty, accelerate the economic and social development of our Country and thus continuously improving the living conditions of the population" (Angop 2017). As result of COREM's efforts and other forces, in December 2016, a ceasefire was decreed by Renamo leader Afonso Dhlakama and relations with Mozambican President Filipe Nyusi improved. Negotiations for a new peace agreement were marked by a handshake between them on August 6, 2017, when Nyusi travelled to Mount Gorongosa for a two-hour meeting with Dhlakama. On August 6, 2019, the definitive peace and national reconciliation agreement between the President of the Republic, Filipe Nyusi and the new leader of the RENAMO, Ossufo Momade, was signed. The act marked the end of the political and military instability that the country had experienced between 2014 and 2016, with RENAMO's refusal to recognize the results of the last general elections (Zacarias and Silva 2020). With this agreement "Mozambique will never return to war" according to Filipe Nyusi, a position reproduced by Ossufo Momade who, in turn, argued that "with this agreement, we seal our commitment to maintain peace and national reconciliation" (Zacarias and Silva 2020). Because of COREM and other forces, Filipe Jacinto Nyusi and Ossufo Momade are the "blessed peacemakers".[9]

This agreement represented a crucial turning point toward the reduction on inequalities in Mozambique that are striking between urban and rural areas. Besides, the agreement has the potential to contribute to "empower and promote the social, economic and political inclusion of all, irrespective of age, sex, disability, race, ethnicity, origin, religion or economic or other status" (United Nations 2015).

CONCLUSION

This chapter examined the role of COREM, the Council of Religions and Peace of Mozambique, an interfaith organization, in search for peace and national reconciliation during the troubled period between 2012 and 2019 where hostilities between the government and RENAMO came to the surface, causing fatalities and destruction of infrastructure. COREM, using the previous experience in which some religious leaders brokered

---

[9] Based on Matthews 5:3 "Blessed are the peacemakers, for they shall be called the sons of God".

the peace process, constantly called for dialogue and the abandonment of guns. It positively influenced the leaders in conflict (first Armando Emílio Guebuza and then Filipe Jacinto Nyusi on the government side and Afonso Dlhakama and later Ossufo Momade on the RENAMO side) to come closer. COREM organized national and international conferences for the promotion of peace and national reconciliation. It participated and was urged to participate in the discussions on the need for a common religious front for national peace and reconciliation. COREM became a strategic actor because its messages of peace were echoed by the leaders of other affiliated organizations. The results of the COREM effort, combined with other efforts, led to the signing of the definitive Accord of Peace and National Reconciliation between Filipe Jacinto Nyusi and Ossufo Momade on 6 August 2019. It is anticipated that this provides a solid foundation for the country to actively pursue and achieve the SDGs and improve the quality of life of the Mozambicans in a very significant way.

REFERENCES

Adam, Yussuf. 2006. Escapar aos dentes de crocodilo e cair na boca de Leopardo: trajectória de Moçambique pós colonial (1975–1990). Maputo: Promédia.

Angop. 2017. Moçambique: PM encoraja confissões religiosas a promover tolerância no país. Available at: http://m.portalangop.co.ao/angola/pt_pt/noticias/africa/2017/9/41/Mocambique-encoraja-confissoes-religiosas-promover-tolerancia-pais,d15241dd-5cf3-4db0-8af3-bc73f060111a.html. Accessed on 13/5/2020.

Beck, Johannes. 2016. Cronologia do conflito entre a RENAMO e o Governo de Moçambique. *DW Africa*, 11.03.2016. Available at: https://www.dw.com/pt-002/cronologia-do-conflito-entre-a-renamo-e-o-governo-de-mo%C3%A7ambique/a-19105846. Accessed on 16/5/2020.

DW África/Correspondentes/LUSA. 2014. Momentos de instabilidade política em Moçambique – uma cronologia. *DW Africa*, 11.03.2016. Available at: https://www.dw.com/pt-002/momentos-de-instabilidade-pol%C3%ADtica-em-mo%C3%A7ambique-uma-cronologia/a-16912568. Accessed on 16/5/2020.

Bonate, Liazzate. 2005. Dispute over Islamic Funeral Rites in Mozambique A Demolidora dos Prazeres by Shaykh Aminuddin Mohamad. *Social Sciences & Missions* 17: 41–59.

Coelho, João Paulo Borges. 2004. Estado, comunidades e calamidades naturais no Moçambique Rural. In Santos, Boaventura de Sousa (org.), *Semear soluções: os caminhos da biodiversidade e de conhecimentos rivais.* Porto: Afrontamento.

COREM. 2014. *Guião dos Líderes Religiosos para a promoção da saúde, educação e protecção da criança.* Maputo: UNICEF.

Geffray, C. 1990. *La cause des armes au Mozambique: une Antropologie de une guerre civile.* Paris: Karthala.

Governo de Moçambique. 2017. *Boletim da República, III Série, N. 72, Sexta-feira, 3 de Novembro de 2017.* Maputo.

Hanlon, Joseph. 2010. Mozambique: 'the war ended 17 years ago, but we are still poor'. *Conflict, Security & Development* 10: 1, 77–102.

Londres/Notícias em Português. 2016. Representante da Unesco defende paz em Moçambique. Available at: http://www.noticiasemportugues.co.uk/texto-diario/mostrar/512356/representante-da-unesco-defende-paz-em-mocambique. Acessesed on 16/5/2020.

Lusa. 2018. Conselho de Religiões de Moçambique lança hoje cimeira sobre paz e reconciliação. Available at: https://noticias.sapo.mz/sociedade/artigos/conselho-de-religioes-de-mocambique-lanca-hoje-cimeira-sobre-paz-e-reconciliacao. Accessed on 11/5/2020.

Morier-Genoud, Eric. 2002. *O Islão em Moçambique após a independência: História de um poder em ascensão.* Paris: Karthala.

Morier-Genoud, Eric. 2013. The Catholic Church in Mozambique under Revolution, War, and Democracy. In Manuel, Paul Christopher; Lyon, Alyanna; Wilcox, Clyde (eds.) *Religion and Politics in a Global Society: Comparative Perspectives from the Portuguese Speaking World.* Maryland: Lexington Books.

Presidência da República. 2017. *Abraço Fraternal: Brochura do diálogo do Presidente da República de Moçambique com as confissões religiosas.* Maputo: Presidência da República.

Ratilal, Prakash. 1990. *Enfrentar o desafio: utilizar a ajuda para terminar a emergência.* Maputo: Globo.

Reisman, Lainie & Lalá, Aly. 2012. *Avaliação do Crime e Violência em Moçambique & Recomendações para a Redução da Violência.* Maputo: OSISA

República de Moçambique. 2003. *Agenda 2025*, Maputo: EloGráfico.

República de Moçambique & União Europeia. 2014. *União Europeia – República de Moçambique Programa Indicativo Nacional, 2014–2020.* Maputo: UE.

Sengulane, Dínis S., & Gonçalves, Jaime Pedro. 1998. A Calling for Peace: Christian Leaders and the Quest for Reconciliation in Mozambique. In Jeremy Armon, Dylan Hendrickson and Alex Vines (eds.), *The Mozambican Peace Process in Perspective*, London and Maputo: Conciliation Resources, Arquivo Histórico de Moçambique.

Silva, C.N. 2017. "Viver a fé em Moçambique: as relações entre a Frelimo e as confissões religiosas", *Ph.D Diss.* Fuliminense: Universidade Federal Fulminense.

Silva, Fernando. 2015. The Role of the Christian Council Of Mozambique on Ending the Civil War (1948–1995). *A paper presented at the Annual CHSSA Conference (University of South Africa, August 14–16, 2014)*, Available at: https://www.academia.edu/7998186/THE_ROLE_OF_THE_CHRISTIAN_COUNCIL_OF_MOZAMBIQUE_ON_ENDING_THE_CIVIL_WAR_1948_1995_. Accessed on 11/5/2020.

Silva, Romeu. 2018. Moçambique: Conselho de Religiões preocupado com conflitos. In *DW*, 26.01.2018. Available at: https://www.dw.com/pt-002/mo%C3%A7ambique-conselho-de-religi%C3%B5es-preocupado-com-conflitos/a-42307317. Accessed on 11/5/2020.

UNICEF. 2014. *As nossas crianças em 2025: Opinião de líderes proeminentes sobre o futuro das crianças em Moçambique.* Maputo: UNICEF.

United Nations. 2015. Transforming Our World: The 2030 Agenda for Sustainable Development. New York: United Nations.

United States Department of State. 2018. *2018 Report on International Religious Freedom: Mozambique.* Available at: https://www.state.gov/wp-content/uploads/2019/05/MOZAMBIQUE-2018-INTERNATIONAL-RELIGIOUS-FREEDOM-REPORT.pdf. Accessed on 11/5/2020.

Vines, Alex. 1996. *Renamo: From Terrorism to Democracy in Mozambique?* London: James Currey.

Vines, Alex. 2019. *As Perspectivas de um Acordo Sustentável entre as Elites em Moçambique À Terceira é de Vez?* London: Chatham House/Africa Programme.

Vines, A., & Wilson, K. 1995. Churches and the Peace Processes in Mozambique. In P. Gifford (ed.), *The Christian Churches and the Democratisation of Africa* (pp. 130–148). (Studies of Religion in Africa; Vol. 12). EJ Brill.

Zacarias, Amós & Silva, Romeu da. 2020. Moçambique: Assinado o acordo de paz definitiva e reconciliação nacional. Available at: https://www.dw.com/pt-002/mo%C3%A7ambique-assinado-o-acordo-de-paz-definitiva-e-reconcilia%C3%A7%C3%A3o-nacional/a-49919241. Accessed on 11/5/2020.

CHAPTER 13

Colonial Marginalities and Post-Colonial Fragments: Inter-Faith Networking for Development in Ghana

Samuel Awuah-Nyamekye and Simon Kofi Appiah

BACKGROUND

Religion is important to development, though the project of modernity dismissed religion as being counterproductive (Deneulin and Rakodi 2011). However, changes in thinking about the overall meaning of development and its dependence on material as well as immaterial factors has rekindled interest in the role of religion in development (Freeman 2012). But before the emergence of the idea of development as progression towards modernity, religion was known to be a major drive for social progress in many communities. The contemporary resurgence of religion in the domain of development is realized through intra- and inter-faith networks, which are collaborations or associations of different faith-based organizations (FBOs) for the purposes of development and other

---

S. Awuah-Nyamekye (✉) • S. K. Appiah
University of Cape Coast, Cape Coast, Ghana
e-mail: s.appiah@ucc.edu.gh

© The Author(s), under exclusive license to Springer Nature Switzerland AG 2022
E. Chitando, I. S. Gusha (eds.), *Interfaith Networks and Development*, Sustainable Development Goals Series,
https://doi.org/10.1007/978-3-030-89807-6_13

231

humanist goals. The UNFPA (2009: 4), however, defines faith-based organizations as "Religious, faith-based groups, and/or faith-inspired groups which operate as registered or unregistered non-profit institutions." The UNDP (2014: 4–5), citing Clarke and Jennings (2008), also defines FBOs as "organizations that derive inspiration and guidance for their activities from the teachings and principles of the faith or from a particular interpretation or school of thought within that faith."

Networking is important because it releases the much-needed collaborative energy through which developmental goals can be realized. That there is something collective about development, in the sense that humans have the capability of improving their life when they come together, is a basic presumption in development discourse (Leys 1996; Rist 2002). Intra-faith networks are ingrained in Ghana, but there is obvious interfaith fragmentation, that is, the exclusion of some religions due to latent colonial hierarchical taxonomies, and lack of cultural historical specific ideologies of development. This fragmentation has been one of the reasons for the mixed results facing the collaboration efforts of religious institutions and FBOs as partners in development (Ndekha 2015). Efforts such as the Inter-Faith Waste Management Initiative (IFAWAMI), working in the area of environmental waste management are too few and in between.

In this chapter, we evaluate interfaith networking in Ghana, identifying its contribution to the national development agenda particularly those that fulfil the Sustainable Development Goals (SDGs), particularly, the Goal 10, which aims at encouraging governments and policy-decision-makers to act in a way that will reduce inequality within and among countries. At the same time, we underscore the significant limitations of the achievements of inter-faith networks as a result of the exclusion of groups of African Traditional Religion (ATR), and until recently groups of Islam. Inaccurately judged as lacking the characteristics, structures, and values expected of FBOs that qualify to be partners in collaborations for development, ATR groups are usually side-lined, or inadvertently ignored as partners in development. Given the tenacity with which traditional religion has held to its own in the face of the dominance of Christianity and Islam in Ghana, it is important to determine how to forge a more integrative paradigm of inter-faith networking, which can augment the contribution of FBOs in advancing Ghana's development agenda with special emphasis on the SDG10.

Introduction

Faith is important to people in Ghana. The three major institutional religions through which people express their faith are African Traditional Religion (ATR), Islam, and Christianity. Work, celebration, peace and conflict resolution, politics, and the general organization of life in Africa are all influenced by religion. People make recourse to religion for health security, success in business, and general well-being. But the belief that the continent is "notoriously religious" has in recent times come under criticism as "the making of a tradition" (p'Bitek 1971; Mudimbe 1988; Platvoet and Van Rinsum 2003; Appiah and Kodah 2020). Nevertheless, Ghana, like the rest of Africa, is overtly religious, and some scholars contest the criticism against the tradition of the 'notoriety' of religion in Africa (Awuah-Nyamekye 2020).

When it comes to development in Ghana, some scholars premise the important role they attribute to religion on a number of arguments. They claim, for example, that religious leaders such as pastors, Imams, traditional priests and clerics of all ranks enjoy significant respect among their followers. They are listened to in important decision-making processes in private life and in society. People look up to them for moral and spiritual guidance, and they are held in high respect as mediators of divine presence and blessing for progress. Thus, leaders of religion serve as effective agents for mobilizing and animating communities in pursuit of development programmes and projects. A stronger argument, however, has been that religion tends to provide a framework, which parallels or, in some cases, precedes scientific frameworks for problem solving and meaning making (Appiah 2018). This means that a people's worldview, which includes religious beliefs, would usually play an important role in their development plan. For these reasons, when development is understood beyond its narrow conceptualization as modernization and economic growth, religion stands tall in the development discourse and activities people undertake in Ghana. It is within this 'religio-centric' space that the link between FBOs and development is defined (Awuah-Nyamekye 2012).

Defining Religion and Development

It is important to establish the senses in which the terms religion and development are used in this chapter. In Ghana, people understand religion nearly always to involve belief in a Supreme Being—God for

Christians, Allah for Muslims, and the 'High' God for ATR, called differently in the different indigenous languages of Ghana. The Ewe of the Volta Region, for instance, say *Mawu*, while the Dagaare of the Upper West Region say *Nawinne* (Awuah-Nyamekye 2020). Members of the three religions believe in the immanence of God and trace details of their daily life to God's divine agency.

Closely related to religious beliefs is the social and cultural understanding of development in Ghana, which is much broader than its western materialistic conceptualization. People in Ghana associate development with holistic well-being rather than mere absence of poverty (Awuah-Nyamekye 2012: 80). Development is something like abundant life (Agbeti 1991: 1), including wealth, fecundity, social recognition, absence of misfortune, good health and long life (Larbi 2002). These meanings inform our use of the terms religion and development. However, it is well known that both concepts are difficult to explain; they are not amenable to any single definition. Hence, avoiding duplications of definitions that only belabour existing epistemological controversies, the first part of the chapter will rather briefly review the philosophy or policy that guided development practices from colonial times to the present. This approach has the potential of accentuating contextualized meanings of religion and development that are relevant to the history of Ghana and thus eschew the search for generalizable but controversial meanings. The second part of the chapter interrogates the arrangements that emerge from this historical review of policy and how they account for what we describe as 'fragmentation' in inter-faith networks for development today. By fragmentation, we mean the subtle continuation of the marginalization of ATR and, until recently, Islam in the formation of FBOs and their activities for development in Ghana. But fragmentation also extends to ideologies of development that drive the activities of the FBOs. In the third part, the chapter will explore possibilities of an integrative approach to networking, which accords faith groups from the three main religions in Ghana their place in the collaboration towards holistic development, which in our view, will help to fulfil the SDG10 agenda—reducing inequalities within communities. The chapter will conclude with a recapitulation of the main ideas and recommendations for the way forward.

Reviewing Inter-Religious Relations for Development in Colonial Ghana

In development studies and social science, there is no consensus on the connection between religion and development. The contest over the exact nature of the religion-development nexus can be categorized under three main perspectives—complementary (Deneulin and Bano 2009), ambivalent (Reuben 2011), and obtrusive (Barro and McCleary 2006; Haynes 2007). In his study of the interface between religion and development in Ghana, Awuah-Nyamekye (2020) endorses the 'ambivalence' perspective which claims that religion is not a panacea to development, but some aspects of religion can contribute while others can be inimical to development. Inter-faith networking, however, would seem to depart from the complementary perspective, believing that religion has the potential to act as an agent of development and support the developmental goals of civil society in deprived communities. The UNFPA even suggests that in contemporary times FBOs' participation in development is not just complementary but critical:

> The case for working with faith-based organizations, as one community among many critical agents of change, is no longer a matter of discussion, but rather, one of considered, systematic and deliberate engagement of the like-minded partners among them. For many years, international development has been a field dominated by largely 'secular' agents of development, with a preference for keeping faith and faith-related matters strictly in the so-called 'private' domains. ... [But now], at a time when basic needs are becoming increasingly harder to provide for more than half of the world's population, we can no longer avoid acknowledging these parallel faith-based development interventions which reach so many and provide so much. (UNFPA 2009: 1)

However, there are reasons why it would be anachronistic to think of networks of faith-based organizations during the colonial period. First, the rapid rise of NGOs and inter-faith networking to partner civil society and governments in the pursuit of social progress is quite recent. It is often traced to the period from the 1980s through the 90s (Deneulin and Bano 2009) to the present. Second, colonial Christianity of the nineteenth century was itself fragmented into antagonistic confessions, transporting to mission territories the vestiges of inter-confessional animosities that had developed across Europe since the period of the Reformation, the thirty-year war and its aftermath. For this reason, mapping colonial missionary work in Ghana, just as one example, reveals concentrations of Christian groupings neatly carved out as confessional enclaves. These were formed by 'first come, first served' logic of the various missionary groups that permeated the then Gold Coast (Agbeti 1987; Beidelman 1982). Catholic missionaries were unwelcome visitors to areas previously evangelized by Presbyterians and vice versa; Anglican-dominated territory was non-accessible to Methodists; and domains of Millenialists entertained no intrusion from other missionary groups. Thus, colonial Christianity was at the outset territorial and, what is worse, this missionary geography tended to be ethnically divisive (but see the *Ghana 2018 Freedom of Religion Report* for a different opinion) because of the cultural constellations of Ghana. Thus, colonial ethnography is tied to the history of Christianity in Ghana and, to some extent, certain inter-ethnic divisions, for better or worse, can be traced along the lines of the history of confessional differentiation and rivalry during the missionary enterprise in Ghana.

The third and, probably, more fundamental reason why it would be anachronistic to think of inter-faith networks during the colonial period, was the denigration of indigenous and other non-Christian religions that existed in Ghana (or Africa for that matter) at the arrival of the colonialists. Islam fared better in the kind of recognition it received, despite the varying representations and attitudes among the colonialists (Weiss 2005). These attitudes ranged from anxiety about Islamic militancy, the dismissal of Islam as a religion suitable only to the weak minds of Africans (especially because it tolerated polygamy), and the deployment of Islam, where suitable, as a tool for enforcing colonial order (Weiss 2005; Wilks 1989; Hiskett 1984). Colonialists found Islam in Kings/Chiefs' palaces in Ghana being used for different purposes—religious, administrative, secretarial and spiritual and medical. Preceding this African encounter, however, were the militant confrontations between Christianity and Islam in Europe. Thus, while the colonialists tolerated Islam and instrumentalized it against the indigenes, it was neither accepted as a religion on equal footing with Christianity, nor applied as a partner in the execution of developmental projects in the colony. Consequently, in view of what is today considered as collaboration of religious groups for development, colonial administration as well as colonial Christianity marginalized Islam.

Unlike Islam, which was paradoxically both ignored and instrumentalized, ATR experienced outright disdain at the hands of colonialists based on erroneous impression that it lacked a founder, possessed neither theology nor sacred books, and had no temples or any system of organization to show. Above all, it engaged in rites and practices that were considered inimical to progress. Colonial Christianity in particular demonized and judged ATR to be barbaric and a good recipe for anarchy. It was, therefore, unthinkable for colonial Christianity to admit ATR into any form of partnership, religious or secular under such circumstances.

The colonialists would eventually achieve substantial economic goals, with Christianity becoming a formidable source of 'western-type' developmental drive in the colony. Provision of emergency needs of missionaries, and social services, some of which included housing, schools, hospitals, health care, and relief services were hallmarks of this drive. For example, the history of education in Ghana traces the first basic, secondary and tertiary educational institutions to the initiative of missionaries (Agbeti, 1991; Awuah-Nyamekye 2010). Today, of the total number of colleges of education, secondary and basic schools, more than half are mission/church-based institutions. The same applies to health institutions, many of which are characteristically located in remote and inaccessible parts of the country. The colonial administration on its part saw to the building of roads, railways, civil administrative institutions and structures, furtherance of air and sea transport and international trade, which was of utmost importance to the colonizers. Yet, these successes were at the expense of the admission of ATR and, until recently, Islam, into the space of civil society as partners for development. The lines were drawn and, on this view, the roots of the invisibility of ATR and to some extent, Islam, in contemporary inter-faith networking for development in Ghana had been laid.

Embedded in this colonial history of development in Ghana are glimmers of specific meanings of development, religion and the nature of inter-religious relations, and the role of religion in development. In the case of development, it meant 'civilization,' which Ellis (2010: 27) notes, is a word designating a transfer of European technical expertise and Christian religion. In its British missionary manifestation, the civilizing mission was often coupled with an aspiration to bring Africa into the world of capitalist free trade, reflecting a contemporary view that the introduction of a monetary economy would transform society by creating markets. In Victorian times, the mission to civilize that emerged in Northern Europe in the late eighteenth century and was married to a Darwinian concept of racial science, was a direct forerunner of the modern idea of development.

As regards the meaning of religion in colonial Ghana, it is clear that its conceptual content was nothing other than Christianity brought by the missionaries from the West. This definition of religion prohibited the development of any inclusive paradigm of inter-religious relations. It implied that only Christianity had a role to play in development, leaving indigenous religions and Islam out of the enterprise.

This colonial contextual meaning of religion explains why it may fail the logic of history to imagine inter-faith networking during the period. But what was the case with development during the same period? Contrary to the idea of inter-faith networking, thinking development in colonial times may not be anachronistic, but it usually entails a certain falsification of the cultural history of Ghana. This is because sources of the academic metropole (Connell 2007) have consistently traced the beginnings of whatever can be considered as development in Africa to the arrival of colonialism, with Christianity serving as an active agent of this ideology among the indigenes (Beidelman 1982; Chidester 2014).

The first problem with this narrative is its conceptualization of development as 'civilization', essentialized as a European/Western category (Lauer and Anyidoho 2012). Thus, to be developed was to aspire towards a European/Western teleology. In this scheme, development assumed a hierarchy of cultures and is marked by the binaries of the power negotiations that justified colonialism. Opposed to this colonial imaginary of development, the period soon after independence saw African leaders reconceive development more in terms of a counter-ideology aimed at cultural and historical liberation, aiming at freedom from external control, and justice in a world-order that placed no group of people in a category above others, in a word, decolonization (Nkrumah 1964, 1966; Kaunda 1962). At this time, then, prosperity was part of development in as much as it served the attainment of dignity of culture and person as a function of total emancipation or liberation.

The second problem about the claim that development began with colonialism is that it is contrary to fact, as evinced in the descriptions of a few of the colonial anthropologists and missionaries, who painted a more positive picture of Ghana than the popular stories of the day. Rattray (1923, 1959) and Parrinder (1961), for instance, staying with indigenous Africans for some time, became familiar with the people and their world-view and thus, began to revise their notes on some of the negative impressions they had previously formed about the peoples. In his conversion from his previous impression about the African faith, Parrinder had this to say:

> It is probably true to say that African religion has been more misunderstood, and has suffered more at the hands of the early writers, than any part of African life. Unhappily old misconceptions linger with us still. (Parrinder 1974: 13)

FRAGMENTED GRID: PATTERNS OF INTER-FAITH NETWORKING IN CONTEMPORARY GHANA

The rapid development and proliferation of FBOs is traced in part to the redirection of funds for development from African governments to NGOs that began in the 1980s (Gifford 1994; Freeman 2012).This shift of donor attention also led to what has been called the "NGO-isation" of the mainline churches (Freeman 2012: 2; citing Gifford 1994: 521), referring to the setting up of offices/departments by mainline churches for rechannelling much of their religious effort to the implementation of development programmes and projects in their communities.

Today, the genre of NGOs/FBOs has sunk so deep into national religious and public culture as to suggest that in Ghana "NGOs and the discourses and practices associated with them [have become] an integral part of the post-colonial public space" (Yarrow 2011: 2). Just like the ubiquitous presence of the various churches and mosques, displaying their emblems and offering invitation to would-be members, so are NGO-insignia, offices, and oftentimes imposing means of transport that hoist their visibility in public spaces of development (Yarrow 2011). To these must be added the "prosperity gospel" approach of the vibrant African Pentecostalism. Freeman (2012: 2) states that the Pentecostal tradition asserts a developmental agenda conceived as part of the gospel message and the will of God for Africa. Yet, paradoxically, in the midst of this massive FBO presence on the development landscape, there is a trail of an intricately interconnected two level fragmentation: a) in the mode of networks, and b) the ideologies of development that characterize FBOs in Ghana. In view of their interconnectedness, these two levels of fragmentation will be discussed together in the paragraphs that follow.

It is not exactly clear which organization represents the first faith-based network for development to be registered in Ghana at the beginning of the 1980s, although some already existing NGOs of the mainline churches metamorphosed and gained vitality with access to international funding. According to Yarrow (2011, citing Nugent 2004), the 'NGO-ization' of Ghana was necessitated by the deep economic and political destabilization that spread across Africa in the 1970s, which led the World Bank to intervene with the Accelerated Development Programme, emphasizing free markets, privatization and reduction of state involvement. For this reason, the first professionally staffed national NGOs were set up with the aim of providing various kinds of 'service', including the provision of water, sanitation, health and educational facilities, to impoverished communities. Many of these organizations were founded by those who had been active in the Young Catholic Movement (Yarrow 2011: 31). The provision of such social amenities by these faith-based groups can be said to be a concrete way of helping to reduce inequality among the citizenry.

However, not all NGOs at the time were church-based or linked to any specific religious institution and though church-based development organizations are also loosely called FBOs, the latter need not be anchored within given institutional religions or confessions. In discussing the idea of fragmentation envisaged here, we use both descriptions—church-based NGOs and FBOs—interchangeably.

The pattern of FBO networking in Ghana displays a clear dominance of *intra*-faith over *inter*-faith networking. As in other parts of Africa, nearly all the faith-based organizations established in Ghana are Christian or Muslim (Weiss 2007) and are connected to the elite of society (Yarrow, 2011). Christian FBOs are associated with mission/mainline churches such as the Catholic, Presbyterian, Methodist or else with non-mainline churches such as the Independent, Charismatic or Pentecostal Christian traditions. To ensure that life in the needy communities improves a bit, some of these FBOs come together to form a common front as is the case with the Christian Health Association of Ghana (CHAG), owned by twenty-five different Christian denominations in a network of 302 facilities dedicated to the provision of health services through hospitals, clinics, and health training centres in the remotest parts of the country. The case of CHAG shows that what is loosely designated as inter-faith networks are mostly *intra*-Christian networks. Similarly, there are Islamic FBOs, which are linked to different Islamic groups "such as the Tijaniyya, the Ahlu's-Sunna [Ahl al-Sunna wa 'l-Jamaa], or the Shia" (Weiss 2007: 12). The *Ghana 2018 International Religious Freedom Report* notes that the "Muslim communities include Sunnis, Ahmadiyya, Shia, and Sufis (USCIRF 2018: 2)." The Islamic Council for Development and

Humanitarian Services (ICODEHS) and the Muslim Relief Association of Ghana (MURAG) are among the most influential Islamic NGOs in Ghana, which operate alongside other less influential and purely local ones (Weiss 2007). But here too, networking is mostly *intra*-Islamic and less oriented towards inter-faith coalitions. An important element about Islamic FBOs, which betrays the intra-religious networking in Ghana, is the fact that scholars have found that many of them developed as a reaction to the marginalization of Islam in public space (Weiss 2007).

The split in the inter-faith grid becomes more visible by realizing that beyond the pattern of intra-religious associations, there are, to the best of our knowledge, no ATR affiliated FBOs. Chiefs and other 'traditional' community leaders are invited to workshops and briefing sessions to garner their support for some specific development programmes. Such, for example, is the case when the Ministry of Gender, Children, and Social Protection (MoGCSP) or the Ministry of Culture and Religious Affairs invites chiefs, queen mothers and their council of elders to participate in stakeholder meetings. But there is no known FBO, operating in affiliation with some acclaimed group of ATR, the *Antoa* shrine, for instance, or on behalf of traditional leaders such as chiefs, who serve as the fulcrum of Traditional Religion in their communities. Sometimes, dictated by the need to gain entry into the communities and to manage the success of their projects through good human relations and diplomacy, Christian and/or Islamic FBOs have found it strategically expedient to collaborate with traditional leaders. Otherwise Traditional Religion remains invisible on the FBO landscape in Ghana.

FBOs in Ghana depend on massive foreign donor support (Kumi 2019). Christian FBOs are supported by big European Church-based organizations, agencies of the United Nations, or of the World Bank, and governments of the developed nations such as USAID. Islamic FBOs on their part receive funding from Islamic states such as Saudi Arabia or individual Islamic philanthropists. The result is that many FBOs are competing for support from the same foreign sources. Factorial determinants of who gets how much funding, and to what purposes also ultimately develop a situation of privileged FBOs, which are more socially and politically influential, as against the less privileged and uninfluential ones. Haynes (2013) found a similar situation of privilege and disparity in his study of FBOs at the United Nations (UN). This situation is intensified today in the face of the challenges regarding FBO sustainability due to the changes in donor policies that have led to a gross reduction of funds since Ghana became a lower middle-income country (Arhin et al. 2018).

External funding may not affect the theology of FBOs, but it does certainly influence their philosophy of development, since he who pays the piper calls the tune. Arhin et al. (2018: 351) have explained this phenomenon using the resource dependency theory proposed by Pfeffer and Salancik (2003). According to Arhin et al., the theory helps to understand how power is exerted by actors who control resources. Regarding NGOs resource dependency results in a "supply-led" relationship in which "donors set the goals of programmes because of NGOs' high dependence for funding" (Arhin et al., 351, citing Abou Assi 2013). The result of this relationship, in the view of Arhin et al., is that NGOs pay more allegiance to their donors than the communities they purport to serve, and their sustainability is threatened in the event of changes in donor policies.

There is an additional concern, which Arhin et al. do not mention directly. It is the case that, in as much as FBOs in Ghana depend on donor funding, they are split between liberal and neo-liberal western technological ideologies of development and the more conservative social and religion-oriented imaginaries of development (Ellis 2010). This aggravates the fragmentation of inter-faith networking, since international Islamic donor agencies are less likely to support Christian FBOs and vice versa, and since both religions are less likely to bring ATR on board with their funds in projects that would otherwise have benefited from and at the same time transformed development inimical elements of the traditional religions. This fragmentation in our view, poses a threat to SDG 10 which aims at reducing inequality globally. It is in close association with this concern that we read the findings of Heaton et al. (2009) that inter-religious disparities in FBO networking and funding tend to manifest parallel disparate political and economic results of FBO interventions in the communities. In their own words:

> Religious differences in socioeconomic outcomes are substantial in Ghana. Mainline Protestants have a significant advantage in education and wealth. Catholics and other Christians have intermediate values on these socioeconomic outcomes. Muslims and those without attachment to formal religious groups have a significant disadvantage. Educational differences are particularly important because they account for some of the differences in wealth; the fact that education differences are evident in rates of school enrolment

signals the likelihood that inequality will persist in the next generation. (Heaton et al. 2009: 83)

Heaton, James, and Oheneba-Sakyi were not writing directly in connection with FBOs. But the differences in religious affiliation and their socioeconomic as well as political implications were designed already in colonial times and the cracks that formed then have carried through the history of development till date. It is worth noting that the element of education, which Heaton et al. single out among others as a reason for the significant socioeconomic differences between the various religious groups is also one of the major areas of FBO interventions till now. As such, the findings of Heaton and others can be interpreted to reveal post-colonial fragments of colonial processes of religious marginalization.

During colonial times, children and youth who did not commit to the call of Christianity could not participate in the educational activities of the missionaries. The so-called heathens could not mix with prospective Christians. The findings of Heaton et al show that this trend has not been broken and that it has great potential of being continued into the next generation. They successfully mapped "current educational behaviour and future prospects of religious differences" by examining enrolment of children of school going age. Their examination found that differences in "enrolment rates by age" indicate that inequalities evident among adults are being reproduced in the next generation. Enrolment rates are highest for Mainline Protestants. Catholics and other Christian groups are not far behind. Muslims have substantially lower rates of enrolment, and the traditional/none group has by far the lowest enrolment (Heaton et al. 2009: 83).

What we are seeing, therefore, is that the fragmentation in inter-faith networking is not just a matter of the effectiveness of FBOs in the development environment of Ghana. It is inadvertently also a question about social, economic and political inclusion and the fact that certain forms of religious differentiation, which are repeated in FBO relations, run the risk of denying some sections of the population their legitimate share in development on the basis of their religious affiliation.

In addition, by excluding ATR from FBO interventions in Ghana, the traditional worldview on which contemporary African Christianity is built (Kiunguyu 2017) tends not only to be marginalized, but it is also problematized as anti-Christian and, therefore, anti-development (Freeman 2012). It is difficult not to notice the colonial overtones of this epistemology of religion, which makes the traditional worldview and culture the reason for Africa's lack of modernity. In one sense, this view provides the basis for understanding the ambivalent role of FBOs in development pertaining to the context of Ghana. First, they stand the risk of contributing to setting the parameters of who gets excluded from the national cake. Second, they also run the risk of offsetting the contextual idea of development as social progress towards total emancipation, which the fathers and mothers of the nation envisaged at independence. Thus, by building on the colonial tradition of the marginalization of Traditional Religion, FBOs in post-colonial Ghana have pursued a technocratic development narrowly focused on material and economic improvement. But they have at the same time contributed to a less liberative trajectory of development. On this point, Ellis appropriately observes that religion continues to play an important role in development in Africa because for Africans "material factors" are only part of their attempts "to bring all the forces that shape their lives under control" (2010: 25). This also corroborates Mbiti and Burleson's argument that

> 'Africans come out of African Religion but they don't take off their traditional religiosity. They come as they are. They come as people whose world view is shaped according to African Religion'. (Mbiti and Burleson 1986: 12, cited in Gathogo 2007: 251)

This is similar to Aylward Shorter's contention that the African Christian does away with remarkably little of his former non-Christian outlook (Shorter 1975: 7 cited in Gathogo 2007: 249).

MENDING THE GRID: EXPLORING INTEGRATIVE INTER-FAITH NETWORKING IN GHANA

The facts of history will not allow a total denial of the role of FBOs in development in Ghana. Neither is it possible to dismiss the successes of their initiative and some attempts in recent time for real inter-religious networking and dialogue for the pursuit of common goals in development. At the same time, the facts of history compel the critical eye to see the cracks that are hampering the desired success of inter-faith networking in development initiatives. Hence the review we have conducted in this chapter is in no way an attempt to gloss over the successes that have been attained in development. However, in studying religion, one of our tasks

13 COLONIAL MARGINALITIES AND POST-COLONIAL FRAGMENTS...   245

is a rigorous re-reading of the experiences of religion and development so as to discover overlooked presuppositions on which inter-faith networks are premised. We have, thus, been concerned in this study to extrapolate a general notion on which the basic blocks of the knowledge that seems to be driving the work of FBOs, particularly their networks for development, are based. FBO networking is more *intra-* than *inter-*religious, leading to inter-religious fragmentation.

Since the fragmentation of inter-faith networking tends to be counter-productive, some steps need to be taken to mend the cracks in the grid. To begin with, it is important for FBOs to be interested in researching into and understanding the cultural and political history underlying the developmental environment in Ghana. What we mean by this is that the interface between religion and development in Ghana is a phenomenal space in which the attempt to apply religion in development makes FBOs participants in structures of power negotiations in Africa. Inter-faith networking can improve by making the understanding of this contested phenomenal space part of the development interventions of FBOs.

We can illustrate the importance of the need for mending the FBO-grid by understanding the contested space of Ghana's development history with the following example. It is generally held, on the one hand, that the elements that drive development in 'traditional' Africa include a strong religious worldview, the institution of chieftaincy, the wisdom of the elders of a society, extended family and kinship ties in a communitarian net, and the institution of taboos (Awuah-Nyamekye 2012). On the other hand, it is argued that these same religio-cultural values retard progress in Africa, causing anachronism, supernaturalism and excessive dependency (Wiredu 1986; Assimeng 1989). Freeman (2012) has pushed this claim much further in his theory of "a Pentecostal ethic." He argues that the success of African Pentecostalism in ushering new patterns of behaviour that are commensurate with neoliberal capitalism in African economies today must be traced in part to Pentecostalism's rejection of traditional religious values and practices. He notes that the "Pentecostal ethic" makes it possible to build up capital, since:

> For many Africans one of the main barriers to accumulating wealth is the pressure to participate in traditional practices, such as rites of passage or rituals of commensality, and the constant demands for financial support from poorer kin. Redistribution, in one form or another, is inherent in most traditional African religions and moral systems, and it makes personal

accumulation virtually impossible. By linking these traditional practices with the devil, … Pentecostalism makes avoidance of them, and separation from more distant kin, intensely and aggressively moral, and thus enables the emergence of previously impossible behaviours. (Freeman 2012: 21)

We have here a situation of double binding, aggravated by a colonial history which anchors preselected attitudes in the religion and development nexus. FBOs seeking inter-faith networking for development in Ghana, thus, need to deal with important questions of ideology to help them integrate Traditional Religion and Islam in their efforts at collaboration for development. The questions that spontaneously meet the eye upon considering Freeman's excerpt, for example, include the following: Is a neoliberal capitalist economy the standard for development and the preferred future for most Africans? To what extent are the neoliberal values of individualism, accumulation of capital to the detriment of kin relations and demonization of participation in traditional community celebrations to be preferred to other developmental alternatives? Granted that neoliberal capitalism is the most beneficial alternative, what cost must African communities pay to attain such an economy? Finally, are traditional religious values factorially more obstructive to neoliberal capitalist development in Africa than international political and economic power structures that hold sway in African countries?

Another way to mend the grid involves devising strategies through which Christian and Islamic FBOs can meet ATR on dialogical terms. Through such dialogue, those elements of Traditional Religion, which are indeed outmoded, and which do not support holistic development can be subjected to criticism and challenged to move towards transformation through the internal dynamics of the religion. For example, improving quantity and quality of education using the agency of traditional religion can function as a catalyst of change for ATR without it being demonized, humiliated and marginalized.

An interesting feature about this demonization by Christians, which we term as a paradox, is that empirical evidence abounds to support the fact that these same Christians return to their roots (indigenous religious rituals) when they fall into deep crises. The observations by Mbiti and Burleson (1986) and Shorter (1975) attest to this fact.

The neglect of African indigenous religions was one of the reasons why the late Osofo Komfoo Damoa, a former Catholic priest, decided to represent indigenous African religion at a conference of religious leaders in

Moscow (in 1981) where he noticed that almost everybody was Muslim, Hindu, Buddhist, or Christian but no one represented African Traditional Religion. A decision, which he actualized by forming the Afrikania Mission, a new religious movement in African indigenous religion in Ghana in 1985.

It is important to note that one of the key recommendations of the Consultative meeting which designed the "Plan of Action for Religious Leaders from Africa to Prevent Incitement to Violence that could lead to Atrocity Crimes" was that "Religious leaders and actors should promote the fundamental value of accepting others as they are, whatever their beliefs, without insisting that others should change their beliefs" (UN Consultative Meeting of Religious Leaders, 2017, p. 3). But it is instructive to note that this recommendation is yet to become effective as indigenous religion in Africa still suffers discrimination from other faiths in Africa.

In the view of Elizabeth Amoah (1998), the indigenous African religious heritage, with its age-long plurality, offers useful insights into the search for a viable inter-faith paradigm, which in our view takes into serious consideration the reality of pluralism in our world today. This, of course, is not the same as saying that all persons have a positive attitude to the indigenous African religions. What this simply means is that African indigenous religion cannot be done away with in any meaningful inter-faith dialogue in Ghana, and for that matter, in Africa.

Conclusion

In this chapter, we briefly traced the trajectory of the nexus between religion and development focusing on the Ghanaian context. We also pointed out the ambivalent nature of this exercise. That is, there is the potential of religion enhancing development, as well as its capacity, from time to time, also to impede development. We further emphasized the much-needed collaborative energy through which the goal of development, particularly, SDG 10 can be achieved. In doing so, we traced the ambivalent results of FBOs to patterns of inter-faith dynamics from the colonial period to the present. Evaluating interfaith networking in Ghana, we found that its contribution to national development agenda has been limited as a result of the marginalization of the host religion—African Traditional Religion.

We also found out that the marginalization of the host religion is paradoxical, given the tolerant and accommodating nature of African

Traditional Religion, which allows it to make a contribution in the search for more inclusive paradigms of inter-faith networks. Besides, Traditional Religion still plays a critical role in the lives of many Ghanaians despite the major inroads that Christianity and Islam have made in Ghana. What this means is that for any meaningful inter-faith network towards development to yield the desired benefits in Ghana, the goal should be inclusivity.

REFERENCES

Abou Assi, K. 2013. Hands in the pockets of mercurial donors: NGO response to shifting funding priorities. *Nonprofit and Voluntary Sector Quarterly* 42(3): 584–602.

Agbeti, J. K. 1987. *West African church history I: Christian missions and church foundations 1482–1919.* Leiden: Brill.

Agbeti J. K. 1991. *West African church history II: Christian missions and theological training 1842–1970.* Leiden: Brill.

Amoah, E. 1998. International Interfaith Centre: Annual Lecture, 1998. Available at: Microsoft Word – International Interfaith Centre Annual Lecture 1998 (issuelab.org).

Appiah, S. K. 2018. Stolberg's Typology of religio-scientific frameworks and science and religion education in Ghana. *Oguaa Journal of Religion and Human Values* 4, 54–70.

Appiah, S. K. and Kodah, K. 2020. I think therefore I am: linking human exploitation to religious irrationality in Kourouma's *Allah Is Not obliged. Religious Studies and Theology* 39 (1): 91–105.

Arhin, A. A., Kumi, E. and Adam, M. S. 2018. Facing the Bullet? Non-Governmental Organisations' (NGOs') Responses to the Changing Aid Landscape in Ghana. *Voluntas* 29, 348–360. Retrieved from: https://doi.org/10.1007/s11266-018-9966-1.

Assimeng, M. 1989. *Religion and social change in West Africa.* Accra: University Press.

Awuah-Nyamekye, S. 2010. Religious education in a democratic state: The case of Ghana. A paper presented at the international conference on religious education in a democratic state, held from 6–8 June at Bar-Ilan University, Faculty of Law. Jeanne & Morris Benin Law Annex Hall 200, Ramat-Gan, Israel.

Awuah-Nyamekye, S. 2012. Religion and development: African Traditional Religion's Perspective. *Religious Studies and Theology* 31(1): 75–90. DOI:https://doi.org/10.1558/rsth.v31i1.75.

Awuah-Nyamekye, S. 2020. The interplay between religion and development in Ghana. In Ezra Chitando, Lovemore Togarasei and Masiiwa. R. Gunda (Eds.), *Religion and development in Africa.* Bamberg: University of Bamberg Press.

Barro, J. R. and McCleary, M. R. 2006. Religion and economy. *Journal of Economic Perspectives* 20(2): 49–72.

13 COLONIAL MARGINALITIES AND POST-COLONIAL FRAGMENTS... 249

Beidelman, T. O. 1982. *Colonial Evangelism: A Socio-Historical Study of an East African Mission at the Grassroots*. Bloomington: Indiana University Press.

Chidester, David. 2014. *Empire of Religion: Imperialism and Comparative Religion*. Chicago: University of Chicago Press.

Clarke, G., & Jennings, M. 2008. *Development, Civil Society and Faith-Based Organizations: Bridging the Sacred and the Secular*. Basingstoke, UK: Palgrave Macmillan.

Connell, Raewyn. 2007. *Southern Theory: The Global Dynamics of Knowledge in Social Science*. Sydney: Allen & Unwin.

Deneulin, S. and Bano, M. 2009. *Religion and development: Re-writing the secular script*. London: Zed Books.

Deneulin, S. and Rakodi, C. 2011. Revisiting religion: Development studies thirty years on. *World Development* 39(1): 45–54.

Ellis, S. 2010. Development and invisible worlds. In B. Bompani, & M. Frahm-Arp (Eds.). *Development and politics from below: Exploring religious spaces in the African State*. New York: Palgrave Macmillan, 23–39.

Freeman, D. 2012. *Pentecostalism and Development: Churches, NGOs and Social Change in Africa*. Basingstoke: Palgrave Macmillan.

Gathogo, J. M. 2009. The Reason for studying African religion in post-colonial Africa. *Currents in Theology and Mission* 36(2): 108–117.

Gifford, P. 1994. Some recent developments in African Christianity. *African Affairs* 93(373): 513–534.

Haynes, J. 2007. *Religion and Development: Conflict or Cooperation?* Basingstoke and New York: Palgrave Macmillan.

Haynes, J. 2013. Faith-based Organizations at the United Nations. EUI Working Paper RSCAS 2013/70. Italy, San Domenico di Fiesole (FI): European University Institute. Available at: https://cadmus.eui.eu/bitstream/handle/1814/28119/RSCAS_2013_70.pdf?sequence=1&isAllowed=y.

Heaton, T., James, S. and Oheneba-Sakyi, Y. 2009. Religion and Socioeconomic Attainment in Ghana. *Review of Religious Research* 51(1): 71–86.

Hiskett, M. 1984. *The development of Islam in West Africa*. London: Longman. https://www.un.org/en/genocideprevention/documents/Plan%20of%20Action%20Advanced%20Copy.pdf.

Kaunda, K. 1962. *Zambia shall be free*. London: Heinemann Books.

Kiunguyu, Kylie 2017. The relevance of indigenous religions in the 21st [Online material] Retrieved from https://thisisafrica.me/african-identities/relevance-african-indigenous-religions-21st-century/.

Kumi, E. 2019. Advancing the sustainable development goals: an analysis of the potential role of philanthropy in Ghana. *Journal of Asian and African Studies* 54(7), 1084–1104.

Larbi, E. K. 2002. The nature of continuity and discontinuity of Ghanaian Pentecostal concept of salvation in African cosmology. *Asian Journal of Pentecostal Studies* 3(1), 87–106

Lauer, H. and Anyidoho, K. 2012. *Reclaiming the human sciences and humanities through African perspectives* (Vol. 1). Accra: Sub-Saharan Publishers

Leys, C. 1996. *The Rise and Fall of Development Theory*, London: James Currey.

Mbiti, J.S. and Burleson, B. W. 1986. *The dialogue of an African theologian with African religion.* Ann Arbor, Michigan: University Microfilms International.

Mudimbe, V. Y. 1988. *The Invention of Africa: Gnosis, Philosophy, and the Order of Knowledge.* Bloomington & Indianapolis: Indiana University Press.

Ndekha, L. W. 2015. Ambivalence in Interreligious Relations in Malawi: Is an African Model of Interreligious Relations Possible? *Journal of theology for Southern Africa* 152: 114–130.

Nkrumah, K. 1964. *Consciencism: Philosophy and the ideology for decolonization with particular reference to the African revolution.* London: Heinemann.

Nkrumah, K. 1966. *Neo-colonialism: The last stage of imperialism.* London: Thomas Nelson.

Nugent, P. 2004. *Africa since Independence.* Basingstoke and New York: Palgrave.

Parrinder, G. 1961. *West African religion: a study of the beliefs and practices of Akan, Ewe, Yoruba, Ibo, and kindred peoples.* Epworth Press.

Parrinder, E.G. 1974. *African Traditional Religion, third Edition.* London: Sheldon Press; 3rd edition.

p'Bitek, O. 1971. *Song of a Prisoner.* New York: Third Press.

Pfeffer, J., & Salancik, G. 2003. *The external control of organizations: A resource dependence perspective.* Stanford, CA: Stanford Business Books.

Platvoet, Jan and Van Rinsum, H. 2003. Is Africa Incurably Religious? Confessing and Contesting an Invention. *Exchange* 32(2): 123–153.

Rattray, R. S. 1923. *Religion and art in Ashanti.* London: Oxford University Press.

Rattray, R. S. 1959. *Ashanti.* London: Oxford University Press.

Reuben, R. 2011. Can religion contribute to development? The road from truth to trust. *Exchange* 40(3), 225–234.

Rist, G. 2002. *The History of Development: From Western Origins to Global Faith.* London and New York: Zed Books.

Shorter, A. 1975. *African Christian theology.* London: Geoffrey Chapmans.

UNDP 2014. *UNDP Guidelines on Engagement with Faith-based Organizations and Religious Leaders.* New York: United Nations Development Program. https://www.undp.org

UNFPA. 2009. Guidelines for engaging Faith-Based Organizations as agents of change. Available at: Microsoft Word – GUIDELINES for FBO Engagement +PM – FINAL CLEAN-2 w LOGO AZZA final final 17 Sep 2009 (unfpa.org).

United Nations Office for Genocide Prevention and Responsibility to Protect. 2017. Plan of Action for Religious Leaders from Africa to Prevent Incitement to Violence that could lead to Atrocity Crimes.

U.S. Commission on Intenational Religious Freedom. 2018. Washington DC: USCIRF. https://www.uscirf.gov/sites/default/files/2018USCIRFAR.pdf

Weiss, H. 2005. Variations in the colonial representation of Islam and Muslims in Northern Ghana, Ca. 1900–1930. *Journal of Muslim Minority Affairs* 25(1): 73–95.

Weiss, H. 2007. The expansion of Muslim NGOs in Ghana. *ISIM Review* 20: 12–13.

Wilks, I. 1989. *Wa and the Wala: Islam and polity in Northwestern Ghana.* Cambridge: Cambridge University Press.

Wiredu, K. (1986). The Question of Violence in Contemporary African Political Thought. *Praxis International*, 6(3): 373–381.

Yarrow, T. (2011). *Development beyond politics: aid, activism and NGOs in Ghana.* New York: Springer.

PART IV

Diverse Themes in Interfaith Networks and Development

CHAPTER 14

Education and Interfaith Development in Northern Nigeria

Ezekiel Abdullahi Babagario

INTRODUCTION

While Nigerian diversity reflects her rich cultural heritage, the people and the various groups that make up the country have coexisted peacefully with one another until the beginning of the twenty-first century when the country started experiencing inter-ethnic and inter-religious conflicts. Apart from the recent activities of the Boko Haram terrorist group, the Nigerian nation recorded a tremendous number of inter-religious (Muslim and Christians) killings in the northern region of the country. Inter-ethnic and inter-religious conflicts have led to the loss of lives and property (Voll 2015). The trend of Muslim-Christian conflicts resulted in polarization, segregation, clashes and wanton destruction in different cities located in the northern part of Nigeria. The activities of the militants such as Boko Haram and some other clashes mentioned here have caused the

E. A. Babagario (✉)
International Center for Interfaith, Peace and Harmony (ICIPH),
Kaduna, Nigeria
e-mail: ebabagario@umass.edu

© The Author(s), under exclusive license to Springer Nature
Switzerland AG 2022
E. Chitando, I. S. Gusha (eds.), *Interfaith Networks and Development*, Sustainable Development Goals Series,
https://doi.org/10.1007/978-3-030-89807-6_14

255

displacement of over three million people, which also created an untold number of displaced persons and Internally Displaced Persons Camps. Thousands of people have been killed as a result of the insurgency, while young girls and women have been abducted and young people were forcefully conscripted. Women and men have been widowed and numerous villages disorganized, leaving a lot of people traumatized (Agbiboa 2014; Torgovnik 2020).

Over the past twenty years (2000–2020), insurgency and communal conflicts have been on the rise in Nigeria. The uprising also affected the education sector which also contributed to the high number of children out-of-school. According to the United Nations Children's Fund (hereinafter referred to as UNICEF) (2018), Nigeria accounts for the highest number of children out of school. Also, the country has a high rate of illiterate youth who are unemployed. Most of the times, youths serve as combatants and foot soldiers for some corrupt politicians and religious leaders who used them during conflicts. In Nigeria, most conflicts often turn into interreligious conflict, whatever the initial cause of the conflict might be. Sometimes rumours which are often not true spread into the community about an attack, but because such rumours had a religious connotation, some people react to it violently. In the end, the result is always conflict which often claims lives and destroys the economic fabric of the community. Religious indoctrination has been on the rise in various places of worship. Youth are often radicalized in turn they take up arms in defence of their faith. This had led to rivalry between Christians and Muslims in parts of northern Nigeria. The incessant interfaith and interethnic conflicts in northern Nigeria showed a clear contrast to my early childhood years in Anglo-Jos, north-central Nigeria.

Growing up in Anglo-Jos North Central Nigeria, my friends and I knew nothing about the differences between the two major faith traditions (Christianity and Islam). We visited each other's place of worship and celebrated each other's religious festivals. Most times we attended the Makarantar Allo (Islamic informal Quranic Schools), while our friends joined us during the Boys Brigade weekly Bible study. Our parents never raised any objection to these practices. One striking aspect of my childhood years is that when we committed an offence at home and our mothers wanted us punished, they took us to the Islamic teacher in the neighbourhood for some strokes of cane. Though an Islamic teacher, he often recited a popular verse credited to King Solomon in the Bible in Proverbs 13:24 "Whoever spares the rod hates their children, but the one who loves their children is careful to discipline them." (New International Version). I grew up to respect this Islamic scholar whom we called the "neighbourhood disciplinarian" without noticing that he was a teacher/ scholar of a faith different from mine.

However, after my university education in the early 1990s, the cordial relationship among our parents declined. We had new religious scholars in the community, both Christians and Muslims, who brought new ideologies which divided the people. Religious differences became noticeable in the community as a result of radicalization by some religious leaders. I came to realize that such division was experienced in other parts of northern Nigeria. Such division pitted the people against one another. In no time, most parts of northern Nigeria started to experience interfaith conflicts. The communal relationship between adherents of the two major religions (Christianity and Islam) declined over minor ideological differences. At the time of writing, in some communities, children grow up without a cordial relationship among themselves because their parents discourage such a relationship, based on religious differences. Settlement in most towns is now based on religious affiliation; most people build or rent houses in areas where their religion is in the majority. Adherents of the two faiths often engage in conflict at the slightest provocation. The emergence of foreign religious leaders in the country contributed to the propensity of the conflict among the people. The people who were once united turned against each other in the name of fighting for God (see Adogame et al. 2020).

However, such intractable conflicts could be overcome through dialogue among the people. Intergroup Dialogue may promote frequent contact among the perpetrators of the conflicts and encourage positive communications. Allport (1954) proposed the theory of intergroup contact to promote respect for people who spent time together. According to the theory, when people from opposing camps interacted positively and frequently over time, it helps reduce tension and conflict (Pettigrew and Tropp 2006; Dixon et al. 2010). To encourage such peaceful coexistence, foreign and local interfaith networks in northern Nigeria contributed immensely in achieving such purpose. In this chapter, I will highlight the activities, achievements and contribution of the International Center for Interfaith, Peace and Harmony (hereinafter referred to as ICIPH) one of the many interfaith networks in northern Nigeria. In doing this, the ICIPH has been laying a solid foundation for the achievement of the SDGs in northern Nigeria.

Brief Historical Background of the ICIPH

Hans Kung (1991: 130) once said, "There will be no peace among the nations without peace among the religions, and there will be no peace among the religions without dialogue among religions." Kung, a great advocate of interfaith understanding, emphasized the need for dialogue among the various religions of the world. Research has shown that in the last forty years, religion has contributed to the rise in conflict more than any other cause (Fox 2014). Lately, interfaith dialogue has become an integral part of Nigeria's social life as a result of the incessant religious conflict in the northern region (Smock 2006). Youth between the ages 12–18 often perpetuate the conflict since most of them are out of school. The high level of illiteracy and poverty among parents tends to be the greatest contributing factor as to why they cannot send their children to school. Instead, most parents allowed these children to attend Quranic schools where they are often indoctrinated. Some politicians and religious clerics have not helped matters; the politicians connive with religious leaders of their faith to incite their followers against their opponents (Usman 1987; Ekanem and Ekefre 2013). Religious conflicts are only visible in the northern region; there are no such tensions in the southern region, which may be a result of the high level of literacy in that region (Ushe 2015; Jegede 2019).

To help foster and promote peaceful coexistence among adherents of the two religions in Nigeria, the government of the then President Olusegun Obasanjo (1999–2003) inaugurated the Nigerian Interreligious Council (hereinafter referred to as NIREC). The mission of this council is to promote peaceful coexistence among the people (Ezegbobelu 2009). Before the emergence of NIREC, there were some interfaith organizations in the country, although little was known about these organizations. However, over the past twenty years, interfaith organizations sprang in parts of northern Nigeria as a result of the incessant conflicts. Some of the interfaith organizations are foreign, while others are local. These interfaith organizations have contributed to peacebuilding efforts in conflict zones. The majority of interfaith organizations in the country were either founded by individuals or by foreign organizations. Of the many interfaith organizations in Nigeria, one stood out as unique because of its organizational structure and the collaboration that facilitated its establishment. The interfaith organization networked with other organizations, both foreign and local, to promote its objectives. The organization was established in partnership with the World Council of Churches (hereinafter referred to as WCC), Royal Jordanian Aal Al-Bayt Institute of Islamic Thought (hereinafter referred to as RABIIT), Jamaátul Nasril Islam (hereinafter referred to as JNI) and Christian Council of Nigeria (hereinafter referred to as CCN). This collaboration gave birth to the ICIPH. This interfaith network contributed to the improvement of peaceful coexistence through networking with some Faith-based Organizations (hereinafter referred to as FBOs).

In line with the many recommendations by the consultants, RABIIT and the WCC in partnership with JNI and CCN decided to establish such an interfaith organization in Nigeria. The vision of the organization is to see that "Nigeria becomes a model of interreligious peace and harmony, where people embrace religious diversity as a strength and work together with mutual understanding, kindness, compassion and respect for the sanctity of life and human dignity, towards the advancement of peace, justice and sustainable development" (ICIPH Newsletter 2017). To achieve this set vision, according to ICIPH, the organization set out on a mission to serve as a platform for the promotion of reconciliation, healing and peaceful coexistence among Nigerians through; fostering meaningful interreligious partnership for harmony; education and sensitization on peaceful co-existence; and sharing of information on interfaith issues, stories of victims of conflicts and examples of good interfaith relations and initiatives (ICIPH Newsletter 2017).

The emergence of ICIPH in northern Nigeria contributed to interfaith dialogue efforts in the region. The networking between ICIPH and some organizations in northern Nigeria contributed to the improved relationships among the people tremendously. ICIPH utilized the availability of some faith-based organizations affiliated with JNI and CCN to introduce sensitization programs in the communities. According to Biodun (2020), ICIPH collaborates with JNI and the Supreme Council of Islamic Affairs (hereinafter referred to as SCIA) with the support of His Eminence, Sultan Abubakar Saad III who doubled as the President of JNI and Amir al-Mu'minin (Commander of the faithful's) on many occasions. Leaders of various sects under the JNI serve as contact persons for the implementation of various programs centred on peace and interfaith dialogue. Unlike CCN, JNI has no established faith-based organizations under its leadership which are directly involved in peacebuilding and interfaith dialogue. However, it has some Islamic scholars who partner with ICIPH to achieve the goal of the centre. On the other hand, CCN has institutions which are involved in peacebuilding and interfaith advocacy in the country. One of such organizations is the Institute of Church and Society (hereinafter referred to as ICS) located in Jos north-central Nigeria as a partner in the peacebuilding effort. Further, the ICS serves as the trauma healing centre for the CCN.

The ICS Jos is an ecumenical Christian organization owned and operated by the CCN and this is the oldest protestant ecumenical organization in Nigeria according to the Director of the institute (Ephraim Simon 2020). The institute is set up to provide an avenue for the Church to relate closely with the society outside of the church environment. The ICS Jos is one of CCN's three institutes which was set up in 1987 to cover the northern part of Nigeria. The ICS in Jos north-central Nigeria covers the 19 states in the Northern part of Nigeria. In tandem with the mission and vision of CCN, the organization provides trauma therapy training and counselling to victims of conflict in northern Nigeria. ICIPH benefitted tremendously from the main programme provided by ICS Jos which is trauma therapy training and counselling to victims of conflicts in northern Nigeria. ICIPH partnered with other organizations as well to promote peacebuilding, trauma healing and education, thereby encouraging development in the region. I shall return to the ICS Jos further below when discussing the achievements of the ICIPH.

ACTIVITIES AND ACHIEVEMENTS OF ICIPH NETWORK IN PEACEBUILDING

Many activities at ICIPH are focused on interreligious enlightenment and understanding, where the followers of the two dominant faiths (Christianity and Islam) meet to discuss and ask questions and arrive at a mutual understanding about each other's beliefs and practices. This is done to dispel stereotyping, mitigate violence, create understanding and enable co-operation and peaceful co-existence despite religious differences. Regardless of the different views about the concept of interfaith and its practice in Nigeria, interfaith activities at ICIPH are carried out to bring about an understanding of religious teachings among followers of the two major faiths.

This provides the best means of reducing tension and minimizing conflicts usually associated with ignorance or misunderstanding of issues connected with one another's religion. Achieving peace in Nigeria is the primary goal of ICIPH. Consequently, its interfaith activities are conducted with utmost sincerity. The centre does not in any way attempt to brush aside differences or push them under the carpet, instead, it rigorously pursues them with responsibility and understanding. From time to time, religious scholars from the two dominant religions are invited to explain doctrinal principles and the position of religious texts concerning peaceful-coexistence in multi-religious communities. These platforms are not created as places for arguments or attacking each other's faith, rather it is facilitated to uphold honesty which is critical to the success of any peace program. During these activities, the real sources of tension such as cultural, social, economic and political differences are highlighted, discussed and dealt with.

Since the emergence of ICIPH, the organization partnered with other interfaith organizations to promote community mobilization for development; advocacy for justice, equity and peace; networking for shared values; a collection of credible data and information; capacity building particularly for youth and women; education for development; use of electronic and print media (ICIPH Newsletter 2017). From inception, ICIPH has goals of promoting peacebuilding and development in northern Nigeria. It seeks to achieve this goal is through education, women empowerment and youth ambassadors training programmes. To this end, the organization designed programmes that have a direct bearing on the people which is centred on education among many others.

According to the former Emir of Kano, His Highness Sanusi Lamido Sanusi, who is also an economist, "Education holds the key to our development. We must continue to give priority attention to the sector because it is the bedrock of any development" (Sanusi II 2017). Since education is the key to national development, priority should be given to the sector to drive development. Lately, northern Nigeria suffered significant economic setbacks as a result of incessant conflicts in the region. It was not surprising that the rate of poverty in northern Nigeria is higher than other regions of the country (World Bank and Bretton Wood Institution 2016). This is because of the high rate of illiteracy in the region as a result of the conflict. UNICEF estimated that there are about 10.5 million children out of school in Nigeria, with the majority from northern Nigeria (UNICEF 2019). These children are either carried out at a young age to older spouses or the boys among them are sent to religious scholars at an informal Quranic school far from their parents. This system of a religious school, called the Almajiri Quranic Schools, does not equip the children with any developmental skills for future use. In some cases, the schools result in indoctrinating/radicalizing the children, thereby opening the avenue of division between these children and people who belong to a different religion from theirs. The lack of basic skills such as literacy and numeracy in the Qur'anic education curriculum prompted UNICEF to consider children attending such schools to be officially out-of-school (Umaru 2013).

Another avenue where children tend to become unproductive to society is through addiction to hard drugs. According to the National Drugs Law Enforcement Agency (hereinafter referred to as NDLEA), use of hard drugs has been on the increase among out-of-school children in northern Nigeria. In most cases, such children turned out to be strategic to the perpetrators of conflicts in the region. ICIPH engaged relevant authorities and some FBOs in the sensitization process by enlightening parents on the dangers of the lack of school enrolment of their children. Through the records available at the centre, ICIPH embarked on visitation to conflict areas for on the spot assessment where the conflict is prevalent. Also, the organization prioritized visitation to Internally Displaced Persons (hereinafter referred to as IDP) camps to understand how the education of children in such camps is organized. This is because ICIPH believed education is the bedrock of development and panacea for peacebuilding.

Realizing the importance of education to national development, ICIPH in collaboration with other organizations embarked on sensitization programmes to IDP camps in conflict areas to assess the level of education in those camps. On discovery that education is given little or no attention in some of the camps, the organization kick started a campaign to draw the attention of the government to the neglect of the education of children in these camps. ICIPH believed education is the bedrock of development, according to the Advocacy and Communication Project Officer of the organization. The dilapidated nature of classes in some of the IDP camps prompted the organization to embark on an advocacy programme drawing the attention of other NGOs on the plight of these children. ICIPH pointed out that to protect the future of the camp children, the children must be provided with structures for conducting classes as against having lessons under trees. Also, volunteer teachers should have a weekend training to be abreast with the requirements of the job. Stipends should be paid to the volunteer teachers and instructional materials be provided for the schools. To encourage these children to advance their education beyond elementary school, ICIPH embarked on a campaign to draw the attention of the Local Government Education Authority (hereinafter referred to as LGEA) to register all schools in IDP camps with the necessary examination/testing bodies. This is to enable the students to write the advanced examination for placement in secondary schools.

On youth and women empowerment, ICIPH designed programmes which would help youth and women to be self-reliant. In most IDP camps where the organization visited, there was an emphasis on the need to empower the women, especially widows through skill acquisition. In partnership with organizations such as the Social Justice and Human Development; Youth Education and Development and Damietta Peace Initiatives, ICIPH introduced skill acquisition workshops for participants in the north-central and north-east region of the country. The workshop had participants from some IDP camps in the area and communities as well. The majority of the participants were either out of school or are unemployed. According to ICIPH Communication and Advocacy Project Officer, such collaboration helped to foster cordial relationship among the people who experienced hardship as a result of conflicts in their communities. Another partnership effort worth mentioning here is the peacebuilding trauma healing centre in Jos operated by ICS which partnered with ICIPH to counsel victims of conflicts in northern Nigeria.

THE PEACEBUILDING AND TRAUMA HEALING CENTRE AT ICS

In its effort to contribute to the peace and development of Nigeria, the CCN developed a concept on ways to partner with the government and other agencies on peacebuilding through trauma counselling and healing. The peacebuilding and trauma healing project seeks to contribute to peacebuilding efforts and sustaining of communities in northern Nigeria through interaction with victims/survivors of conflicts. The overall goal is to ensure peace is sustained in communities across northern Nigeria. Through this project, churches under the CCN worked hand-in-hand with other faith groups and community leaders in Nigeria to build peaceful and sustainable communities, as well as counselling traumatized individuals. The Centre has been used as means of giving hope and support to the victims/survivors of conflicts. This has assisted the devastated individuals in overcoming traumatic experiences to return and rebuild their communities which were destabilized by the violence.

According to the Director of the Center, the project trained Islamic clerics, Christian leaders and community leaders in the 19 states of the northern part of Nigeria and Abuja. These trainees were drawn from CCN member churches, Islamic group from SCLA and the JNI. At the time of the study, a total of three hundred trainees were trained on basic peace and counselling skills from these groups in batches. The training incorporated trauma healing skills so that the trained individual is developed and equipped to help those who are traumatized in their communities (Ephraim Simon 2020).

Another target group in this project were the traumatized individuals in various IDP camps across the north-east region of the country. A report published in 2014 stated that 3.3 million Nigerians are internally displaced by conflict. The report further stated that the number of internally displaced persons in Nigeria is approximately a third of the IDPs in Africa and 10% in the world (Eweka and Olusegun 2016). These internally displaced Nigerians have lost everything in their lives to the conflict. The project gave these individuals succour through counselling therapy, advice, encouragement and support. The project also contributed immensely to peacebuilding efforts and sustainability of communities in Nigeria, especially the northern region. ICIPH and ICS worked hand in hand with other faith groups and community leaders in various communities to build bridges by ensuring peace and sustainable development through restoring harmony in northern Nigeria.

Contribution of ICIPH to Development in Northern Nigeria through Peacebuilding

Peace is believed to be one of the highest of human values (Jimoh 2018). There can be no meaningful development without peaceful coexistence among the people. According to Igbafe (2014), development cannot be reduced to economic and technological development alone. Rather, it is a process that encompasses emancipation which reduces inequality, deprivation, gender biases, racial discrimination, oppression, poverty and corruption. If development is limited to economic and technological advancement, then it renders the argument that peace is one of the highest of human values untenable. A society cannot be considered developed when the citizenry cannot lay claim to components of social justice such as freedom at the same time achieving their sets goals with their resources (Rodney 1972).

One of the best ways to promote the concept of peace and development in northern Nigeria is to understand the underlying factors to interfaith/communal conflicts in the region (Smock 2001). ICIPH decided to use education and public enlightenment through the two faiths to create awareness among the people. According to ICIPH, identification of the causes of conflict and its impact on the communities is one of the key factors to averting conflicts. The organization further pointed out that, there is a need for experts and government to identify the many root causes of the various conflicts experienced in the communities. This could be achieved through sensitization programmes using conflict analysis tools such as Community Peace Action Network. Also, ICIPH envisaged the use of local and national media in conflict prevention. According to the Advocacy and communication project officer, the media is very important in combating conflicts in the communities. The media could play prominent roles in sensitizing the youth and students in the communities. To encourage the participation of women in peacebuilding efforts, ICIPH promoted programmes where women were trained as peace advocators. In northern Nigeria (as in many parts of the world), mothers spend more time with the children than the fathers. As such, encouraging women to participate as peacebuilders is believed to be important in the peacebuilding efforts. ICIPH encouraged women to be self-reliance and advocates of good governance in their communities. In partnership with women wings of faith-based organizations, ICIPH trained more women in trauma therapy and counselling skills so they could attend to victims of conflicts.

ICIPH has also run sensitization programmes on good governance. According to George-Genyi (2013), good governance is an antidote for peace and security in Nigeria. This assertion seems to align with Amartya Sen's position that development is most times promoted by a balanced democratic institution (Sen 1999). This position only points to the fact that the government officials at all levels in northern Nigeria have prominent roles to play in achieving meaningful development. One of such roles is interfaith education.

Interfaith Education and Development in Northern Nigeria

As seen above, the incessant interreligious conflicts over the years affected the socioeconomic development of northern Nigeria. The wanton destruction of properties of small businesses is a major setback to development. Youth who are to be leaders of tomorrow are denied an education because in some cases schools are closed for months because of unrest in the communities as a result of conflicts. In some cases, parents contribute to the problems as they failed to enrol their children in school. The majority of the parents have used religion as the basis for refusal to send their children to school. For some of these parents, western education corrupts the traditional and religious values of their people. In some cases, the education of the girl-child is forbidden, because it is considered a waste of resources to train them since they will be married out to another family(Babagario 2016). All of these factors and many others contributed to the high rate of illiteracy in northern Nigeria and at the same time, it is believed to have contributed to the incessant conflicts in the region.

Education is power, it is an avenue where enlightenment is passed from one generation to the other. The importance of continuous dialogue among the people in northern Nigeria cannot be overemphasized. Politics and religion succeeded in dividing the people along religious lines. The division affected the cordial relationship experienced by the people in the past. Also, the division prompts people to relocate to communities they feel safe with people from the same faith. Such divisions contributed to people not listening to each other because each side adopts the concept of 'us' and 'them'. The education sector has been neglected by previous governments in the country. Some of the schools lack even basic infrastructure for conducive learning. In some schools, students sit on the floor to study, while others take lessons under a tree. This type of environment is discouraging to both the teachers and students. The environment often results in some students staying away from school.

According to the agenda of the SDGs), education is to play a vital role in the promotion of sustainable development in the world. One of the targets of SDG 4 (7) pointed out that by 2030, there is need to "…ensure that all learners acquire the knowledge and skills needed to promote sustainable development, including, among others, through education for sustainable development and sustainable lifestyles, human rights, gender equality, promotion of a culture of peace and non-violence, global citizenship and appreciation of cultural diversity and culture's contribution to sustainable development (United Nations General Assembly 2016)" However, some parents cling to the teachings of their religion which are often misrepresented by some religious scholars in collaboration with corrupt politicians as an excuse for not enrolling their children in schools. In some families, two or even three generations are often wasted without education. The policy of the government on education is that all children must compulsorily attend the first nine years of school. However, many parents flout such decisions and no parent is ever prosecuted for violating such orders. Gwamna (2010) pointed out that the high rate of illiteracy in northern Nigeria is believed to be one of the major contributors to interfaith conflicts in the region. ICIPH used the influence of religious leaders in their network to encourage school enrolment.

Since the religious leaders are influential in the communities, ICIPH believed they could help to sensitize their followers to enrol their children/wards in schools. The network pushed for the inclusion in school curriculum subjects that will encourage peaceful coexistence among the children in schools and the communities. ICIPH thinks that interfaith education should be encouraged in schools. However, it can only be achieved when parents are sensitized on the need to educate their children with the government providing a conducive environment. An atmosphere of interfaith dialogue will best suit the purpose of promoting interfaith understanding and peaceful coexistence. ICIPH is aware of the importance of such dialogue hence it has made it one of its cardinal principles.

Interfaith Dialogue is a perfect tool that can help in resolving conflicts and misunderstanding. Adopting Allport's (1954) 'Intergroup contact theory' dialogue could be considered a process whereby peace can be achieved among warring parties. According to the Communication and Advocacy Project Officer at ICIPH, the government and community leaders should encourage frequent dialogue among the people. This could be achieved by bringing them together often they may understand what causes the disaffection among them. ICIPH believes this dialogue should not be restricted to religious leaders and parents alone. The youth should be included in the dialogue process because they are the future leaders of the country. Educational institutions need to embrace the interfaith education (IFE) curriculum to encourage dialogue among students/youth in schools and communities.

Nigeria is not exempted from the many challenges interfaith dialogue faces. According to Ashafa and Wuye (1999), the most common challenge interfaith dialogue faces in Nigeria is the lack of IFE teachers that are trained in interfaith dialogue. The authors think that since most of the perpetrators of religious violence in Nigeria are the youth of school going age, teacher training colleges should endeavour to include interfaith curriculum into the education system. This way, religious education teachers will reach out to the students, and at a tender age, they will be groomed to respect each other. Since religion is an integral part of the Nigerian society, and research has shown that some adherents are often willing to fight and die for their faith, emphasis should be placed on interfaith education. This will help youth in northern Nigeria to imbibe the spirit of respect for each other in schools and the community. According to Sampson (2011), the only way to establish a desirable scenario of religious harmony within Nigeria is through the creation and sustenance of a neo-religious educational praxis. Such a measure would create a culture of multi-religiosity for children to understand, pursue, and appreciate.

By establishing a neo-religious educational praxis, we would also be able to re-orient and re-educate the adult population as well. Religious education curricula have been part of the education system in Nigeria at all levels. The curricula are only focused on students' faith tradition; leaving the students ignorant of other faith traditions. Research has shown that most of the youth who perpetrate an act of religious conflict are either ignorant or illiterate (Gwamna 2010). In many countries where conflicts or crises were experienced, education was used to create enlightenment among the youth who are mostly used as combatants. Albert (1999: 5) posits, "Education is seen as one of the cornerstones of this peacebuilding process." Education often serves as a panacea for peace if used in the right way. Sirleaf, J. asserts, "Quality education is central to peace, and peace should be at the heart of education. We owe it to all our children to make both a reality" (Sirleaf 2008: 3) (99). According to ICIPH, education is very important to peacebuilding effort in northern Nigeria. Also, the organization suggested that the government should consider the integration of western education into the Almajiri religious education system in northern Nigeria. Respect for each other's religious beliefs should be incorporated into the education curriculum to teach the children about faiths different from their own.

CONCLUSION

Most Nigerians consider themselves to be religious. Parents try to train their children in their faith traditions. Failure to do is considered by many as a dis-service to the children and community since it is assumed that the children will become irresponsible in society. Since religion is very important to most parents, it would only be proper if such religion is taught with wide world-view rather than a secluded view. ICIPH has always reiterated the fact that religious institutions should be encouraged to preach themes that promote unity among the people rather than dividing them. The organization frowned at the government's usual response to outbreaks of violence in Nigeria, over the last few years. Using the data collected and archived at the centre, ICIPH believes that the government and religious institutions should always retrieve such information and use it for public enlightenment. In the past, the government sets up many commissions of inquiries to determine the immediate and remote causes of religious conflicts and violence in different parts of the country, but regrettably, Nigerians are constantly kept in the dark as to the findings and implementations of recommendations from such commissions. Only a few of such commissions have published their reports, and even when they have, their recommendations have rarely been acted upon or have led to prosecutions. Regarding events in northern Nigeria, there can be no meaningful development without reconciliation. To show its seriousness in handling, preventing, reducing and ending religious conflicts in northern Nigeria, the government must, in the spirit of justice and accountability, publish the findings of previous and subsequent commissions of inquiries while diligently acting upon recommendations made by such commissions. The reports of such commission will educate others of the many dangers of conflicts and its adverse effect on development. Moreover, it may be helpful also in teaching interfaith education in schools. According to President Buhari of Nigeria: "Peace, security, unity and harmony are prerequisites for development in Africa" (Africa Day 2020 address). Peace is vital to the security of any nation. Education is vital to the development, however, there can be no meaningful education without peaceful coexistence among the people. The role of religious leaders cannot be overemphasized in the community. ICIPH encourages religious leaders to embrace a more progressive outlook than a sectarian one. Such religious leaders should contribute to the promotion of interfaith dialogue/education in northern Nigeria which is very crucial and important at this moment of national development. Religion has divided the people for a long time through misinterpretation of religious texts, as such interfaith organizations have prominent roles to play in promoting peace in the communities that may lead to the socio-economic development of the region (Babagario 2016). To improve peaceful coexistence among the people, ICIPH called on the government with the help of interfaith organizations to create an atmosphere where interfaith education/awareness be encouraged in the communities. This way, youth who were indoctrinated by religious leaders could learn about other faiths at the same time respect their views without necessarily believing their doctrines. Through various activities outlined in this chapter, ICIPH as an interfaith network is contributing towards various SDGs, including SDG 16 on, "Peace, justice and strong institutions," SDG 4 on "Achieving inclusive and quality education for all..." and 10, "reduced inequalities."

REFERENCES

Adogame, A., Adeboye, O. and Williams, C. L.. Eds. 2020. *Fighting in God's Name: Religion and Conflict in Local-Global Perspectives.* Lanham, MD: Lexington Books.

Agbiboa, D. 2014. Why Boko Haram Kidnaps Women and Young Girls in Northeastern Nigeria. *Conflict Trends* 3: 51–56.

Albert, I. O. 1999. *The Socio-Cultural Politics and Religious Conflicts-Inter-Ethnic and Religious Conflicts Resolution in Nigeria.* Lagos: Evans Press.

Allport, G. W. 1954. *The Nature of Prejudice.* Reading, MA: Addison-Wesley Publishing Company.

Ashafa, M. N. and Wuye, J. 1999. *The Pastor and the Imam: Responding to Conflict.* Lagos, Nigeria: Ibrash Publications.

Babagario, E. A. 2016. Religion as a Catalyst for Peacebuilding in Jos, Plateau State North Central Nigeria. In: Irvin-Erickson, D. and Phan, P. (eds.), *Violence, Religion, Peacemaking. Interreligious Studies in Theory and Practice.* New York: Palgrave Macmillan.

Dixon, J. Tropp (et al.) 2010. Let Them Eat Harmony: Prejudice-Reduction Strategies and Attitudes of Historically Disadvantaged Groups. *Current Direction in Psychological Science* 19: 76–80.

Ekanem, S. A. and Ekefre, E. N. 2013. Education and Religious Intolerance in Nigeria: The Need for Essencism as a Philosophy. *Journal of Educational and Social Research* 3(2): 303–310.

Eweka, O. and Olusegun, T. O. 2016. Management of Internally Displaced Peons in Africa: Comparing Nigeria and Cameroon. *African Research Review: An International Multidisciplinary Journal* 10(1). 40: 193–210.

Ezegbobelu, E. E. 2009. *Challenges of Interreligious Dialogue between Christian and the Muslim communities in Nigeria.* Frankfurt: Peter Lang GmbH Internationaler Verlag der Wissenschaften.

Fox, J. 2014. Religion and Intrastate Conflict. In: Newman, E. and DeRouen, K. (eds) *Routledge Handbook of Civil Wars.* New York, NY: Routledge: pp. 157–172.

George-Genyi, M. E. 2013. Good Governance: Antidote for Peace and Security in Nigeria. *European Journal of Business and Social Sciences* 2(2): 56–65.

Gwamna, D. J. 2010. *Religion and Politics in Nigeria.* Bukuru: ACTS Bookshop.

ICIPH Newsletter. 2017. March edition. Kaduna: Nigeria.

Igbafe, M. L. 2014. *Core Issues and Theories in Philosophy of Development.* Ekpoma: A Inno Publication.

Jegede, O. P. 2019. Implications of Religious Conflicts on Peace, National Security and Development in Nigeria. *Ilorin Journal of Religious Studies* 9(1), 53–70.

Jimoh, A. K. 2018. Peace Development and Development for Peace: Philosophy for Integral and National Development in Nigeria. *PACEM Journal of Peace and Development* 1(1): 13–24.

Kung, H. 1991. *Global Responsibility: In Search of a New World Ethic.* Michigan: Crossroad Publishing Company.

Pettigrew, T. F and Tropp, L. R. 2006. A Meta-analytic Test of Intergroup Contact Theory. *Journal of Personality and Social Psychology* 90: 751–783.

Rodney, W. 1972. *How Europe Underdeveloped Africa.* London: Bogle-Louverture.

Sampson, I. T. 2011. Religious Violence in Nigeria: Causal Diagnoses and Strategic Recommendations to the State and Religious Communities. Retrieved from: http://www.ajol.info/index.php/ajcr/article/viewFile/78703/69042 on 03/03/2015.

Sanusi II, M. S. 2017. 50th Anniversary of the Creation of Kano State. In *United Nations SDG Advocates.* Retrieved from: unsdgadvocates.org/emir-of-kano.

Sen, A. 1999. *Development as Freedom.* Oxford: Oxford University Press.

Sirleaf, E. J. 2008. Where Peace Begins: Education's Role in Conflict Prevention and Peacebuilding. In: *Save the Children.* London: International Save the Children Alliance.

Smock, D. 2001. *Interfaith Dialogue.* Washington, DC: USIP.

Smock, D. R. 2006. Mediating between Christians and Muslims in Plateau State, Nigeria. In: Smock, D. R. (ed). *Religious Contributions to Peacemaking: When Religion brings Peace, Not War.* Washington, DC: United States Institute for Peace: pp. 17–20.

272 E. A. BABAGARIO

Torgovnik, J. 2020. Six Years after #BringBackOurGirls, Freed Chibok Captives Face Fresh Danger. *The Wall Street Journal.*

Umaru, T.B. 2013. The Challenges for Tolerance and Peaceful Coexistence between Christians and Muslims in Northern Nigeria. In: Svartvik, J. and Wirén, J. (eds.) *Religious Stereotyping and Interreligious Relations.* New York: Palgrave Macmillan: pp. 123–133.

Ushe, U. M. 2015. Religious Conflicts and Education in Nigeria: Implications for National Security. *Journal of Education and Practice* 6(2): 117–129.

Usman, B. 1987. *The Manipulation of Religion in Nigeria, 1977–1987.* Kaduna: Vanguard Printers and Publishers.

Voll, J. O. 2015. Boko Haram: Religion and Violence in the 21st Century. *Religions* 6(4): 1182–1202.

UNICEF. 2019. '*Education*' Unicef Nigeria. Retrieved from https://www.unicef.org/nigeria/education#:~:text=One%20in%20every%20five%20of,years%20are%20not%20in%20school. on 11/21/2021

World Bank and Bretton Wood Institution. 2016. Advancing Social Protection in a Dynamic Nigeria. World Bank.

INTERVIEWS

Biodun, A. A. 2020. International Center for Interfaith, Peace and Harmony. Kaduna: Nigeria.

Ephraim Simon. 2020. Institute of Church and Society. Jos: Nigeria.

CHAPTER 15

Addressing Environmental Issues Through Interfaith Dialogue: A Case of the Southern African Faith Communities' Environmental Institute (SAFCEI)

Tapiwa H. Gusha and Ishanesu Sextus Gusha

INTRODUCTION

The issues of environmental crisis cannot be ignored in the discussion on sustainable development in any society. This explains why in terms of the United Nations Sustainable Development Goals, eight of them are linked to the environment and these are; No Poverty (1), Zero Hunger (2), Good Health and Well Being (3), Clean Water and Sanitation (6), Affordable and Clean Energy (7), Climate Action (13), Life Below Water (14), and Life on Land (15). SDG 10 is not isolated from the above mentioned SDGs and these are the very things that are affecting equality

---

T. H. Gusha (✉)
Anglican Diocese of Winnipeg, Winnipeg, MB, Canada

I. S. Gusha
Anglican Diocese in Europe, Palma de Mallorca, Spain

© The Author(s), under exclusive license to Springer Nature Switzerland AG 2022
E. Chitando, I. S. Gusha (eds.), *Interfaith Networks and Development*, Sustainable Development Goals Series,
https://doi.org/10.1007/978-3-030-89807-6_15

273

among nations and communities. Sometimes decisions on environmental issues that affect the local communities are made without including or consulting these communities. It is within this context that this chapter discusses the contribution of the Southern African Faith Communities' Environmental Institute (hereinafter referred to as SAFCEI) towards confronting environmental issues affecting Southern and East Africa. The chapter discusses the historical background of SAFCEI, governance, initiatives and then finally the evaluation of their work.

The Historical Background of SAFCEI

SAFCEI is a reputable interfaith organisation in Southern Africa that has been in existence since 2005 and is based in Cape Town, South Africa. According to the organisation's website, "it is committed to supporting faith leaders and their communities in Southern Africa to increase awareness, understanding and action on eco-justice, sustainable living and climate change" (*safcei.org*). The work of SAFCEI is, therefore, two-pronged, that is, empowering leaders and engaging communities. Three terms, namely, eco-justice, sustainable living, and climate change, need to be unpacked before going further. Emily Hill defines the term 'eco-justice' as, "the recognition that human and environmental rights are indivisible-that humans are, in fact, part of nature, and that injustice against either party are mutually reinforcing" (Hill 2016: 11). We are in a world where the subject of environmental degradation is topical in academic discourse. Poor farming practices, unethical extraction of minerals, and selfish business practices are contributing towards the degradation of the environment. Countries in Africa are imbued with natural resources yet these countries remain poor. Therefore, in our quest to address SDG 10, one cannot ignore the issues of unethical extraction of minerals and selfish business practices. Ethan Lowenstein, Rebecca Martusewicz, and Lisa Voelker echo that, "the world is facing enormous ecological and social problems-top soil loss, overfishing and acidification of oceans, loss of potable water, and access to safe food sources and global change are just the tip of the iceberg" (Lowenstein et al. 2010: 100). As we discuss eco-justice later, these are some of the concrete issues confronting the world and communities. We need to understand that eco-justice has four basic norms and Dieter T. Hessel mentions them as:

1. A deep respect for the diversity of creation on earth: this means active solidarity with other people and creatures.
2. Ecologically sustainable lifestyles that utilize 'ecologically and socially appropriate technology'
3. Establishing 'basic forms and definite ceilings' for consumption, so that there is equitable distribution of resources among humans and all can enjoy sufficient standards of living.

   This is the target of SDG 10.1 that is on progressively achieving and sustaining income growth of the bottom 40% of the population. The majority of these poor people are the ones who are custodians of these precious resources. For example, many people in the Marange area in Zimbabwe are poor yet their homes are built on diamond fields.
4. Radically more democratic decision making; a recognition that decisions about use of the commons-our communal air, water, and soil, must be made by all segments of society and must further the common good (Hessel 2007; *http://fore.yale.edu/disciplines/ethics/eco-justice/*). The question is, how can we empower and promote the social, economic and political inclusion of all irrespective of age, sex, disability, race, ethnicity, origin, religion or economic or other status in the context where such decisions are made for them by other people?

Harry Lehmann and Sudhir Chella Rajan define 'Sustainable Living' as "a complex multi-level phenomenon which comprises the following integrated perspectives of social and socio-cultural transformation towards sustainability; sustainable use of products; sustainable consumption behaviour; sustainable consumption patterns and sustainable lifestyle (Lehmann and Rajan 2015: 6). The following six basic categories comprise sustainable living: shelter, food, power, water, transportation, and waste. The fact is that the earth is facing challenges to sustain the current levels of excessive consumption that is being experienced in the first world countries (Alexander 2012: 292). Climate Change is a term that is being frequently referred to in most discourses that have to do with the environment. It is frightening to learn that the world temperatures are consistently rising. According to Nicola Scafetta, "since 1900 the global surface temperature of the earth has risen by 0.8 degrees celcius" (Scafetta 2010: 71). This is the context in which the term global warming is being employed by environmentalists. C. K. Uejio et al. define the term 'Climate Change' as, "a systematic change in the long term state of the atmosphere over multiple decades or longer" (Uejio et al. 2015: 5).

The three terms defined above shape the scope of the purpose of the SAFCEI. The SAFCEI was launched in 2005 and this was an outcome of the multi-faith environmental conference that was held in that same year in South Africa. Instead of just having that conference, there was a feeling that something long-term should be established as a way of consistently engaging environmental issues affecting the communities of Southern Africa. This was the birth of the SAFCEI. As a multi-faith organisation, at the time of writing the SAFCEI enjoyed the membership from the following religions; African Traditional Religions, the Baha'i Faith, Buddhism, Hinduism, Islam, Judaism, Quakers, and Christianity. The emphasis of SAFCEI is, "the spiritual and moral imperative to care for the earth and the community of all life" (*safcei.org/about-us/*). The organisation is driven by the vision; "people of faith caring for the living earth" (*safcei.org/about-us/*). Its mission reads; "As an institute of many faiths, we are united in our diversity through our shared commitment to caring for the living earth" (*safcei.org/about-us/*). Finally, the objectives of SAFCEI are to:

1. Raise environmental awareness
2. Engage in formulating policy & ethical guidelines within our faith communities
3. Facilitate environmental responsibility & action
4. Confront environmental & socio-economic injustices
5. Support environmental training and learning. (*safcei.org/about-us/*)

GOVERNANCE

The SAFCEI has a clear and well-structured governance which is at three levels (all these are with reference to the time of writing). The first level is the patron of the organisation, who was the retired Anglican bishop, Bishop Geoff Davies (2013). He was now in his old age but remained passionate about the environment. The next level of leadership was composed of the Board of Directors and these were; Francesca De Gasparis (Executive Director-Ex Officio Member), Kirtanya Lutchminarayan (Hinduism), Sister Usha Jevan (Brahma Kumaris), Shaun Cozett (Anglican), Clare Hendry (Christian), Moulana Shuaib Appleby (Muslim), Venerable Tsondru Sonam (Buddhism), Stephen Jacobs (Jewish), and Dr. Braam

Hanekom (Dutch Reformed Church). The composition of the members of the board of directors is testimony to the attempt to fulfil SDG 10.2 on the inclusion of all regardless of race and religion. The majority of religions are represented in the board of directors with the exception of ATR. Below the Board of Directors were the energetic office staff members and these are the drivers of the organisation who are on the ground. The staff members were mainly female and this complemented the Board of Directors which was mainly comprised of males. Having gone through the historical background and governance of the organisation, now we need to move to the organisation's initiatives and this is the core of the chapter.

The SAFCEI Initiatives

The initiatives of the SAFCEI are arranged in different thematic areas in line with the organisation's vision and mission. In terms of initiatives, the SAFCEI seeks with people of faith to:

1. Raise environmental awareness.
2. Promote environmental responsibility and action.
3. Facilitate and support environmental advocacy.
4. Confront injustices and advance eco-and socio-economic justice
5. Influence and formulate environmental policies and ethical guidelines. (*safcei.org. about-us*)

To accomplish all these initiatives, the SAFCEI engages in networking, training, learning, research, and action. Ultimately, the goal is to replenish the living earth in a way that is informed by prayer, contemplation, and meditation. The outcome is that the leaders should become the agents of change. In this section, we are discussing these initiatives in the context of their impact on sustainable development.

Faith Leader Environmental Advocacy Training (FLEAT) Programme

The FLEAT programme is designed to capacitate the leaders of different religious communities to become good stewards of the living world. The acronym 'FLEAT' stands for, Faith Leader Environmental Advocacy

Training. How is the programme structured? According to the organisation's website, "the programme includes training, learning, and follow-up with faith leaders who are selected for their interest and desire to develop on eco-faith approach with their faith communities" (*safcei.org/project/fleat/*). The trained leaders are equipped to respond to challenging situations arising from environmental degradation, climate change, and to develop advocacy tools for eco-justice. They do all this work with their faith communities so as to achieve sustainable results.

The inaugural FLEAT Group One training was done in Harare in 2015 and the theme of the training was 'Water scarcity in Southern Africa'. Since the inaugural training in 2015, the SAFCEI has made milestone achievements and here is a snapshot of their achievements with the FLEAT programme:

- Zambia: 150 community members trained in organic farming.
- Zimbabwe: Environment Day held in 5 schools with 180 multi-faith learners, resulting in the formation of environmental clubs, tree planting, and energy and water saving at schools.
- Kenya: 70 people involved in a coastal clean-up for World Wildlife Day; FLEAT members ran a schools programme of talks on protecting the environment; CYNESA organised a Green Room at a UN Conference in Kenya.
- Tanzania: 40 additional faith leaders were educated on climate change, and 1200 congregants, including climate change projects with a Maasai community and workshops for youth on climate change and poverty.
- Malawi: FLEAT faith leaders planted 132,000 trees through a joint Christian and Muslim initiative with congregations in Jali District. (*safcei.org/project/fleat/*)

The acronym 'CYNESA', stands for Catholic Youth Network for Environmental Sustainability in Africa. To date, the SAFCEI has done more than 30 FLEAT Advocacy trainings in different countries in Southern and East Africa.

Eco-Audit

In 2018, the SAFCEI produced an *Eco-Audit User Guide*, which is a self-help eco-audit booklet to be used by congregations and individual families. The booklet helps congregations and individuals in identifying and measuring energy and water use and waste production. The purpose of eco-audits is to, "create awareness, encourage action and save money and the environment" (*SAFCEI Eco-Audit. User Guide for Faith Communities* 2018: 3). Energy audit is important in addressing economic issues especially among poor communities. In a bid to progressively achieve and sustain income growth of the bottom 40% of the population in line with SDG 10, one cannot underestimate the impact of huge electricity and water bills. A good energy audit will go a long way in cutting expenditure on those with poor income already. It is a 19 pages comprehensive and friendly user guide that can be used even by a non-expert person. The user guide gives step-by-step eco-audit. Here are the four steps of carrying an eco-audit:

1. Collect information: energy and water consumption, waste generation and site description.
2. Identify and understand service costs (electricity, water and waste removal)
3. Prioritise and act for efficiency and resilience.
4. Evaluate the cost savings and benefits to the environment and plan further action. (*SAFCEI Eco-Audit. User Guide for Faith Communities* 2018: 4)

Many companies and religious organisations waste lot of money and resources in poor eco-audit. Here are some of the issues raised by the user guide in terms of eco-audit; (1) How much energy is used by the company or family? Why would an organisation buy high fuel consumption vehicles for the management to use as transport from home to work? In many organisations the management use big cars that consume more fuel for driving to work and sometimes at the expense of the tax payer's money. It is the tax of this bottom 40% of the population who happen to constitute the bulk of the working class. Instead of this tax being channelled towards improving the infrastructure of the country, the tax are being used to support the luxury life styles of the elite in the managerial positions. This remains the fundamental source of inequalities in many societies. This is one area that needs to be addressed as different governments in the region seek to reform the economies of their families. How much electricity is used in the organisation? Are the electricity bulbs energy servers? Many companies use high voltage bulbs in a context where electricity is scarce. What type of geysers are being used in the organisation? Many organisations are still using high voltage electric geysers in the age of solar geysers. This applies to all appliances that need power. Does the organisation have an audit of such appliances? (2) In terms of water, does the organisation consistently check for leaks and drips? How much water is used by the toilets and sinks? Some organisations are still using the old urinary systems that use lot of water. (3) In terms of waste management, is the organisation avoiding packaging items in packs that are not recyclable? Is the organisation separating recyclable and non-recyclable wastes?

The User guide also addresses issues to do with land management audit. How are the homes, offices and faith centres cared for? The major encouragement is on greening spaces. According to the guide, "trees and shrubs clean and cool the air, dampen sound, absorb pollutions and provides habitants for other than human creatures" (*SAFCEI Eco-Audit. User Guide for Faith Communities* 2018: 13). In the eco-audit, organisations are discouraged from having hard surfaces. The issue concrete paving on the whole premise is discouraged. There should be a high percentage of indigenous vegetation on the property. The place should be friendly to wild creatures such as birds, insects, and small reptiles. Organic litter should be kept for mulching and properties should have compost heaps. These are just summaries of eco-audit areas that are covered by the user guide.

Green Your Life

The SAFCEI also runs a programme for families called, 'Green Your Life.' The argument is that for people to change or transform the world, that change or transformation should start at home. How can people initiate that change from their homes? People should live in harmony with nature through greening their lives. The proposal is that people are to make every Monday a Green Monday in their homes by skipping meat and dairy products for the day. It is a simple practice but an effective one. Just imagine one billion people abstaining meat and dairy products for a day and how many animals will be saved on that day? The programme also involves making homemade bread cooked from sun stoves and serve plastics and electricity.

ENERGY JUSTICE

McCauley et al. (2013: 1) define 'energy justice' as "providing all individuals across all areas with safe, affordable and sustainable energy" (McCauley et al. 2013: 1). Energy crisis in a common feature in some African countries and load shedding of power takes almost 8–10 hours a day. Energy is the bedrock of development in any country and failure to have affordable and sustainable energy is a recipe for lack of development. Thus, "SAFCEI is committed to energy justice and to ensuring that people of faith are informed about our energy choices, and the right to participate in decisions that affect us" (*safcei.org*). The SAFCEI opposes nuclear energy, uranium mining and fracking, and instead support just energy development. Faith leaders are therefore encouraged to advocate for energy justice in their faith communities by opposing unethical energy projects that harm the environment. These are discriminatory laws, policies and practices that condemned by SDG 10.4. They appears attractive and progressive in terms of solving people's problems hence they create long term life threatening problems for the local communities there by disempowering them. The SAFCEI also opposes any energy policy that impacts negatively on the environment. In 2014, the South African government entered into a nuclear deal with a Russian state owned company to establish a nuclear company in South Africa as a way of increasing energy in the country. However, the deal was entered without following proper procedures like passing through parliament channels and this means that the electorate was not involved. The SAFCEI and Earthlife Africa Johannesburg in October, 2015, took the matter to court. According a report, "On 26 April 2017, after a campaign inside the courtroom and in the public arena, with public meetings and workshops, protests and marches, the Western Cape High Court found that the nuclear deal and the various associated energy procurement processes, were both illegal and unconstitutional" (*safcei.org*). The issue was not only about following procedures, but they were many socio-economic and environmental concerns such as:

- The R1-trillion nuclear deal would have tied the country into unnecessary debt well into the foreseeable future. Such a fiscal engagement put the country into a serious debt that will affect future generations. In opposing such an engagement, SAFCEI is embodying SDG 10.4 on the adopting of policies especially fiscal, wage and social protection policies and progressively achieve greater equality.

- Stopping further government corruption and poor decisions in the energy sector, and to hold the Executive accountable for its decisions.
- Promoting energy justice and civil participation, since citizens were excluded from having a say in decisions which will affect them in future.
- South Africa's energy policy is outdated and must be interrogated and participatively updated.
- Progress in renewable energy technology has sped up and costs have dropped significantly, so we should be investing in renewable energy instead.
- Evidence has shown that nuclear energy is NOT clean, NOT affordable and NOT sustainable. (*safcei.org*)

The court case was won because of the collective effort of the civil society and non-governmental organisation partners, and also individual citizens. However, the war was far from over as another nuclear deal was on cards. "The environmental impact assessment (EIA) for a new nuclear plant to be built at Koeberg, near Cape Town in the Western Cape, was given the green light" (*safcei.org*). SAFCEI had to mobilize the community to appeal through the minister to reverse the deal. Seven hundred letters of appeal were gathered and handed over to the minister. The government had to put plans on halt while SAFCEI was to keep an eye on the possible corrupt deals on the matter.

Keep the Karoo Frack-Free

SAFCEI's role of being the environmental watchdog for the community did not end with the fight against nuclear projects, but they had another battle in Karoo. Karoo is a vast semi-desert region stretching more than 400,000 square kilometres covering the three provinces of the Eastern, Northern and Western Cape. It is one of the tourist attraction area well known for the beautiful botanical gardens. The other government project was on cards and this time around, it was not a nuclear power station but gas extraction project through a process known as fracking.

Hydraulic fracking is:

The process of forcing natural gas or oil from layers of shale rock deep below the earth's surface. Wells are drilled 5 kilometres deep into the ground and then turned horizontally for 2–3 kilometres. Millions of litres of water, mixed with sand and chemicals, are injected into the wells at high pressure. The shale is cracked open and sand and liquid are forced into the tiny cracks. Natural gas, trapped in the rock, is released and returns to the surface with the fracking fluids. (*safcei.org*)

The questions to be asked are; in what ways is the process a hazard to the environment? In ways does the project affect sustainable development, especially when it creates jobs and revenue? SAFCEI sees the project in many ways not as a solution to climate change. The positive thing is that, shale gas is methane and it burns cleaner that coal and other fossil fuels.

However, SAFCEI sees fracking not as a solution to climate change because methane is still a fossil fuel. Fossil fuels are greenhouse gases that trap heat in the atmosphere 20 times more effectively than carbon dioxide (CO^2). This has the following negative consequences of the environment and communities. First, yes, there is promise of job creation but that is exaggerated. Infrastructure is likely to improve, but SAFCEI argues that "actual fracking jobs will be short term, and mostly done by external specialists" (*safcei.org*). Second, fracking affects water issues and that is not welcome news in a country with water scarcity like South Africa. Fracking is likely to have a serious impact on the water catchments in all the areas where it takes place. The argument of SAFCEI is:

Water used in the fracking process is mixed with a cocktail of chemicals which fracking companies are reluctant to name because some are highly poisonous. Some are known to persist in the environment, accumulating in food chains posing risks to human health and ecosystems. Pollution and contamination of water will have wide-ranging impacts on agriculture and human livelihoods that are dependent on the land. (*safcei.org*)

The side effects of the environmental degradation will be threat to human and animal health. The effects are insurmountable and apart from methane in the atmosphere, ground and surface water can be contaminated with methane, arsenic, radioactive minerals, a variety of metals, fracking chemicals and salty brine. It is argued that "some fracking chemicals are carcinogenic (they cause cancer). On-site, workers must be protected from silica dust, which causes silicosis, an incurable and fatal lung disease" (*safcei.org*). In the same region, SAFCEI had to fight government's efforts to do a uranium mining project. Several protests against the government were organised by SAFCEI and other anti-nuclear activists. Munyaradzi Makoni writes:

> Anti-nuclear energy activists are up in arms, and have taken to vigils outside South Africa's parliament in Cape Town to protest against President Jacob Zuma's push for nuclear development. As the protests mount, the Southern African Faith Communities' Environment Institute (SAFCEI), an interdenominational faith-based environment initiative led by Bishop Geoff Davies, has said the government's nuclear policy is not only foolish but immoral. (Makoni 2015)

The protests yielded the desired results in 2017 when the mining company finally gave up the projects after spending more than USD$10 million on legal feels and consultants.

Food and Climate Justice

SAFCEI also takes seriously the issue of food and climate justice. Firstly, SAFCEI raises awareness against bad consumerism culture and toxic farming practices that result in poor quality food. Second, SAFCEI fights for animal rights especially bad animal husbandry practices. One notable campaign that SAFCEI was involved was the fight of cage-free eggs. In poultry, there is massive production of eggs through the cage system. This is process whereby, each layer is confined in a tiny cage without any moving space and food and water are accessed through a tiny hole. The laid egg then roles down the cage to outside tray for picking. The system is viewed by many activists as being cruel to the freedom of movement of animals. SAFCEI had to lobby for companies in the food industry not to purchase such eggs as they promote the oppression of animals. The response was positive as:

> On 20th September, Wyndham Destinations and Wyndham Hotels & Resorts both published a strong global cage-free commitment online following a public campaign by the Open Wing Alliance, a coalition of 70 major animal protection organisations. In these policies, Wyndham Destinations and Wyndham Hotels & Resorts commit to sourcing 100% cage-free eggs and egg products for every single one of their locations worldwide by 2025. They promise to provide annual progress reporting to

15 ADDRESSING ENVIRONMENTAL ISSUES THROUGH INTERFAITH... 285

ensure they meet their deadline and will translate their commitment and progress into multiple languages. (*safcei.org*)

This was a milestone achievement because these two multinational companies are major players in the hospitality industry with nearly 40 brands, thousands of locations, and a presence in over 100 countries. The outcome of such a success was that this significantly reduced the suffering of millions of egg-laying hens and sets a global precedent that cages are no longer acceptable. As a follow-up to this commitment, SAFCEI in partnership with Open Wing Alliance (OWA) successfully hosted the second annual Africa Regional Summit in Cape Town from 16th to 18th September 2017. Twenty-four attendees from thirteen organisations representing four countries attended the three-day summit. The attendees had to spend three full days workshopping, networking, and strategizing on how to bring about a cage–free Africa. The collective testimony from attendees was that:

> We were excited to meet many activists and organizations new to the cause and were able to learn about the OWA's resources, the theory of change behind corporate campaigning, the role Africa plays in the global cage–free movement, and more! Additionally, we were able to collectively take part in the Wyndham campaign, letting the hospitality giant know that Africa will not support companies that cage hens. This event was very inspiring and we are excited to see all the great work these groups will be doing in the coming year! (*safcei.org*)

SAFCEI is one such interfaith organisation that functions as both capacity builder and community watchdog on environmental issues. As SAFCEI alumni, we gladly term SAFCEI, 'the 21st century prophet/ prophetess of environment and sustainable development in Southern and East Africa.' Having explored the story of SAFCEI, this chapter ends with evaluating their initiatives since every story has its successes and challenges.

SUCCESSES

It is a fact that SAFCEI has a success story to tell and this section highlights some of the successes. Since its inception, SAFCEI has managed to bring together leaders of different religions to tackle environmental issues. It is not easy to bring together people of different faiths but SAFCEI has managed it. The organisation has also managed to train many leaders and faith communities on environmental advocacy. These leaders have become vehicles of change on environmental sustainability. For example, many churches in the Anglican Diocese of Harare are now carrying eco-audits. The Diocese of Harare through SAFCEI initiatives established the environmental desk and with a chaplain appointed by the bishop. The church now dedicates the whole month of September as the season of creation where the liturgy is dedicated towards certain environmental themes. SAFCEI also managed to mobilize the communities against harmful government projects that have a bearing on the environment. Notably, they managed to block the South African government from carrying certain energy programmes such as the nuclear power station, Karoo Fracking and the Uranium mining projects that had a negative impact of the environment. This saved people's health and wellbeing. All these successes were crowned by the winning of an international award by the SAFCEI staff for outstanding work on protecting the environment. In 2018, SAFCEI's Executive Director, Francesca de Gasparis, says "SAFCEI is immensely proud of Liz and Makoma, and the recognition they are receiving for their work on the nuclear deal, with the Goldman Environmental Prize. We commend their tenacity and commitment to blowing the lid off the secret and corrupt nuclear energy deal—which would have bankrupted South Africa and set us back generations in terms of development" (https://allafrica.com/stories/201804230857.html). That was statement of the Executive Director on the celebrations of their receiving of the awards.

CHALLENGES

There have been some challenges in SAFCEI's work as an interfaith environmental organisation. First, they have been viewed by the government as the enemies of the state and it is not easy to operate in a context where one's initiatives are not appreciated by the supreme authorities of the country. Second, they received negative publicity and blackmailing by the business tycoons who benefitted from extracting from the environment. In a world of profiteering, people make money from deals that harm the environment, for example, gold panning. These are the people who dislike organisations that advocate for ethical practices in dealing with the environment. SAFCEI is one such organisation that has to endure strained relationships with certain sections of the community. This leads to the third challenge of lack of funding. Over the years, SAFCEI has struggled with funding as business communities are not forthcoming. Their funding is mainly from faith communities and other well wishes with passion on the environment. This has slowed down their initiatives but though they are frustrating tactics they continue to soldier on. Regardless of these challenges, their story remains a success.

Conclusion

This chapter concludes that SAFCEI is one such home grown organisation that has made a meaningful contribution to the livelihoods of communities in Southern and East Africa. They are dealing with an important aspect of sustainable development which is environment. Today, the entire world is shut down because of the COVID-19 virus and the environment cannot be left out as one of the possible causes of the pandemic. The existence of such organisation is necessary for the realisations of the 2030 Sustainable Development Goals and promotion of the reduction of inequalities within and among the countries as stipulated by SDG 10.

References

Alexander, Samuel. 2012. "Degrowth Implies Voluntary Simplicity: Overcoming Barriers to Sustainable Consumption." *Simplicity Institute Report 12b, 2012.* http://simplicityinstitute.org/wpcontent/uploads/2011/04/OvercomingB arrierstoSustainableConsumptionReport-12b.pdf (Assessed on 03/04/2020).

Geoff, Davies. SAFCEI. (Southern African Faith Communities' Environment Institute). In *ANVIL 29 (1).* September 2013.

Hessel, Dieter T.. *Eco-Justice Ethics. The Forum on Religion and Ecology at Yale,* 2007. http://fore.yale.edu/disciplines/ethics/eco-justice/ (Assessed on 02/04/2020).

Lehmann, Harry and Sudhir Chella Rajan. 2015. Sustainable Lifestyles Pathways and Choices for India and Germany. *Policy Paper.* Berlin: Deutsche Gesellschaft für Internationale Zusammenarbeit (GIZ) GmbH.

Hill, Emily C. 2016. Christianity and the Development of Eco-Justice. *Pomona Senior Theses.* http://scholarship.claremont.edu/pomona_theses/142 (Accessed on 02/04/2020).

Lowenstein, Ethan, Martusewicz Rebecca and Voelker, Lisa. 2010. Developing Teachers' Capacity for EcoJustice Education and Community-Based Learning. *Teacher Education Quarterly.* 99–118.

Makoni, Munyaradzi. 2015. "One Tune, Different Hymns—Tackling Climate Change in South Africa. Africa Climate Wire." http://www.ipsnews.net/2015/07/one-tune-different-hymns-tackling-climate-change-in-south-africa/. Jul 28.

McCauley, D., Heffron, R. J., Stephan, H., & Jenkins, K. 2013. Advancing energy justice: The triumvirate of tenets and systems thinking. *International Energy Law Review* 32: 107–110.

SAFCEI Eco-Audit. User Guide for Faith Communities. 2018.

Scafetta N. 2010. "Climate Change and Its causes: A Discussion about Some Key Issues," *La Chimica e l'Industria 1*, pp. 70–75.

Uejio, C.K., Tamerius, J.D., Wertz, K. & Konchar, K.M. 2015. "Primer on climate science." In G. Luber & J. Lemery (Eds.), *Global Climate Change and Human Health*. San Francisco, CA: Jossey-Bass.

WEBSITES

https://safcei.org/ (Accessed 21/11/2019).

https://safcei.org/knowledge-base/eco-audit-user-guide/ (Accessed 21/11/2019).

https://safcei.org/project/what-you-can-do-at-home/ (Accessed 21/11/2019).

https://www.greenafricadirectory.org/listing/the-southern-african-faith-communities-environment-institute/ (Accessed 22/11/2019).

https://allafrica.com/stories/201804230857.html.23 APRIL 2018. (Accessed 22/11/2019).

CHAPTER 16

Interfaith Networks, the African Diaspora and Development: The Case of the United Kingdom

Nomatter Sande

Introduction

The phenomenon of the global movement of people is continuing to be topical in global development discourses. Whenever people move, they carry their religion with them. Religious diversity in the world is rising due to the movement of people (Kristen 2016). Besides, there is growth in the spread of religions across the globe. The predictions are that Christianity will grow to 2.9 billion in 2050, about 2.8 billion Muslims, 16 million Jews; affiliations to Hindu, and Buddhist communities would increase (Pew Foundation 2015). Alongside these helpful statistics, it is important to acknowledge that the international diaspora communities are gaining attention because of the increase in migration across the globe. The international migrants are persons living in a country other than where they are born, and in 2019, the international migrants reached 272 million

---

N. Sande (✉)
University of South Africa, Pretoria, South Africa

© The Author(s), under exclusive license to Springer Nature
Switzerland AG 2022
E. Chitando, I. S. Gusha (eds.), *Interfaith Networks and Development*, Sustainable Development Goals Series,
https://doi.org/10.1007/978-3-030-89807-6_16

289

worldwide, compared to 153 million in 1990 (United Nations International Migration Report, 2019). Statistically, Europe has the largest number of migrants (82 million), North America (59 million) and North Africa and Western Asia (49 million).

In particular, the United Kingdom has remained a viable destination for migration and this study focuses on the African diaspora communities. At the time of writing, the United Kingdom was increasingly becoming more multicultural and interfaith society. Some of the potential problems of multicultural and multi-faith community is the emergence of violence, terrorism and radicalism. Religious beliefs have been implicated for supporting these problems. Literature shows that the United Kingdom has used the 'interfaith dialogues' as a mitigatory approach to end the deployment of religion in terrorism.

There has been limited focus on interfaith networks and their role in meeting the Sustainable Development Goals (SDG10) reducing inequalities (within and among countries) in particular, or development in general. The faith-based organisations have a role to play in development. Faith issues are important to development because religion influences the behaviour of the followers (Taylor 2006). Both the role of interfaith networks to develop and the meaning of development is different to contexts. While interfaith dialogues are important in the case of the United Kingdom, and perhaps is a form of development, there is a need to question the connections between interfaith networks, diaspora communities and development. The meaning of development tends to be influenced by context. Therefore, this study theorises what interfaith networks must consider being relevant to development in African diaspora communities and reduce inequalities using the United Kingdom as a case study.

Conceptual Framework

This study used 'interfaith dialogue' as a conceptual framework. Interfaith dialogue is a process of engaging diverse faiths to understand one another. Grant and Osanloo (2014) argued that conceptual framework describes the relationship between concepts beings studied and how these relate to one another. Interfaith networks and development are the concepts that are the main variables. Both interfaith networks and development are contested variables and they should be narrowed to specific areas. This study limits interfaith networks and development to the United Kingdom and the African diaspora communities. In this study, I use 'interfaith dialogue' as constructivist communication to understand interfaith networks as an engagement with difference. The Platform for Intercultural Europe and Culture Action Europe (2010) argued that dialogue goes beyond religious diversity expressions and formulates new things. I use the concept of 'interfaith dialogue' as the initial entry to understand interfaith networks in Diaspora settings such as the United Kingdom, which reduce inequalities in Africa (SDG10).

The principle of interfaith dialogue argue that each participant should be learning from others to change or grow (Swidler 2013). Interfaith dialogues help to identify and construct how interfaith networks respond to development. Keaton and Soukup (2009) proposed a pluralistic conceptualisation of interfaith dialogue. Thus, the conceptual framework of interfaith dialogue shows that it recognises how diverse religions can work together and end negative issues and enhance development to communities.

THE NATURE OF INTERFAITH NETWORKS AND DEVELOPMENT IN THE UNITED KINGDOM

Depending on the context, the nature of interfaith networks and development is different. Within some contexts such as the United Kingdom, the nature of development focuses on engagement, integration and dialogue. According to Ramli and Awang (2014), dialogue brings a conversation between people of different backgrounds and aims to identify differences and similarities that help people learn and understand one another. Accordingly, this resonates with SDG10.2, which seek to "empower and promote social...inclusion" (United Nations 2015: 31). The term 'interfaith' is commonly used in the United Kingdom to describe diverse religions. Further, terms like interreligious and multi-religious are used interchangeably. Nevertheless, the common underlying element is about a dialogue amongst people of different faiths. Although the United Kingdom uses the term interfaith but in reality, it does not constitute a 'movement' (Lewis and Dando 2015). The problem with interfaith movement in Britain is that it is often misunderstood and little appreciated and has a poor image than its United States counterpart.

In this chapter, I do not single out particular networks unless otherwise but, the focus is to give an overall picture of the trajectories of interfaith networks in the United Kingdom. While there has been some work about interfaith in the United Kingdom from as early as 1936, the September 11, 2001 United States of America bombing and the July 7, 2005 in London placed a priority on interreligious relations and a sense of 'urgency' (Wingate 2005). From 1987 registered interfaith networks were 30, increased to 100 in 2000 and shot up to 240 in 2010 (Pearce 2012). The first coordinated Interfaith network in the United Kingdom was established in 1987, and the focus was dedicated to interreligious relations. There has a special appreciation of religious issues within the United Kingdom government. For instance, in 2003 the Home Office Race Equality Unit was reconfigured to incorporate the Faith Communities Unit, to deal with the 'civic version of faith' (McLoughlin 2010).

Succinctly, Lewis and Dando (2015: 5) argued that "to enable religions, separately and together, to engage the socially excluded, facilitate consultation between them and the state, and promote 'social cohesion', money was made available by different government departments". This shows that in the United Kingdom there is intentional support to interfaith networks through defined areas of achievement. Lewis and Dando (2015) argued that the interfaith movement focused on faith leaders than individuals or communities. The Three Faiths Forum (3FF) was started in 1997 focusing on the Abrahamic religions. However, in 2004 it focused on schools and how to enhance interfaith understanding amongst the younger generations. This approach extended to Christians, Muslims and Jewish people. The agenda increased to involve the atheists, humanists and other minority religions. In 2007, the 3FF managed to extend its focus to deal with undergraduate leadership scheme. Such innovations managed to see a shift from the issue of interfaith dialogues to action dedicated to younger audiences.

The British Muslim communities formed a council called the Muslim Council of Britain (MCB) in 1997. Lewis (2007: 67) argued that legal advisory role of this body remains 'work in progress.' The then Labour government welcomed the MCB. The MCB pressed to receive state funding for Muslim schools and this was granted in 1998. By 2020, there are some twelve state-funded Islamic schools and more than 160 private schools (Lewis and Dando 2015: 9). Working together, the MCB, Church of England and other faiths persuaded the government in 2001 to make a decennial census on religion. This was previously done in 1851. The results of the census showed that 76.8% of Britons were affiliated to religion. As such, 'faith', alongside 'race' was included in the state's management of minority communities. Another milestone achievement was recorded in 2003, when the Sikhs and Jews, together with the MCB, witnessed the religious discrimination outlawed in employment.

In 2006, the 'Race and Religious Hatred Act' was put in place. This Act made incitement to religious hatred and offence. The United Kingdom government-funded a campaign against anti-terrorism under the banner 'PREVENT'. The project was sponsored £60 million and ran from 2007 to 2010. 'Faith Communities Capacity Building Fund' was allocated £13.8 million in 2006, £7.5 million in 2008. This "was easily the largest single investment ever made in British Muslim civil society" (O'Toole et al. 2013: 20). However, this type of funding triggered suspicion whether the United Kingdom government was brokering a peace treaty with MCB. The impact was noted when other faiths reacted against the Muslim organisations. Other funding related to MCB included to the Young Muslim Advisory Group (YMAG) and the National Muslim Women's Advisory Group (NMWAG) was formed to "circumvent first-generation older male gatekeepers" (O'Toole et al. 2013: 22). Further, in 2010 the 'Single Equality Act' was put in place. This Act brought together other aspects like the anti-discrimination laws, and the Equalities and Human Rights Commission (EHCR). According to O'Toole et al. (2013: 1–10) the United Kingdom enacted "religious legislation which goes beyond EU directives or indeed anything found in Europe".

The uniqueness of the interfaith network is the existence of the Church of England. The Church of England is institutionalised and has a greater role to play in religious issues. In 2011 the Church of England gave £5 million in 2011 towards the interfaith networks. This shows that the Church of England has been working as a voice for other religions within the United Kingdom. Also, Lewis and Dando (2015) argued that for over 40 years the Church of England has been involved in interfaith discourses to the extent that there are specialised interfaith advisers stationed at most dioceses. The role of these interfaith advisers is to help the clergy, policy makers and churches leaders with skills that help them to engage with people from other faiths. Besides, there are Chaplains from the Church of England at different institutions and prisons. The Islamic institution has begun to offer Muslim chaplains as well. The curriculum for theology in different universities and colleges now includes Islamic studies. Another funding of £5 million was invested to boost the grassroots interfaith social projects in 2011; this project was given to the 'Near Neighbours Programme'. The money was distributed to institutions like the Christian

294   N. SANDE

Muslim Forum (CMF), The Council of Christians and Jews (CCJ) and Hindu Christian Forum (HCF).

KEY ISSUES RELEVANT TO INTERFAITH NETWORKS, THE AFRICAN DIASPORA AND DEVELOPMENT

The foregoing discussion shows that most interfaith networks in the United Kingdom focus on the integration of and avoidance of religious extremism. This can be summarised as the major nature of the contributions of interfaith networks to development. Relating to ethnic minorities in the United Kingdom some trajectories can be noticed. According to Peach (2005), the British discourse about minorities has changed from colour around the 1950s to race around 1980s, ethnicity in the 1990s and to religion. This chapter focuses on the second descendant Africans tracing from the second and third waves of African migrants. According to Cohen (2008), the second wave is characterised by anti-colonial and anti-apartheid struggles, civil wars and ethnic conflict. The third wave is associated with the deterioration of socio-economic conditions in diverse African nations between 1980 and 1990.

African diaspora communities within the United Kingdom face diverse challenges which include but are not limited to an imbalance in resources and social engagements. Besides, migrants bring their religions to host nations and perhaps hang on to one religion. Bringing together experiences and faiths has the potential not only to support integration but to enhance development. Therefore, it is critical to explore the nature of the contributions to development by African diaspora communities.

It seems many Africans in diaspora from different parts the world are dedicated to issues that promote Africans. From both coordinated or sporadic perspectives, Africans strive to discuss their culture and traditions, setting up networks, blogs, websites and development projects. Such dispositions show that there can be several factors that are critical to understanding how African diaspora communities conceptualise development. Van Hear et al. (2004) cited in Bond For International Development (2015: 10) argued that "positive integration, economic prosperity and sense of belonging are key factors to determine the extent to which diaspora communities will act as development agents". To appreciate how interfaith networks can be relevant to development in African diaspora communities, this chapter reflects on the following factors that seem to bedevil the African diaspora communities: financial remittances, generation gaps and communications, identity and religious affiliations.

Financial Remittances

The nature of the contribution to the development of the African diaspora communities in the United Kingdom is heavily contested. Bond (2015: 7) argued that "a clear and accurate picture of their actual engagement in civic life and key policy areas, including development, has not yet emerged". A possible explanation of this might be that the population of African diaspora communities is too low. Maurice (2014) argued that statistically about 2.8 million people in the United Kingdom come from diaspora communities and this is roughly 4.4% of the total British population. The majority of the migrants recorded were from, Nigeria, Kenya, South Africa and Zimbabwe. Although politically, this population's contribution to development is insignificant, their international contribution financially is notable. In 2013, the formal remittances were estimated at £2.5 billion (The Independent 2013). The African diaspora communities are known to support their families, friends, hospital medications and education. Thus, it is critical to reducing remittance costs for migrants. The SDG10.c suggested that by 2030, the migrant's transaction costs should subside to 3% and eliminate the existing higher 5% remittances corridors (United Nations 2015: 31).

It seems possible that there is a great affinity that the African diaspora communities are natural partners to international development. What is interesting to note is that the Black Africans have the propensity to remit their money to homelands (Department for International Development 2013). For instance, the African diaspora communities contribute greatly to their sending nations through remittances, business initiatives and professional contributions. In the religious context, the African diaspora communities contribute tithes, offerings, donations and even volunteering their time, thereby contributing to international development. An implication of this is the possibility that age, religion, economic prosperity, integration, identity and sense of belonging determine the level of community engagement. It is possible, therefore, that faith groups have values embedded within their religious beliefs which make a distinct understanding of development.

In developing countries development is skewed because of the impact on poverty, exploitation by the developed countries and unequal global

296   N. SANDE

economic system. The SDG10.a suggested that there should be special and different "treatment for developing countries, in accordance with the World Trade Organisation agreements" (United Nations 2015: 31). Since this chapter has showed that the approach of the United Kingdom interfaith networks is helpful, there is need to uphold this model. Hence, it could conceivably be hypothesised that interfaith networks can fund programmes that enhance African diaspora communities. In this case, the developing nations are places of opportunities, innovation or learning ground. Regardless of the generation gaps, the African diaspora communities have a sense of a desire to change the status quo for their homelands. At times, the African diaspora feels that their contributions for development are misappropriated by politicians in Africa. Therefore, interfaith networks can act as bridges for the good governance of the African diaspora communities' resources.

Generational Gaps and Communication

Most people receive their religious faith through their families. The nature of the relations between generations is important to diaspora communities. The first generation migrant tends to maintain a strong link with their homelands and remit finances regularly. The first generation diaspora migrant exhibit Afromania and Afrophilia. Commenting from an interview with a fashion designer, Brandellero (2007) defined Afromania as finding African prints or images everywhere. I define Afrophilia as a deep desire for anything which represent and stand for Africa. The concept of development in this context is motivated by their first-hand experience of the homeland and its challenges. In this way, they tend to have a positive attitude towards their countries of ancestry. The second generation tends to support their ancestral homeland because of their parents' influence. They either join their parents to remit support to their homelands or even start business projects in their homelands. Their worry of development is skewed towards the country of origin than the host nations. The use of social media helps this generation to understand and be abreast to events in the countries of ancestry. "Religion and places are mutually influential" (Knott 2010: 476). The third and fourth generation migrants are likely to have a different perspective on their ancestral homelands. There is also some negative stereotyping, especially of the third and fourth generation diaspora Africans by fellow African counterparts for their lack of understanding of African-ess.

The African diaspora communities have added advantage in transmitting the information. Diaspora communities connect instantaneously, continuously and dynamically to their sending nations (The Economist 2011). Both the environment and common experiences within the host nations make people trust each other. Therefore, it is probable that they end up making connections across the ethnic divide. In this case, the diaspora communities can be described as communities of care. It follows, therefore, that development in the context of inter faiths involves the relationship between religious institutions and leaders in public life. It can thus be suggested that for interfaith networks to work in the African diaspora communities the issue of safe space and environment is critical. The lived experiences of some African diaspora communities are diverse because of the nature of the migration processes. The reason for migrating to the United Kingdom include but not limited to enhancing professional opportunities, political asylum seekers, and family reunions. In general, therefore, it seems that interfaith networks should consider creating a positive, hopeful and peaceful environment that helps for engagement. It may be the case therefore that within the African diaspora communities, interfaith networks should promote a favourable and conducive environment that promote their interfaith dialogues. "In the context of a world in which religious-based difference is seen as a threat, interfaith dialogue is viewed as a potential harmonising and accommodating framework to support unity within the diversity of humankind" (Atkinson 2019: 47).

However, the question is whether this is the same concept or not when it comes to developed countries? Answering this question helps to understand the role of the interfaith networks in the diaspora context and what it means to contribute to development. This notion is based on the notion that diaspora communities expand through networks and potentially linking other countries across the nations. To this end, the SDG10.7 focuses to "facilitate orderly, safe, regular and responsible migration and mobility of people, including through implementation of planned and well-managed migration policies" (United Nations 2015: 31). As such, interfaith activities are viable opportunities to offer global development as opposed to developing the host nations. Religion has, and continues to play a critical role in migration processes and matters. Although the African diaspora communities are diverse, they share a common ground when it comes to the interconnection of developing countries through their heritage. Because of the increasing religious diversity of the United Kingdom, interfaith engagement is important.

Identity

Understanding the role of the identity of African diaspora communities helps to know how and why these communities should be involved in development. The diversity of the United Kingdom population makes visible dual ethnicity and national identities are a key component of life. African diasporas can be regarded as people of multiple identities. Be this as it may be, 'faith' is regarded as one component which is beyond ethnicity and nationality. Hence, interfaith networks have ability to context other areas that relate to development which include but not limited to contraception, gay rights, abortion, capital punishment, gender, equality, freedom, HIV and AIDS. Further, religion has had a positive attitude to development issues like helping to topple authoritarian regimes and enhancing human rights (Medhurst 1992; Moreno 2007; De Gruchy 1995). Africans who either came to Europe at a young age or born in Europe struggle with two identities. One instinct makes them identify themselves as members of the host countries. It is therefore likely that such a connection exists between interfaith and identity. The SDG10.2 focuses on promoting social equality respective of age, sex, disability, race, ethnicity and origin (United Nations 2015: 31). Thus, interfaith networks should consider issues of identity as well as a relationship which makes identity. Most interfaith dialogue is facilitated where there are shared community relationship. It is important therefore for the interfaith networks when considering engagement with the African diaspora communities to create a mutual relationship among people of diverse backgrounds. A phenomenological approach is strategic, especially in the United Kingdom where there are diverse religious persuasions, including the secular atheists, humanist and agnostics. It may be the case therefore that that interfaith excludes other groups which do not mention 'faith' but are spiritual and non-religious. Prothero (2010) argued that there is a perception that the secular population are not part of faiths. However, some people are now moving away from mainline Abrahamic faiths to spirituality, hence the need to embrace a more elastic approach towards "faith" and "interfaith."

Religious Affiliations

According to Sunak and Rajaswaran (2014), many British diaspora communities practise religion as part of their lives. Interfaith teaching from diverse religions can shape the lives of the people and help them to contribute towards development. Most faith teachings enhance the principles of development. For instance, most religions emphasise the issue of justice, compassion, reconciliation and stewardship. When upheld, such teachings help to promote development. Further, charity work such as giving offerings, tithes or *zakat* in religious shrines goes a long way to foster notions of development. Although some development organisations attempt to avoid faith and religion because they view it as a barrier to development, there is need to adopt a more progressive stance. According to Tettey (2007), there is a continuous engagement between members of African Independent churches with the socio-economic and political concerns in Africa. The western tradition seems to make a distinction between religion and state, thereby excluding them on matters of development. Perhaps, when they are allowed to participate then they are supposed not to mention their faith issues. There are other faith values which defend the secular and materialistic world and thereby do not want to engage with interfaith official donors. However, the World Health Organization (2007) argued that about 40% of health services in sub-Saharan Africa and up to 70% in other African countries are provided by faith groups.

These findings suggest that the acknowledgement of African Traditional Religions is critical for accommodating the African diaspora communities. Beversluis (2000: 127) argued that one of the rules for interfaith dialogue is that "dialogue is seeking understanding of other persons' beliefs". Interfaith networks in the African diaspora have a role in contributing towards meeting the SDG10.2 which seeks to empower and promote religion or economic or other status (United Nations 2015) in particular and development in general. In developing countries, diverse forms of spiritual practices and faiths play a significant role in the lives of the people. Faith groups situated in diverse parts tend to instil trust and confidence in the people and seem to turn to them in times of need and crisis (Narayan et al. 2000).

Conclusion

This chapter sought to use the United Kingdom as a case study to theorise what interfaith networks must consider being as relevant to development for African diaspora communities. The chapter showed that the effects of global migration have created diaspora communities within host nations. Such a phenomenon has contributed to the increase in the diversity of faiths because people always migrate with their religions. Existing literature shows that religion has been blamed for violence, terrorism and radicalisation. However, interfaith networks have the potential to contribute to development in different contexts. This chapter shows that the United Kingdom has remained focussed on interfaith dialogues, integration and working together as foundations for development. This goes a long way in overcoming inequality, as envisaged by SDG10. The chapter also illustrated the holistic approach that the interfaith networks within the United Kingdom have adopted. There is also a robust investment into the interfaith networks from the government of the United Kingdom, while African diaspora communities within the United Kingdom have been contributing to global development through financial remittances to their sending nations. This chapter has identified a gap when it comes to understanding how African diaspora communities perceive as development. It suggested that for interfaith networks to engage the African diaspora communities in matters of development they should pay attention to factors such as financial remittance, generation gaps, communications, identity and religion. Taken together, these results contribute to understanding what interfaith networks can do to be relevant to development in the context of African diaspora communities and fulfilling SDG10 to reduce inequalities.

References

Atkinson, Michael. 2019. Interfaith Dialogue and Comparative Theology: A Theoretical Approach to a Practical Dilemma. *The Journal of Social Encounters* 3(1): 47–57.

Beversluis, J. 2000. *Sourcebook of the World's Religions*. Novato, CA: New World.

Bond For International Development. 2015. What is Development Means to Diaspora Communities. *2015 European Year for Development*.

Brandellero, A. 2007. *Crossing Cultural Boarders: Migrants and Ethnic Diversity in the Cultural Industries*. Amsterdam: University of Amsterdam.

Cohen, R. 2008. *Global Diasporas*. London: Routledge.

De Gruchy, J. 1995. *Christianity and Democracy: A Theology for a Just World*. Cambridge: Cambridge University Press.

Grant, C. and Osanloo, A. 2014. Understanding, Selecting, and Integrating a Theoretical Framework in Dissertation Research: Creating the Blueprint for 'House'. *Administrative Issues Journal: Connecting Education, Practice and Research*: 12–22.

16 INTERFAITH NETWORKS, THE AFRICAN DIASPORA AND DEVELOPMENT... 301

Keaton, J. A. and Soukup, C. 2009. Dialogue and Religious Otherness: Toward a Model of Pluralistic Interfaith Dialogue. *Journal of International and Intercultural Communication* 2(2): 168–187.

Knott, K. 2010. Geography, Space and the Sacred. In J.R. Hinnells (ed) *The Routledge Companion to the Study of Religion.* Abingdon and New York: Routledge: 476–491.

Kristen, Allen. 2016. Achieving Interfaith Maturity Through University Interfaith Programmes in the United Kingdom. *Cogent Education* 3(1): 1261578. https://doi.org/10.1080/2331186X.2016.1261578

Lewis, Philip. 2007. *Young, British and Muslim.* London: Continuum.

Lewis and Dando, C. Baker. (ed.). 2015. The Interfaith Movement. *Temple Tracts* 5(1): 1–22. https://williamtemplefoundation.org.uk/wp-content/uploads/2017/02/The-Interfaith-Movement_Lewis-Dando.pdf.

Maurice, N. 2014. *Voices of the Diaspora: A New Vision, Building Understanding through International Links for Development (BUILD), United Kingdom.*

McLoughlin, Sian. 2010. From Race to Faith Relations, the Local to the National Level: The State and Muslim Organisations in Britain. In A. Kreienbrink and M. Bodenstei (eds), *Muslim Organisations and the State: European Perspectives.* Nurnberg: Bundesamt fur Migration und Fluchtlinge.

Medhurst, K. 1992. Politics and Religion in Latin America. In G. Moyser, ed. *Politics and Religion in the Modern World.* London: Routledge.

Moreno, A. 2007. Engaged Citizenship: The Catholic Bishops' Conference of the Philippines in the Post-authoritarian Philippines. In G. Clarke et al, eds. *Development, Civil Society and Faith-based Organisations.* Basingstoke: Palgrave Macmillan.

Narayan, D. (et al.) 2000. Voices of the Poor: Can Anyone Hear Us? *World Bank.* Oxford University Press.

O'Toole, T. (et al.) 2013. *Taking Part: Muslim Participation in Contemporary Governance.* Bristol: University of Bristol.

Peach, Ceri. 2005. Britain's Muslim Population: An Overview. In Tahir Abbas (ed.), *Muslim Britain: Communities Under Stress.* London: Zed Books.

Pearce, Brian. 2012. The Inter Faith Network and the Development of Inter Faith Relations in Britain. In Woodhead, Linda and Rebecca Catto, eds. *Religion and Change in Modern Britain.* Oxon and New York: Routledge.

Pew Foundation. 2015. *The Future of World Religions: Population Growth Projections, 2010–2050.* Washington, DC: Pew Research Center.

Platform for Intercultural Europe & Culture Action Europe. 2010. *Concepts in Practice Intercultural Dialogue as an Objective in the EU Culture Programme 2007–2013. Platform for Intercultural Europe & Culture Action Europe.*

Prothero, S. 2010. *God is Not One: The Eight Rival Religions that Run the World and Why Their Differences Matter.* New York.

Ramli, Ahmad F. and Awang, J. 2014 The Practices and Approaches of Interfaith Dialogue at Leicester, UK. *Journal of Human Development and Communication* 3: 1–16.

Sunak, R. and Rajaswaran, S. 2014. *Portrait of Modern Britain, Policy Exchange*.

Swidler, L. (2013). Dialogue Principles. http://dialogueinstitute.org/dialogue-principles/.

Taylor, N. 2006. Working Together? Challenges and Opportunities for International Development Agencies and the Church in the Response to AIDS in Africa. In *Tearfund*. London.

Tettey, W. J. 2007. Transnationalism, Religion and the African Diaspora in Canada: An Examination of Ghanaians and Ghanaian Churches. In K. J. Olupona and R. Gemignani (Eds.), *African Immigrant Religions in America*. New York: New York University Press, pp. 321–364.

The Economist. 2011. Weaving the World Together (19 November 2011). www.economist.com/node/21538700.

The Independent. 2013. Remittances Could Be as Sustainable as International Development Finance. blogs.independent.co.uk/2013/06/15/remittancescould-be-as-sustainable-as-international-developmentfinance.

United Nations. 2015. Transforming Our World: The 2030 agenda for Sustainable Development. A/RES/70/1.

United Nations. 2019. International Migration 2019. Department of Economics and Social Affairs Population Division, United Nations Publications. ST/ESA/SER.A/438.

Van Hear, N., Pieke, F. and Vertovec, S. 2004. The Contribution of UK-based Diasporas to Development and Poverty Reduction. In *A Report by the ESRC Centre on Migration, Policy and Society (COMPAS)*. University of Oxford for the Department for International Development.

Wingate, Andrew. 2005. *Celebrating Difference, Staying Faithful: How to Live in a Multi-faith World*. London: Darton, Longman and Todd.

World Health Organization. 2007. Towards Primary Health Care: Renewing Partnerships with Faith-based Communities and Services. Geneva: WHO.

INDEX

A
Abortion, 12
Abrahamic faiths, 298
Activists, 5
Advocacy, 277, 278
Africa, 30, 31
Africa Conference of Churches, 86
African diaspora, 290
African Independent churches, 299
African Traditional Religion, 139, 140
Afromania, 296
Afrophilia, 296
Agreement, 226
Agriculture, 122
Allah, 139
Amharic, 7
Amnesty, 219
Anachronism, 245
Anglophone, 82
Anthropocentric, 8
Anti-apartheid, 294
Anti-colonial, 294

Anti-development, 243
Arts, 5
Austria, 68, 69
Awareness, 276, 277

B
Baha'i, 50
BOFABONETHA, 150
Boko Haram, 255
Botswana, 149
Brahma Kumaris, 221, 222
Buddhist, 50

C
Capacity building, 180
Catholic Youth Network for
    Environmental Sustainability
    (CYNESA), 278
Ceasefire, 226
Central African Republic, 78

© The Author(s), under exclusive license to Springer Nature
Switzerland AG 2022
E. Chitando, I. S. Gusha (eds.), *Interfaith Networks and
Development*, Sustainable Development Goals Series,
https://doi.org/10.1007/978-3-030-89807-6

304   INDEX

Child Protection Unit, 191
Christian, 50
Church of England, 292, 293
Civilization, 238
Climate, 274
Coexistence, 85
Colonial, 231
Confucian, 50
Constitutionalism, 183
Contraception, 12
Corruption, 264
COVID-19, 3
Culture, 102, 239

D
Development, 4–7
Dialogue, 30
Discrimination, 126, 264
Diversity, 144
Domestic Violence Act, 131

E
Eco-audit, 279
Education, 242, 243
Energy, 273
Energy justice, 281
Ethnicity, 75
Ethnography, 236
European Union (EU), 204
Extremism, 112

F
Faith, 47, 48
Faith-Based Organizations, 187
Faith Leader Environmental Advocacy
    Training (FLEAT), 277, 278
Family, 131
Francophone, 82
FRELIMO, 216

G
Gays, 151
Gender, 47
Gender-based violence, 138
Gender minorities, 150
Governance, 183
Greek Orthodox Church, 221, 222

H
Health, 47
Heterosexuals, 151
HIV/AIDS, 177
Homogenous, 109
Homosexual, 151
Humanities, 5
Human rights, 104
Hunger, 273
Hydraulic fracking, 282

I
Identity, 109
Inclusion, 29
Inclusive, 81
Inequality, 100
Initiatives, 66
Intercultural, 30
Inter-ethnic, 236
Interface, 4
Interfaith, 3, 4

J
Jains, 119
Judaism, 66
Justice, 117–127

K
KAICIID, 68
Kenya, 52

L
Lesbians, 151
Liberation, 9

M
Media, 30
Migration, 289, 290
Mozambique, 215
Multicultural, 290
Multifaith, 137

N
Networks, 3

O
Oppression, 264

P
Pan-African, 81, 82
Partnership, 86
Phenomenological approach, 298
Pluralism, 100
Policymakers, 28, 52
Post-colonial, 231
Poverty, 264
PROCMURA, 83–85
Prosperity gospel, 239
Protestant, 218

Q
Quaker(s), 119, 276
Quran, 139

R
Radicalization, 101
Religions, 28, 29

RENAMO, 216
Researchers, 5
Roman Catholic Church, 177

S
SAFCEI, 274
Sanitation, 273
Saudi Arabia, 69
Scriptural, 7
Seventh-day, 119
Sex Education, 187
Sexual diversity, 150
Sikhs, 119
Social media, 127
Social network analysis, 28
South Africa, 3
Spain, 69
Supernaturalism, 245
Sustainable Development Goals
(SDGs), 4

T
Taboo, 151
Tanzania, 118, 119
Terrorism, 290
Transformed masculinity, 150
Typology, 10

U
Uganda, 52, 175
United Nations (UN), 4
United Religions Initiative (URI), 29
United States Institute of Peace
(USIP), 7

W
War, 87
Wellbeing, 108

306 INDEX

Women, 101, 102
World Council of Churches
(WCC), 82

Y
YouTube, 137

Z
Zakat, 299
Zambia, 199, 200
Zambia Interfaith
Networking Group
(ZINGO), 199–201
Zimbabwe, 278